G000152192

Endorsements for *Peace Beyo*

Vijay Mehta's book *Peace Beyond Borders* is an important contribution to the urgent and ongoing debate on Europe's future. The book gives hope by acknowledging the Union's difficulties but suggesting new ways in which Europe can overcome these by adopting a new, demilitarized, strategic approach to expansion, internal migration and the refugee crisis. This book is a must-read for all those citizens wishing to find ways to end wars, demilitarize both Europe and our world, and build peace – a necessary base for prosperity for all the human family.

Mairead Corrigan Maguire, *Nobel Peace Prize Laureate, 1976, Founder, Peace People, Belfast, Northern Ireland*

As stated in your own remarks, 'there is a risk that Europe's great peace-promoting project will start to unravel.' Robert Schumann, one of the founders of the European Union, said that 'we must invent Europe'. In the last decades, because of a lack of leadership and an extreme neoliberal influence, the progress of a truly European Union has been strongly reduced. There is no political and economic union – only monetary – and no common foreign policy, including the role of NATO in security. This book can contribute to substantially decrease this risk and pave the way for a more equitable and peaceful world.

Federico Mayor Zaragoza, *Former Director General UNESCO; President, Foundation, Culture of Peace, Madrid, Spain*

Mehta offers strong arguments that regional coherence and unification based on a minimum degree of solidarity are substantial factors to secure stability and, ultimately, peace. His appraisal of achievements through European integration cannot be dismissed lightly and should be a warning to those cultivating anti-European sentiments of national isolationism. The book deserves recognition for a fascinating study of Europe.

Henning Melber, *Director emeritus of The Dag Hammarskjöld Foundation, Sweden. Extraordinary Professor at the University of Pretoria and the University of the Free State*

Too often the case in Britain for our membership of the EU is made in the narrow economic terms of what's good for business and good for jobs. This excellent book is refreshingly different. It is about how the EU should be a force for peace and good in our troubled world.

Lord Roger Liddle, *Special Advisor and Consultant on European Matters and Author of* The Europe Dilemma, *UK*

I think the argument of your book is similar to a position I have argued for some years: namely, that the EU's greatest achievement is not economic co-operation and the regional machinery, but the establishment of a culture of peace within Europe, although not beyond Europe.

Richard Anderson Falk, *Former UN Special Rapporteur on Palestinian Human Rights, Professor Emeritus of International Law at Princeton University, US*

I do wish that your book will be highly successful as I fully agree with the direction of your thoughts as laid out.

Prof Dr Jürgen Elvert, *Jean-Monnet Chair of European History and AIAS-COFUND Fellow of Aarhus University, Denmark*

Vijay Mehta's wise, historically informed, presently encompassing, future-oriented, practical *Peace Beyond Borders* should be read by educators, leaders, the public and media commentators everywhere who favour human evolution toward a killing-free world. This pioneering book speaks for itself and will need no words from me or anyone when readers find it.

Glenn D Paige, *Chair, Governing Council, Center for Global Nonkilling, Honolulu, Hawaii*

Vijay Mehta's book is a timely, important and stimulating volume. That the regional approach to international peace and prosperity has much to commend it has also, for a long time, been my view. Europe has indeed made great strides, and has been seen as an example for other continents and regions to follow, as skilfully depicted in the book. At the same time, there are great strains, as Vijay has mentioned.

Peter Van Den Dungen, *Author and Emeritus Professor, School of Social and International Studies, University of Bradford, UK*

This book is an important contribution to how we should think and talk about the European Union today. The accurate claim that the Union brings peace to Europe has in recent years too often become a cliché, trivialized by repetition. Vijay Mehta powerfully reminds us that peace can never be taken for granted and demonstrates to us, logically and eloquently, the Union's continuing role in assuring peace for Europe. Anyone unsure how to vote in the forthcoming European referendum should read this book.

Brendan Donnelly, *Director, Federal Trust and former MEP*

At this time, when the European Union faces unprecedented economic and political challenges from the Eurozone, refugee crises and populist nationalism, Vijay Mehta's reminder and re-affirmation of the EU's foundation ideals and unequalled record as peace-builder between historic enemies is hugely relevant for current geopolitics. Rejecting conventional notions of an uneasy post-1945 peace based on Cold War nuclear balance, he instead identifies 10 positive 'Peace Promoting Factors' which stabilized the continent after the catastrophic 1914-45 era – with EU ideals and institutions as focus and builder of the new peaceful order. Mehta cogently argues that the EU can be an inspiration and model for regional peace-building structures around the world, very positively contributing to world peace. Rich in original angles on European affairs, *Peace Beyond Borders* is a ground-breaking analysis of the EU and its global role, deserving the widest readership among policymakers and the general public. With Britain's EU referendum looming and continent-wide debate on Europe's future raging, Mehta's refreshingly innovative and positive appraisal is very welcome and timely.

Rev Brian Cooper, *Co-ordinator and Uniting for Peace Churches and Interfaith Secretary, Edinburgh, UK*

PEACE BEYOND BORDERS

How the EU brought peace to Europe
and how exporting it would end
conflicts around the world

VIJAY MEHTA

Peace Beyond Borders:
How the EU brought peace to Europe and how exporting it
would end conflicts around the world
First published in 2016 by
Catapult
an imprint of New Internationalist Publications Ltd
The Old Music Hall
106-108 Cowley Road
Oxford OX4 1JE, UK
newint.org

Design and cover design: Ian Nixon, New Internationalist

Printed by T J International Limited, Cornwall, UK
who hold environmental accreditation ISO 14001.

MIX
Paper from
responsible sources
FSC® C013056

British Library Cataloguing-in-Publication Data
A catalogue record for this book is available from the British
Library.
Library of Congress Cataloging-in-Publication Data.
A catalog record for this book is available from the Library of
Congress.

ISBN 978-1-78026-376-2
(ISBN ebook 978-1-78026-377-9)

*To peace visionaries whose tireless efforts
made war unthinkable in Europe.*

*To Shanti, Sanjay, Renu, Ajay, Vimal, Ritika, Sheetal, Mahir, Dhairya,
Shivika and Vandika. Life would be burdensome without your love.*

Contents

Preface and acknowledgements

At the time of writing this book, Europe was in the news for all the wrong reasons. The Eurozone crisis, an influx of migrants and refugees, war in Ukraine and the debt crisis in Greece dominated the headlines. The UK's impending referendum on European Union (EU) membership added to the bloc's woes.

Little attention was being devoted to the EU's positive effects, other than a sterile and polarizing debate over the benefits of free trade. No-one seemed to ask why the European continent, which not so long ago was the crucible of global conflict, was now assumed to be so peaceful.

This book has identified 10 pro-peace functions that dispelled the mutual antagonism that was once the hallmark of European countries. These include enshrined democracy, open borders, soft power, shared values, human rights, the rule of law and multiculturalism, all of which have made the EU a model of peaceful coexistence. The book argues that by following these same paths, the rest of the world can also become peaceful. The book is an appreciation of the EU's efforts to make war unthinkable in Europe, but it is also intended to reiterate the fact that peace is a condition of life without which humanity could not have existed or developed.

Peace in Europe has been forged through co-operation, unity and rule of law, not because of NATO or the US security paradigm, which is based on aggressive military force. It was not NATO or any other military alliance that drove Europe's institutional alignment and economic integration, but the European Coal and Steel Community (ECSC), then the European Economic Community (EEC), and then finally the European Union. These were the bodies that eliminated the causes of recrimination that hitherto found violent expression between European states.

For the past 70 years, European nations have avoided going to war with one another, a feat never before achieved in

European history. The 2012 Nobel Peace Prize was awarded to the European Union (EU) 'for over six decades of [having] contributed to the advancement of peace and reconciliation, democracy and human rights in Europe' by a unanimous decision of the Norwegian Nobel Committee.

Without question, there are aspects of the EU that need reform. First and foremost, the EU must abandon its alliance with NATO and end the US veto over its foreign affairs. Countries at peace with one another do not require expensive weapon programmes. Nor do they require the backing of a military pact which damages the EU's credibility as the greatest soft power in the world.

One advantage of being a member of the EU is that all 28 countries receive access to a giant common market, the biggest trading bloc in the world, in which trading across borders benefits businesses small and large and which has made the majority of EU citizens affluent by global standards.

As a peace activist, my desire is to bring the EU's oasis of peace and prosperity to other continents. This book is an attempt to explore the prospect of EU-like structures being created in Africa, the Americas, Asia and Oceania and the Middle East to end some of the bloodiest and most intractable conflicts facing the world today.

Writing the book has been a fascinating journey over the past two years, a virtual tour of the world, exploring continents, their distinct cultures, traditions and values. What has motivated me throughout is the fact that the ideas of great thinkers, past and present, have contributed to the world of peace, prosperity and harmony in which some of us live today. The book is my humble attempt to follow in the footsteps of those remarkable giants who changed the world, and to offer a radical vision to end war and build peace to make the 21st century a peaceful one and change history along the way.

The book has already started an educational campaign, 'Europe for Peace – Count me in', highlighting the EU's peace endeavours. This highlights how the EU has created mechanisms to prevent conflicts before they begin, and how these impact all areas of society. It explains the dangers to peace and stability that a disintegrating EU would present. It argues that issues like the refugee crisis and increasing terrorism can only be tackled through mutual co-operation and shared responsibility. And it stresses the need for reform at home and in Europe, particularly with regards to the austerity agenda, the influence of NATO on defence policy, and the problem of ordinary people feeling removed from EU decision-making – none of this can be done without giving the public a seat at the table.

I owe an immense debt of gratitude to José Ramos-Horta for taking the time from his busy schedule to write a very wonderful and valuable foreword to my book.

Thanks to Jo Lateu and Daniel Raymond-Barker at New Internationalist Publications for guidance and advice on the editing, production and publicity of the book.

Thanks to James Brazier for extensive research, including giving me temporary relief to be away from my desk. Thanks to Raceme and Natasha Wort for formatting the notes, bringing the book together and making it ready for publication.

I'm indebted to Shanti, Renu, Sanjay and Ajay for their continuous love and their support for tolerating my absence and making my time free to think and write.

Vijay Mehta
20 April 2016

Foreword

By José Ramos-Horta

Just a few decades ago, two generations of Europeans were already discussing the genesis and merits of Europe as a political project. The parents were born in the aftermath of the Second World War, their sons and daughters after the Carnation revolution that brought down the Portuguese dictatorship.

For the younger group, the European Community, as it was still called, was above all an economic alliance and a trading agreement, while for older folk, Europe's raison d'être was above all the maintenance of peace in the world's single most war-ridden region in history.

As time goes by, this latter's view seems to be lost on an increasing number of Europeans – non-Europeans tend to be much more positive about Europe, just as they are much more aware of the fact that it actually means something to be European.

As the former leader of the European Green Party, Dany Cohn-Bendit, once said: 'Send young Europeans off to Asia, Africa or the Americas for a while and then to a different European country... Upon returning to the old continent they will at once realize just how European they feel.'

In 2009, and again in 2010, I nominated the European Union for the Nobel Peace Prize. What inspired or motivated me to write a long submission to the Nobel Peace Committee in Oslo nominating the European Union for this award?

I am very much Timorese, born and growing up in as remote as an island can be, but I am also European. My grandfather and father, very active members of the much-feared anarchist bands who resorted to homemade bombs in their fight against fascism in the Iberian Peninsula, were exiled to the then-Portuguese Timor in the early 1930s. The farthest and most-forgotten colony was for centuries mostly useful for its famed native sandalwood, its unique Arabica coffee, and as a penal colony for disposable political dissidents.

The Europe I nominated for the Nobel Peace Prize was the group of nations that were able to heal their war wounds together, reconciling themselves with each other as well as with the rest of the world after centuries of slavery and colonialism and, as they re-emerged and regained affluence, began to share their wealth among themselves and many poorer countries of the South.

Of course, the EU's depressingly overbearing bureaucracy and the lack of accountability of swaths of its officialdom continually contribute to undermine its institutions. Still, let us not throw out the baby with the bathwater.
The construction of Europe is undoubtedly the single most ambitious, exciting and, so far, successful political project since the founding and consolidation of the United States of America, if not of all time.

This book, by an astute non-European observer, uses this unprecedented, extraordinary experience as the centrepiece of a carefully crafted theory on the construction and maintenance of peace and prosperity on a global scale.
It is my hope that many non-Europeans will use it as a source of inspiration as they attempt to carve out long-lasting peace in other parts of the world.

It is my hope furthermore that the overarching message of this book will be heard by Europeans and that they too will use it as an opportunity to reflect on the long list of unprecedented achievements of this Union they have built, from trust and peace among nations, economic truce and open borders to permanent dialogue and multiculturalism.
Many of these achievements are taken for granted nowadays, especially by so-called 'sovereignists' and nationalists. But make no mistake. They can subside and indeed they will, if the construction of Europe comes to a halt.

Bob Kagan was right to point out that, historically, Europe's Kantian project of perpetual peace among member states was facilitated by America's more Hobbesian worldview. But now it is up to Europe to assume full responsibility for its heritage.

Some seem to think that too much Europe has hurt, has brought Europe to its knees. To the contrary, it is not enough Europe that is putting all these achievements at risk today. What we call the refugee crisis would not be one if each European nation were welcoming its fair share of refugees.

What can be done to infuse or restore the sense of shared identity and destiny that seems to be increasingly lacking among Europeans these days?

This, surely, must be the single most important question European leaders should be asking themselves. Indeed, it is the only one worth asking these days.

José Ramos-Horta is a Nobel Peace Prize Laureate (1996). Between 2001 and 2012 his roles in Timor-Leste included Senior Minister and Minister for Foreign Affairs, Minister of Defence, President and Prime Minister. He was Chair of the High Level Independent Panel on UN Peace Operations from 2014-15; Co-Chair of the Independent Commission on Multilateralism at the International Peace Institute in New York (2015-16); and Under-Secretary-General, Special Representative and Head of the UN Integrated Peace Building Office in Guinea-Bissau (UNIOBIS) (2013-14).

Introduction –
An idea whose time has come

The United Kingdom, one of the European Union's largest and most important members, announced an in-out referendum vote on EU membership to take place in June 2016. Many, perhaps a majority, of British citizens wish to see the EU as little more than a trading bloc. Their government has promised to negotiate looser ties.

In the eyes of its opponents, Brussels is an ineffectual, overstaffed and overpaid bureaucracy, a 'gravy train' that exists only for the benefit of its hirelings, Eurocrats who scheme endlessly to strip powers from member states. All the while, migration across the EU serves only the interests of mendicant Eastern Europeans, blighting the countries to which they move.

These accusations, found across the continent, have created a surge in support for anti-EU and anti-immigration parties across Europe. Efforts to counter such rhetoric have tended to swing on economic arguments that not everyone finds convincing or comprehensible. In the process, a wider point has gone ignored.

Peace and prosperity go hand in hand. This much is known. It is curious that so much intellectual energy is devoted to studying the causes of prosperity, when so little is devoted to understanding the causes of peace. When peace is established, prosperity tends to take care of itself.

Famously, peace does not mean just the absence of war. A society is at peace only when its motives for war are gone. How to achieve this state is the most fundamental question faced by humankind.

This book answers that question.

It argues in Chapters 1 and 2 that wars and militarism make humanity less safe rather than protecting us. It takes as its example what historically has been the planet's most violent continent – Europe. Today, this historical truth is almost forgotten, a testament to the remarkable change in Europe's inter-state relations after 1945. Until that point, war was a perpetual fact of European life. What changed?

Put simply, European countries systematically cancelled their own motives for war. They understood that war has causes, and that these causes can be identified and managed intelligently before they reach critical mass. Chapters 1 and 2 dispense with alternative explanations for peace, such as the threat of mutually assured destruction or the security 'guarantee' provided by NATO and the US. Instead, it identifies the 10 mechanisms that dispelled Europe's internal belligerence:

Enshrined Democracy and Rule of Law
Economic Truce
Open Borders and Human Ties
Soft Power and Shared Values
Permanent Discussion, Dialogue and Diplomacy
Financial Incentives and Support
Veto and Consensus Building
Resistance to External Interference
Rules, Human Rights and Multiculturalism
Mutual Trust and Peaceful Coexistence

It is possible to give specific examples of how these 10 factors prevented inter-state conflict during the latter half of the 20th century by defusing European flashpoints. These included the territorial dispute between Spain and the UK over Gibraltar; the dispute between the UK and Ireland over the six counties of Ulster; and the secessionist movements in Scotland, Spain and Belgium.

The framework that delivered these 10 mechanisms is today known as the European Union. The EU grew out of smaller and less ambitious regional bodies such as the European Coal and Steel Community (ECSC) and then the European Economic Community (EEC). The 10 principles of peaceful co-existence accreted around these structures within a few decades.

The EU ensures that its members co-operate peacefully. The ECSC and EEC were founded on the principle that tying former arch-enemies together economically would bring about their reconciliation. Today's EU is not perfect, but it represents the most successful experiment in international co-operation.

It is possible to export the European model of regional integration as a means of securing peace elsewhere. At present, there is a system of sovereign states which generally works well in looking after the interests of its own country and its citizens. International relationships are less stable, however, and they often descend into violent conflicts.

The need is pressing. The second half of the 20th century began as a bi-polar contest between two superpowers, and ended with one superpower, the US, as global leader. The 21st century, however, has ushered in a multi-polar world. Every continent and subcontinent will demand an equal voice with the US and the EU. How can this enormous, destabilizing shift be managed peacefully?

Competition between superpowers risks a nuclear war. The US, China, India, Russia, Brazil and the EU cannot be the six corners of a new Cold War. Excluding from global power the roughly two billion people who live outside the 'giants' is unjust. They risk becoming the victims of proxy wars fought between the giants, of the kind that peppered the latter 20th century. This dynamic has already plunged Ukraine into civil conflict. Parts of Africa and the Middle East are on fire and under the grip of proxy wars.

The answer is to replicate Western Europe's 10 pro-peace factors on other continents. A new regionalism is required to ensure that large neighbours live harmoniously alongside smaller ones. This book examines the progress being made towards EU-like institutions in Africa, North and South America, Asia, Oceania and the Middle East. It finds that regionalism is already well-established on some continents, but that in others its absence is feeding directly into violence. In some, Samuel Huntington's 'clash of civilizations' concept has become a self-fulfilling prophesy. The book explores the ever-growing conflict between Islam and the West and how it can be tackled.

Africa has already made strides. Chapter 3 illustrates how the African Union (AU) has reduced the scope for the kind of military coup that so blighted the continent's post-independence history, by shunning those leaders who seize power by force. The AU has also become a conduit for the sharing of knowledge between African countries and the creation of infrastructure for mutual prosperity, such as Ethiopia's giant renaissance dam. The block has also been instrumental in preventing Egypt's opposition to that project from descending into war.

Asia is a continent like no other, comprising half of humanity and being best understood not as a unit but as three sub-continents: those of South Asia, South-East Asia, and Confucian cultures surrounding China. It is on these sub-continents that experiments with regional union are now being overlaid. The Association of South-East Asian Nations (ASEAN) is easily the most successful, as explored in Chapter 4. Integrating giants such as India and China poses a knottier problem.

South America, quietly and outside the global spotlight, has achieved even more. Chapter 5 demonstrates how the body known as UNASUR is emerging as a strong and credible regional union that will soon allow the continent to speak with a single voice. Given South America's troubled history with the US, equalizing that relationship is likely to reap dividends for both sides.

Surprisingly, North America, discussed in Chapter 6, is itself still experimenting with its own regional unions. The provincial model offered by Canada is one from which the US and Europe can learn. Canada has retained a provincial autonomy that has mostly been lost in the US, where the federal government has accumulated vast power relative to the states. This slide back from federalism into a unitary super-state is a major driver of violence and militarism in the US, with inefficient and militaristic central solutions being imposed from Washington DC. The country is in urgent need of a federal revival, to ensure that local problems find local remedies.

Australasia, in Chapter 7, presents a daunting challenge to efforts towards regional unity. There is no more diverse region on earth: by some measures Australians are the world's wealthiest nation, but they share their continent with cultures little changed since the Bronze Age. Forging a regional union that accommodates those cultural differences is the only sure way of preventing conflicts of the kind seen in Timor-Leste (East Timor) and Papua New Guinea.

The Middle East is already wracked by those who seek to impose regional unity at the point of a gun. Those fighting for an Islamic State, or Caliphate, draw upon a very real desire among the Muslim faithful for unity, in order to create a strong state able to resist the malign influence of the Western powers who, for so long, have supported dictators across the Middle East, West Asia and North Africa. Those dictators now face a choice: either fulfil this desire towards Muslim unity through peaceful channels, or face oblivion at the hands of the expanding pro-Caliphate movement. All this is discussed in Chapter 8, devoted to Islam and the Middle East.

In Chapter 9, the book also explores the exorbitant privilege created by the current international system, creating inequality and economic injustice which are detrimental to global peace. The world of financial systems is tilted towards wealthy US and Western countries. For lasting peace, a new international order needs to break the shackles of neo-colonialism, political tyranny, economic exploitation and financial speculation in which income, resources and opportunities are justly distributed between and within countries.

In this regard, the emergence of the BRICS (Brazil, Russia, India, China and South Africa) group of countries is a welcome addition to the international scene. It can act as a force for good, ending the unilateralism of the US and EU, opening a level playing field for developing countries. Rather than superpower rivalry and Cold Wars, however, the BRICS, like the US and the EU, have a responsibility to lead in the creation of EU-like regional structures that give a voice to all humanity, not just those lucky enough to be born within the largest states.

Chapter 10 – The Anglo-Paradox – examines the vast internal and external threats now facing the European Union. It locates these in the EU's continued willingness to act not in its own interests, but as a strategic device of the US-led NATO, rushing in to 'capture' territory in Eastern Europe from Putin's Russia. This over-hasty growth has led Russia once again to view the West as a rival, not a friend. It has also created vast inequalities within the EU, resulting in unmanageable population flows and a surge of rightwing resistance to European integration.

The book concludes with support of the European Union against its critics. It argues that whatever the troubles of the Eurozone, peace is a necessary foundation for prosperity and that economic arguments against the EU will always fall at this hurdle. Acknowledging the union's difficulties, it suggests new ways in which the EU can overcome its growing pains and Euroscepticism in general, by adopting a new, demilitarized strategic approach to expansion and internal migration.

The positive benefits of the longest period of peace in Europe's history should be evident to EU citizens. They enjoy the fruits of a prosperity achieved through greater economic co-operation, trade, and the free flow of goods, services, people and capital across borders. Never before have Europeans as a whole been able to look at each other as on the same team.

None of this is to say that the EU faces a smooth future. On the contrary, if it is to survive and prosper, the union must detach itself from US strategic imperatives. So too must every similar project. The 21st century will be an era of multi-polarity, but it cannot be defined by a new superpower struggle without risking the future of humanity itself. Instead, the spread of EU-like regional unions, working amicably within a reformed UN, is the last, best hope for peace in our time. For peace, the critical aim must therefore be to ensure that the new international system does not degenerate into a new superpower competition, with smaller countries as mere pawns. Instead, the continents must unite around those same 10 principles that brought peace to Europe. Only then will humankind's capacity for conflict be finally contained.

Chapter 1 – Uniting for Peace

This chapter assesses the sudden decline of inter-state war in Europe after 1945. It considers and refutes common explanations such as cultural change, the influence of NATO and the threat of mutually assured destruction. Instead, it identifies 10 specific mechanisms that pre-empted war and thus created a permanent peace. These institutions are today administered by the European Union, which plays a vital but generally unheralded role in upholding Europe's 21st-century peace.

In the summer of 1814, as British forces burnt down the White House on one continent, and exiled the French emperor Napoleon Bonaparte on another, Norwegian insurgents were rallying against their Swedish masters. Earlier that year, Norway had fallen under the control of the powerful Swedish king after the Danes, Norway's former masters, made the mistake of siding with the defeated Bonaparte.

The Napoleonic Wars entangled countries such as Norway and Sweden, as well as Switzerland and the Netherlands, which today are bywords for liberal peacefulness. They were part of a continuum of war between England and France that stretched far into the past. Multiple Anglo-French conflicts marked each and every century after the Norman conquest of England in 1066. The cycle only ended after Napoleon's defeat, as France and Britain shifted to wars of colonial expansion.

The Norwegian rebels were led by Prince Christian Frederik. He rallied insurgents in the Gudbrandsdalen valley and the Dovre mountains, before convening an assembly to write a constitution for an independent Norway. That assembly elected him king, and he set about seeking allies among the Great Powers of Europe in a desperate attempt to find a protector against Sweden's overbearing military might.

It was to no avail. That summer, as the first steam train entered service in England and Beethoven premiered his 8th Symphony in Vienna, the powerful Swedes crushed

Norway's independence revolt. The Swedes had no intention of relinquishing more territory. Five years earlier, they had themselves suffered defeat in war, losing the eastern third of their territory to the newly autonomous Finland, a country which now existed within the confines of the Russian empire. Later, in 1918, Finland would fight its own bitter civil war between Russian-backed communists and German-backed conservatives. Around one per cent of Finns would perish in that conflict, many in appalling conditions.[1]

Sweden's victory over Norway was not to last. In 1905, the year that Albert Einstein published his theory of relativity and Teddy Roosevelt entered the White House, Norway's parliament again declared independence and readied for battle. Thousands of heavily armed Swedish troops mobilized at the border. Norway placed its navy on a war-footing. Germany's emperor suggested that the Swedes should strike down the Norwegians 'with a fist of iron'.

The crisis gripped the international media. In Great Britain, *The Spectator* reported the situation with the same chilly analytical remove that marks the reporting of foreign wars today; Norway, it said, was internally homogeneous and had little loyalty to Sweden's ruling Bernadotte dynasty, but the newspaper cast doubt on the country's ability to operate independently, without Swedish military protection.[2]

In the US, the *Chicago Tribune* covered the crisis in great detail.[3] It reported that Norwegian-Americans were in full sympathy with the separatists. It speculated that the reason Norway was able to declare independence was because at the time, Russia was fighting – and losing – a war with Japan in the Far East. This was the first time an Asian power would defeat a European one.[4]

All this was soon crowded from memory by the two world wars. Today, Scandinavia is so renowned for its stability as to make the very idea of 'Norwegian insurgents' mildly amusing, even though the events of 1905 fall only just outside living memory, and even though such Norwegian rebels also fought the Nazi-backed regime of Vidkun Quisling in the 1940s.

Modern Europeans struggle to comprehend quite how violent their past really was. A complacency has crept in. Younger generations assume that peace in Europe is a natural state of affairs, one that needs no work to be sustained.

This book argues the opposite. It argues that without constant maintenance, peace collapses quickly into war. That far from the world being safer than in times past, it is at very great risk of its most destructive conflict, and that the complacency surrounding the nature of peace is a critical factor in this risk. It argues that peace, to be permanent, relies on the kind of regional institutions erected after the Second World War.

Today, these institutions are consolidated in the European Union. Its regional integration mirrors a much older concept, that of federalism. The concepts are closely related. A federation ensures the political stability of large countries by devolving powers to constituent states. Regionalism is the same process in reverse: independent states pool their sovereignty in order to create peace and prosperity through a commonwealth and a union.

After the Second World War, humanity's minds were focused on how to prevent a conflict of that scale breaking out for a third time. The advent of nuclear weapons lent a terrified urgency to the debate. In 1947, the World Federalist Movement was formed from long-established civil-society groups to advocate for a new international system that strengthened common structures along federal lines.

Its animating rationale was the idea that humankind could not survive another world war. Two years previously, atomic bombs had destroyed entire Japanese cities – and they were small devices compared to those in development. The limitation of national sovereignty to prevent nuclear war was a founding principle of the movement. In the words of US President Woodrow Wilson:

There must be, not a balance of power, but a community of power; not organized rivalries, but an organized common peace.[5]

Such powerful support was not to last. As the public became habituated to the idea of nuclear arsenals, a complacency set in. Today, the risk of nuclear war is rarely discussed, and when it is, it is dismissed as unlikely. Even as recently as the 1980s, few were so sanguine. Nuclear apocalypse was a common theme of novels, songs and films. The campaign for nuclear disarmament was front-page news, illustrated by the University of Chicago's Doomsday Clock. Today, there is near-silence.

Yet viewed rationally, the threat is greater today than it was in the 1980s. The US and Russian nuclear stockpiles are smaller than they once were, but they are still easily enough to destroy every major city in the northern hemisphere. Politically, the situation is far less stable. The old Soviet Communist Party, a gerontocracy with its own mechanism for replacing leaders, is gone. Today's Russia is led by Vladimir Putin, a relatively young man who has controlled Russia since 1999, longer than any Soviet leader except Brezhnev or Stalin.

Russia and the US are declining powers, with little hope of recovering their 20th-century supremacy. Given Russia's shrinking population, a nuclear war would be proportionally more devastating for the urbanized and prosperous US and EU; it would 'level the playing field'. That Putin considers such a conflict to be a viable possibility was attested by his opposition to a planned US anti-missile shield in Eastern Europe; in 2007, Russia responded by testing missiles with multiple warheads designed to beat the system.[6] Sabre-rattling by NATO and neo-conservatives in the US and Europe has damaged relations with Russia still further, and has also damaged hopes for nuclear disarmament – for pro-bomb leaders in the West, Russia is a useful pretext for retaining these weapons of mass destruction.[7]

Nuclear war is no less realistic today than it was in 1969 or 1989, and it is arguably more so. The number of countries with nuclear weapons has increased, with warheads spreading to troubled nations such as Pakistan and North Korea. China has proved it is possible to combine rapid economic growth with authoritarian politics, striking a blow to the spread of democracy in the process. It has vastly expanded its own military might. In the Middle East and North Africa, the entire system of nation-states shows signs of dissolution, amid widespread public disillusion with autocratic 'national' leaders. Unless new, stabilizing factors come to the fore, the world stands on the brink of chaos. It faces an era of drone warfare, national collapse, cyber attacks, polonium poisoning, and the hydra-like phenomenon of state-backed insurgency that combines with the threat posed by non-state actors such as Boko Haram, al-Qaeda, the Taliban and the Islamic State. This is why the creation of new regional unions has become so important. As Europe has demonstrated, such unions are the surest path to lasting peace.

The EU and its predecessors, beginning with the European Coal and Steel Community in 1951, created a legal framework inside to align the interests of its members. This unglamorous, often dull work served to eliminate the competition over territory and resources that propelled the era of European imperial expansion. It created a commonwealth, allowing the warlike European states to pool their available resources for mutual benefit.

There is plenty of evidence that EU membership acts as a brake on potential conflicts. It is a mistake to believe that no flashpoints exist in Europe. There are still territorial disputes between Austria and Italy over the latter's German-speaking South Tyrol region, or Portugal's claim to Spanish-held Olivença, or between Spain and the UK over the status of Gibraltar, or between London and Dublin over the status of Northern Ireland. Separatist movements operate, mostly peacefully, in many EU countries. In previous centuries, war was a frequent outcome of such disputes.

Evidence of the EU's pro-peace influence in Gibraltar, part of Spain captured by Britain in 1704, is particularly strong. The regional union acts as a 'referee' between Britain and Spain on questions of law.[8] It pressures them into de-escalating any planned reprisals against one another.[9] It ensures Gibraltar's economic survival by enforcing free trade with Spain while also 'softening' the disputed border.[10] The EU acts as a forum in which the two sides can frequently air their grievances and negotiate with one another. Perhaps most importantly, the EU ensures that bilateral relations between Spain and the UK are so broad and dense that armed conflict would inflict acute disruption to both sides.

Courtesy of the EU's liberalization of travel and rights of residence, more than one million Britons live in Spain, bringing their skills and pensions into its economy. Hundreds of thousands of Spanish nationals reside in the UK. These factors mitigate against armed confrontation by ensuring economic interdependence and reminding the parties of each other's humanity, as an everyday fact rather than a theoretical abstraction. By contrast, the outbreak of the Falklands War between the UK and Argentina in 1982 demonstrated how such small territories can become a *casus belli* between countries with little to bind them.

Northern Ireland offers another important example of the EU's pacifying influence. There, voting patterns run along confessional lines, to the benefit of the Protestant majority. For decades this eroded the civil rights of the North's large Catholic minority, which identified more with the Republic of Ireland than with the British state. Violence inflicted by the Irish Republican Army (IRA) in pursuit of a united Ireland stoked bloody reprisals by the British army and Protestant paramilitary organizations. The province became militarized.

Yet by the turn of the millennium, it was hard to see what the IRA was fighting for. The EU's pursuit of 'ever closer union' increased the freedom of the Irish, Northern and Southern, to live and work wherever they pleased on the island, or indeed further afield. Customs checks on the border ended in 1993 as a result of the European common market (even during the Troubles, cross-border movement was freer than in the rest of Europe).

Twenty years later, anyone wishing to move across the border for business or leisure faced very few obstacles. Most large shops in Northern Ireland accepted Euro banknotes as well as Sterling, and citizens of the Irish Republic who wished to work in the UK could do so in virtually any capacity; some even enlisted with the British army.[11] The EU played a major role in bringing this about.

Katy Hayward, a sociologist and borders expert at Queen's University Belfast, noted that the transformation of the Irish border was 'integrally connected' to the role of the EU.[12] A 1984 report submitted to the European Community by rapporteur Niels Haagerup found that, contrary to some assumptions, the conflict was driven primarily not by the Protestant-Catholic divide, but by conflicting *national* identities.[13] He noted that the IRA, denounced by the Catholic Church, actually had a 'vaguely Marxist position'.

Haagerup's recommendation was for the EEC to focus on improving Ireland's economy on both sides of the border. The chances of the British and Irish governments combining to do so were bleak, at that point: as Hayward notes, their frosty relationship continued after the UK's accession to the EEC in 1973, with the Irish government portraying European unity as a precursor to a united Irish state.

However, rather than entrenching separation, the two governments' common EEC and later EU membership meant that they 'came to identify and build on common ground in many policy areas'. This, Hayward noted, was 'largely a consequence of the normal functioning of the EU's institutions rather than any particular EU effort'. Put another way, the British and Irish had so many shared interests that they inevitably became partners within a European setting.

A second strand of Haagerup's recommendations, regarding poverty, was also important. The EU poured money into Ireland to reduce the poverty that, as elsewhere in the world, fed violence by limiting economic opportunities. Between 1995 and 2013, the three EU PEACE Programmes poured over two billion Euros into the six counties of Ulster alone.[14] From being among the poorest parts of Europe when Haagerup wrote his report, three decades later Northern Ireland was relatively wealthy.[15]

The EU received little credit for its role in Ireland's peace. The media tended to emphasize the mediation of US President Bill Clinton, and his close partnership with UK Prime Minister Tony Blair. They were charismatic figures, whereas the EU's influence did not have an individual human face. But without its financial support, and the transformation it brought about in Anglo-Irish relations, the Good Friday Agreement of 1998 would never have come to pass.

The EU's practical role in securing peace can be broken down into the following 10 mechanisms:

1. Enshrined Democracy and Rule of Law

First and foremost, the EU maintains democratic standards. To become a member, a country must elect its governments, and those governments must operate according to the rule of law. Leaders are held accountable to their own statutes, by independent judges. Backsliding is punished.

Countries such as Spain, Portugal and Greece were military dictatorships until as recently as the mid-1970s, and it was only after they returned to civilian rule that they were permitted into the EU (then the EEC), an objective which in Portugal, for one, became a touchstone of unity between otherwise disparate civilian parties.

Research by Philip Levitz at Princeton University found that the prospect of EU membership not only fostered democracy in post-Soviet Eastern Europe but also bolstered post-membership mechanisms to ensure there was no backsliding into autocracy. These included conditional EU financing and 'peer pressure' from existing members.

Full democracy still eludes even the EU, in the sense of fully inclusive, representative, responsive and accountable governance of the people, by the people. Further work is needed to achieve non-corrupt electoral democracy and to prevent control of governments by business interests, while neutralizing excesses of state power. Yet even imperfect democracy is the indispensable underpinning of peace.

Democracy is one of Europe's shared values, traceable

back to ancient Greece. Shared values build on the common intellectual heritage of Europeans, accumulated over 3,000 years, that encompasses everything from Greek philosophy, the use of Latin as *lingua franca*, to the Reformation and the Enlightenment. The rise of Hollywood and US soft power in the 20th century sometimes distracted Europeans from their shared heritage, but the EU makes a conscious effort to remind them, for instance by nominating European capitals of culture.

2. Economic Truce

Democracy sets the conditions for the EU's second tier of pro-peace mechanisms. By forcing members to open their borders to trade, the EU ensures that disputed territories such as Gibraltar cannot be embargoed or otherwise pushed into the kind of desperate financial straits that force a war. Napoleon, for instance, imposed the so-called Continental Blockade on Britain from 1806-14.

'Truce' is an appropriate term. Even today, states weaponize the use of customs inspections and border tariffs. Such tactics can be seen in the battle between Russia and the EU for influence in Eastern Europe. Former Soviet countries that leant towards EU membership would suddenly find their key exports to Russia being embargoed on 'health grounds', a fate that befell Moldovan wine in November 2013.[16] Or they would see the previously beneficial terms of Russian gas imports shifted to a more punishing regime, as Armenia found in June of that year.[17] In Ukraine, Putin pulled both these levers, while also pledging extensive aid in return for its joining his new Eurasian Economic Union.[18] The Economic Truce condition can therefore be seen as a form of disarmament, by preventing trade controls being used as a weapon.

3. Open Borders and Human Ties

Thirdly, by opening borders, the EU blurs the lines between separate nations and disputed territories. It lessens the requirement for, say, the Northern Irish to identify exclusively either with Britain or with the Republic of Ireland. This reduces the need for governments to employ heavy-handed security methods to preserve national integrity.

Open borders also reduce the appeal of separatism. There is little chance of Catalan, Scottish or Flemish separatists resorting to armed insurrection, because they do not wish to exit the EU – they only wish to be 'independent' of Spain, Britain and Belgium respectively. In other words, they are not proposing to change life all that much. This lowers the political stakes considerably, in comparison to those many countries where separatism entails an entirely new system of rights and responsibilities, and where separatist militants fight the state.

Furthermore, by enabling the free flow of people as well as goods, the EU makes it difficult to demonize other nationalities with propaganda. Although the British and Spanish governments argue fiercely over Gibraltar, the human connections between the countries are so dense that resorting to war would be enormously disruptive to both sides, in a way that ordinary citizens of the countries would feel deeply.

4. Soft Power and Shared Values

The EU works to make Europeans feel more European. Standardizing the design of car number plates and passports, and by branding Europe with the blue and gold flag and the single currency, the EU encourages its citizens to identify with Europe and, thus, with one another.

Even the most hardened Eurosceptics tend to cheer for the European team in golf's Ryder Cup, and the Eurovision Song Contest is one of the most-watched non-sporting events in the world. Such events serve to encourage Europeans to think of themselves as a united group, rather than disparate tribes.

5. Permanent Discussion, Dialogue and Diplomacy

Mandatory participation in EU forums makes it very difficult for one member to sever diplomatic relations with another (a usual precursor to war). No matter how poor Greece's relations with Germany become, for instance, they will continue to interact in Brussels. This permanent framework also allows previously alienated member governments to discover interests they share with governments otherwise viewed as adversaries, as was the case between the UK and Ireland. Even the most contentious legislation surrounding territorial disputes, fishing quotas and agricultural subsidies are discussed in the European Parliament and decisions are taken in a peaceful manner.

6. Financial Incentives and Support

By collecting revenue from member states, the EU can concentrate financial resources on localized poverty of the type that contributed to violence in Northern Ireland. This is the case even when the governments of the affected states are at loggerheads. Crucially, however, member governments still retain enough fiscal power to address local and national spending priorities.

The money handed over to the EU goes towards funding development schemes, addressing social issues and research programmes across member states. Rather than challenging the cohesion of member states, EU regional spending actually strengthens them, by closing the gap between rich and poor regions. The EU has dedicated more than €30 billion to the development of southern Italy, for example, which lags far behind the industrialized north.[19] Ensuring some degree of regional equality prevents the poverty and inequality being exploited by violent political movements.

Econometrics also help to reduce the scope for discontent. The EU gathers statistical data on the prosperity of its members, producing comparative statistics that make it clear when one locality is falling behind. This heightens pressure on member states to ensure that they address regional disparities, and allows EU institutions to allocate their own funding.

Not all the financial decisions taken by EU members are conducive to peace. The group's wealth has encouraged EU members to spend huge amounts on their military budgets. Combined, the EU spends over €170 billion a year on its military, second to the US but much more than China, Russia, or India. The EU's military spend has fallen in recent years, but leaders are under heavy pressure from the US to spend more.

7. Veto and Consensus Building

Government policies that affect the union as a whole must be agreed at a European level. This need for consensus, although sometimes frustrating, prevents one member embarking on a political collision course with other members. It also prevents the agglomeration of strong factions or coalitions within the union of the kind that fought the First World War.

In the words of Anand Menon, Professor of European Politics and Foreign Affairs at King's College London:

Rather than being the all-powerful behemoth frequently alluded to by its critics, the European Union is a fragile – indeed perhaps uniquely fragile – political system. It relies on the consent of member states without whose acquiescence decisions would neither be taken nor implemented... The flip side of this is that member states decisively shape what the EU can and cannot do.[20]

8. Resistance to External Interference

The factors above impede any outside power from setting up or sponsoring proxy governments in member states. This prevents the kind of puppet dictators and monarchs that have torn apart much of the developing world, or the level of corruption and opacity that allows foreign intelligence agencies to buy the services of ministers and generals. The union's common financial mechanisms (Factor 6) also make it difficult for a China or US to buy the loyalty of member states with aid packages.

Historically, puppet states have been particularly prone to conflict and human rights abuses. Modern Iran, for instance, vets its political candidates before elections. One reason for this is that the US government has allocated $30 million for Iranian 'opposition groups'.[21] This is a considerable sum in any election campaign and could easily allow the CIA to 'buy' victory for its preferred Iranian candidates, discrediting genuine pro-democracy movements in the process. This gives Iran's government an excuse to deal violently with them, as it did during the country's 'colour revolution' of 2009.

It is a mistake to think that Western Europe is somehow immune to such behaviour. There is evidence that, during the 1970s, militant groups such as West Germany's Red Army Faction (the Baader-Meinhof gang), were infiltrated by the Stasi, communist East Germany's secret police.[22] Today, the infiltrators are more likely to be wealthy and rootless multinational corporations.

Such companies spend billions on lobbyists whose sole *raison d'être* is to influence elected officials in ways that do not reflect the will of the electorate. These corrupt tactics work best in small, financially weak states, where corporations can pay off politicians and then pollute and exploit their way to profit – a particular specialism of mining companies operating in the southern hemisphere. As we shall see, local responses to such pollution and disruption are often violent.

The EU helps prevent this state of affairs. Its sheer size, coupled with the need for cross-national consensus, makes it difficult for corporations to get what they want by paying off a few apex decision-makers. And because of the EU's size and importance, and indeed because of its necessarily slow machinery, its major decisions attract enormous levels of scrutiny. This allows for democratic objections to be raised in plenty of time, for instance to any free-trade deal in which corporations may try to weaken democratic controls.

9. Rules, Human Rights and Multiculturalism

The European Human Rights Act makes it difficult for governments to treat ethnic, religious or regional minorities so unfairly that they resort to violence. Such rebellions were once common in Europe. The Bohemian Revolt that sparked the Thirty Years War began with Protestants in what is today the Czech Republic rising up against the Catholic Holy Roman Empire, which they feared was about to crush their religious freedoms.[23]

In modern Europe, the legal sanctity of individual rights ensures that no such rebellions occur. Similarly, the standardization of working conditions and safety practices also served to prevent the violent discontent of previous centuries arising from class conflict. Historically, these have ranged in severity from the Paris commune and Luddite attacks on factories, to the French and Russian revolutions.

The EU, through its charter of fundamental rights and community spirit, fosters tolerance among its members. The shared values concept encourages secularism, peace, cosmopolitanism and multilateralism. Its multilateral organizations mediate between states and thus guarantee international law and establish respect and co-operation between people of diverse physical appearance, culture and belief systems, averting any hatred, division and conflicts.

There is also a learning function at play. Before standards and rules can be set, countries must examine each others' experiences to discover better ways of approaching problems. Such mutual learning serves to remind all concerned of the benefits of co-operation, in almost any field.

10. Mutual Trust and Peaceful Coexistence

The founding visionaries of the EU, who went through two of the deadliest wars in history, did not want their continent to descend again into war, destroying humanity and civilizations built over millennia. Mutual trust is the tenth and final factor and it is a by-product of the first nine, which have consolidated mutual trust between the member states.

This allows for innovations that would once have been unthinkable. Qualified Majority Voting (QMV), for instance, has weakened the veto power of governments in many areas, in a way that those governments would once have rejected. It established a virtuous circle, whereby QMV allows the first nine factors to be strengthened more readily, binding more tightly the strings that support the long European peace.

These 10 mechanisms are similar to those that nation-states

developed to avert internal conflicts. Europe's countries were themselves forged from smaller units. Germany only became a unified nation-state in 1871; before that, the Germanies were a weak association of princes, dukes, archdukes, bishops, and margraves under the Holy Roman Empire, which collapsed after its defeat by Napoleon's forces at Austerlitz. Later, under the leadership of the notoriously militaristic Prussians, the united Germany changed the balance of power in Europe, leading to the world wars of the 20th century.

Even more recently, the reunification of Germany in 1990 ended four decades of mutual suspicion and espionage. East German border guards were notorious for shooting their compatriots who tried to flee to West Germany across the Berlin Wall. The peaceful removal of this barrier, overseen by political giants Soviet President Mikhail Gorbachev and German Chancellor Helmut Kohl, was actually opposed by many Europeans who feared the consequences of a united Germany, including the leaders of France and Britain.[24] Today, however, such misgivings are mostly forgotten.

This urge to unite against the power of other nation-states propelled the creation of the current international system, but there were other factors at work. Faster communications – paved roads, railways, the telegraph and eventually the telephone and internet – allowed the administration of a much wider area, where once fiefdoms were small because they lacked the bureaucratic capacity to grow further.

All this demonstrates how the EEC and then the EU transformed Western Europe from being a particularly warlike region to a particularly peaceful one. Alternative explanations for the long peace exist, but they do not withstand scrutiny. One is the concept of mutually assured destruction (MAD): the idea that nuclear weapons provided a catastrophic deterrent to warfare in the 20th century. This deterrent operated within a Cold War context in which the US and the USSR operated as global 'police' who regulated the behaviour of states within their spheres of influence, such as the members of NATO and the Warsaw Pact.

It is an argument that does not hold water. The nuclear 'umbrella' failed to restrain those who wielded nuclear weapons. Far from the Cold War being 'cold', the nuclear-armed superpowers launched 'hot' wars in Korea, Vietnam, Afghanistan, Algeria, the Falkland Islands and Panama. They fought wars that were avoided by non-nuclear states such as the Netherlands, Spain, Portugal, Italy, Sweden and Austria.

When it was too dangerous for the US, Chinese and Soviets to fight each other directly, they sought out proxy wars in far-flung corners of the world. The Soviets funnelled guns and Cuban troops to Angola's MPLA.[25] The US used third parties to arm their UNITA rivals.[26] Hundreds of thousands of Angolan civilians died as a result. Nuclear weapons did not protect them. If anything, MAD made the world more dangerous for smaller countries, including those in Europe, by sucking in countries far removed from the actual belligerents.

A second argument is that a sort of cultural enlightenment took hold after the world wars. War became socially unacceptable. Violence diminished between states just as it diminished on the streets and in homes. Reaching for a weapon was no longer seen as an acceptable solution to any problem facing civilized peoples. The connection between masculinity and physical force has been severed, and feminine values are ascendant.

The trouble with this argument is that it overlooks the extraordinary growth in state violence, mass incarceration and coercion, even in the West. The newfound willingness of governments to secretly monitor, secretly try, secretly imprison and secretly torture anyone suspected of terrorism would shock a time traveller even from the mid-1990s. The 1993 film *In the Name of the Father* won multiple Oscars for depicting the British state's violation of a suspected Irish terrorist's human rights.

Yet by today's standards, in a world of black prisons, legal torture and Guantánamo Bay, the treatment of Irish prisoners such as the Guildford Four seems almost humane. One British Muslim was held in Guantánamo for nearly 14 years before being released. There has been no cultural enlightenment. If anything, the European public has become more callous, and more accepting of militarized security.

A third argument postulates that it was not the EU, but rather the spread of democracy that pacified the once warlike European continent. Electorates rarely, if ever, seek war with a neighbour; therefore, democratic governments likewise shun wars with other democracies due to their obeisance to popular opinion. Democratization has led to the popular (albeit now-defunct) notion that countries where you can buy a McDonald's burger do not wage war upon one another. By this rationale, the EU is irrelevant to Europe's peace.

Democracy is important to peace, but this argument overlooks the EU's vital role in securing Europe's democratization. The EU's support for democracy is just one of its many practical pro-peace functions.

It is true that technology has played a role in Europe's peace. Strong regional unions such as the EU were made possible by advances in communication and administration. Mass education, particularly in the fields of literacy and language, enabled civil servants to exchange information quickly and clearly through the new communication architecture. Computerized bureaucracy allowed records to be maintained and consulted with ease, reducing the scope for protracted misunderstanding or dispute. Cheap airfares reduced the cost of physically moving long distances.

Administration underwent a slow process of technical improvement. A central government's strength is closely connected to its ability to raise taxes, but efficient taxation turns on concepts such as percentages, which require a large body of people who understand what they are and how to calculate them. This requires education. Britain imposed its first income tax in 1799, as a temporary measure to fund the war against Napoleon. More complex taxes require even higher levels of general education; Britain did not introduce a value-added tax until 1973.

Progressive, sophisticated taxation allows governments to

collect revenue in a way that is fair and that does not skew the markets for certain goods. This increases prosperity and reduces popular resistance to sharing wealth between nations (though it does not eliminate it entirely, as we shall see later). These taxes support the bureaucratic infrastructure needed to govern continental-sized unions.

From a teleological perspective, the evolution of nation-states into regional unions has the air of historical inevitability. Many scholars locate the origins of sovereignty in the 17th-century Peace of Westphalia, the moment European states accepted the idea of non-interference in each others' affairs. By casting the protective net over a wider area, regional unions such as the EU bring a lasting peace to entire continents, ensuring that wars between Britain and France – once an inevitable feature of European life – are today no more likely than wars between Texas and Louisiana.

Herein lies a paradox. The continents most desperately in need of regional unity and the 10 peace-promoting mechanisms listed above are also those most lacking the administrative and communications capacity to build those unions. That situation is changing, however. As the UN's 2014 Human Development Report put it:

Most people in most countries have been doing steadily better in human development. Advances in technology, education and incomes hold ever-greater promise for longer, healthier, more secure lives. Globalization has on balance produced major human development gains, especially in many countries of the South.

As communication technology spreads, hand in hand with the educational resources needed for modern administration, so too does the scope for replicating Europe's peaceful experiment elsewhere. This book examines the prospects of EU-like structures being created in Africa, the Americas, Asia, Australasia and the Middle East, and how they might serve to end some of the bloodiest and most intractable conflicts facing the world today, while averting those of the future.

1 Sylvelin, Sini, 2004, 'The Victims of the Finnish Civil War', Finnish Institutions Research Paper, FAST Area Studies Program, Department of Translation Studies, University of Tampere. **2** Unknown author, 1905, 'The Future of Sweden and Norway', *The Spectator,* 3 June, archives. **3** Unknown author, 1905, 'Sweden Yields to Norway's Act', *Chicago Tribune,* 8 June. **4** Unknown author, 1905, 'Sweden Averts Danger of War', *Chicago Tribune,* 17 September. **5** Address to the Senate of the United States, 22 January 1917, 'A World League for Peace' **6** Stott, Michael, 2007, 'Russia tests new rocket to beat missile defenses', Reuters, 29 May. **7** Winchester, Levi, 2015, 'Putin 'will use nuclear blackmail on Britain' if Trident is scrapped, warns ex-ambassador', *Daily Express,* 25 April. **8** Unknown author, 2013, 'Spain's Gibraltar checks lawful – EU', BBC News, 15 November. **9** Doncel, Luis, 2013, 'Bruselas avisa a España que los controles a Gibraltar deben ser "proporcionados"', *El Pais,* 5 August. **10** Gonzalez, Miguel and Sevillano, Elena G, 2014, 'Las denuncias medioambientales contra Gibraltar no prosperan en Bruselas', 25 July. **11** Riegel, Ralph, 2013, 'Number of Irish recruits joining British Army is down by half', *Irish Independent,* 5 December. **12** Hayward, Katy, 2011, 'The EU and the transformation of the Irish border', Conciliation Resources, permanent URL: www.c-r.org/accord-article/eu-and-transformation-irish-border **13** Report on behalf of the Political Affairs Committee, 1984, European Parliament Working Documents, 19 March. **14** Potter, Michael and Egerton, Leigh, 2011, 'The EU PEACE and INTERREG Programmes in Northern Ireland', Research and Information Service Briefing Paper, Northern Ireland Assembly, 14 October. **15** Eurostat, Gross domestic product (GDP) per inhabitant, in purchasing power standard (PPS), by NUTS 2 regions, 2013 (% of the EU average, EU = 100) **16** TJ, 2013, 'Why has Russia banned Moldovan wine?', *The Economist,* 25 November. **17** Grigoryan, Marianna, 2013, 'Armenia: Could a Gas Price Hike Have Political Implications?', Eurasianet.org, 10 June. **18** Park, Jeanne, 2014, 'The European Union's Eastern Partnership', CFR Backgrounders, Council on Foreign Relations, 14 March. **19** EU Regional Policy press release, 'Bridging the divide between Italy's North and South: Commissioner Creţu in Calabria and Sicily', 24 April 2015. **20** Menon, Anand, 2015, 'The Five Things Everyone Should Know About the European Union', 8 April, www.socialeurope.eu/2015/04/the-five-things-everyone-should-know-about-the-european-union/ **21** Appropriations committee report to US Senate, S. Rept. 113-81 - DEPARTMENT OF STATE, FOREIGN OPERATIONS, AND RELATED PROGRAMS APPROPRIATIONS BILL, 2014 **22** Pidd, Helen, 2011, 'Baader-Meinhof terrorist may have worked for the Stasi', *The Guardian,* 1 August. **23** Ogilvie, Sheilagh, 1992, 'Germany and the Seventeenth Century Crisis', *The Historical Journal,* Cambridge University Press. **24** Interview with former French Foreign Minister Roland Dumas, *Der Spiegel,* 14 September 2009. **25** p144-50, Birmingham, David, *A History of Postcolonial Lusophone Africa,* ed. Chabal, Patrick, 2002, Indiana University Press. **26** p167, *ibid*

Chapter 2 – Team Europe (European Union)

An assessment of the criticisms levelled against the EU, weighed against the economic gains generated by the absence of armed conflict from 1945 onwards. Using historical economic analysis, this chapter demonstrates that the peace-prosperity binary is so significant as effectively to end the economic debate over the benefits or otherwise of EU membership. Without peace, there can be no prosperity.

The role of pan-European political institutions in the long peace after 1945 is not acknowledged by the European Union's many critics. All they would concede, by force of reason and fact, is that such institutions have not rendered Europe *more* prone to internecine war. They would argue that the 10 practical mechanisms listed in Chapter 1 made no difference to why Britain and Spain refrained from fighting over Gibraltar, or in reducing separatist violence in the Basque country and Northern Ireland, or preventing separatism elsewhere from escalating into insurgency, or sustaining democracy in post-communist Eastern Europe. They would maintain that the Nobel Peace Prize handed to the EU in 2012 was a biased and self-congratulatory gesture.

These critics locate the explanation for Europe's long peace not in shared institutions, but in the North Atlantic Treaty Organization (NATO) and the security blanket thrown over Western Europe by the US and its military. On hearing of the 2012 Nobel Prize, Britain's former foreign secretary Malcolm Rifkind said that NATO deserved it more, and that at the very least the two organizations should have shared the award.[1]

Rifkind's argument assumed that the communist Soviet Union posed the greatest security threat to Western Europe in the latter 20th century. It assumed that, had it not been for the NATO alliance, the Soviet Army would have invaded West Germany, France, Britain, Ireland, the Iberian peninsula, Italy,

Scandinavia, the Low Countries, Greece and the Mediterranean islands, either in a single grand manoeuvre or by picking off countries one at a time, while the others spectated. This Stalinist military sweep would have been achieved despite the Soviet Union's manpower shortages; it suffered proportionally more deaths in the Second World War than the wealthier and more populous countries of Western Europe.[2] The argument also supposes that the Soviet forces would have overcome resistance from the many millions of heavily armed, battle-hardened veterans of two World Wars, fighting on the ground, in their own countries, against Joseph Stalin's unattractive totalitarian regime. A type of resistance that the Nazis had been unable to crush.

Having subjugated Western Europe in a way that no previous Russian empire had done (or attempted), communism's victory would then be assured.

How plausible one finds this thesis is a matter of opinion. One cannot prove or disprove a counterfactual history. Declassified Soviet archives suggested that there were indeed plans for an invasion of Western Europe, but that these were only to be activated if NATO attacked Russia first.[3] Stalin, the most menacing of the Soviet leaders, died in 1956 and his successors were less expansionist. The Soviets' 1968 invasion of Czechoslovakia was to prevent an already-communist state from reforming, rather than to force communism on new European territory.

What is less debatable is that historically Western Europeans have posed a greater threat to each other than external forces have posed to them. European governments have inflicted more violence against European populations than any other force. So before worrying about Russia, it is important to explain why, by the time of the Cold War, Western Europeans no longer needed to worry about other Western Europeans.

The existence of NATO cannot explain why Western European governments refrained from fighting each other after 1945, to the point that today, such a conflict is highly implausible. NATO was geared towards the external threat, not towards internal harmony. This was equally true of the Warsaw Pact, NATO's Eastern Bloc counterpart. The Soviet Union invaded Czechoslovakia despite both being Pact signatories. Hungary, invaded by the Soviets in 1956, was also a member.

Likewise, NATO's charter explicitly included French Algeria within its collective defence. This did not prevent a brutal war between French forces and Algerian nationalists in the 1950s and 1960s, nor the military-inspired collapse of the French Fourth Republic in 1958. NATO membership did not deter Britain and France from invading Egypt during the Suez Crisis of 1956, despite the opposition of other members, including the US, and even though Article 1 of the NATO charter requires members to seek peaceful resolution to such disputes.

France, one of Europe's leading powers, quit NATO's military joint command in 1966 and expelled foreign troops from its territory. Europe did not become more conflict prone as a result. If anything, France became less so. It disentangled from Vietnam just as the US entangled itself, and it avoided the kind of colonial-style war that the British fought in the South Atlantic in 1982, even though the French military often intervened in its former African colonies.

There was clearly more to Europe's peace than NATO. What was it? One clue was offered by the words of British Prime Minister Neville Chamberlain, two days before he led Britain into the Second World War:

We have no quarrel with the German people, except that they allow themselves to be governed by a Nazi government.

Chamberlain is often derided as a failed peacemaker who gave way to Winston Churchill. Yet his words contained a truth that should be axiomatic. Wars are waged not by peoples but by the governments that represent them – and represent them only imperfectly, if at all. Peace, therefore, rests on governments co-operating with one another.

NATO's charter recognized this. Article 2 required that

members develop peaceful and friendly international relations by strengthening their free institutions, bringing about a better understanding of the principles upon which these institutions are founded, and promoting conditions of stability and well-being. They must seek to eliminate conflict in their international economic policies and encourage economic collaboration between any or all member countries.

These laudable aims could not be achieved by NATO or any other military alliance, however. It was not NATO that drove Europe's institutional alignment and economic integration, but the European Coal and Steel Community, and then the European Economic Community, and finally the European Union. These were the bodies that eliminated the sources of recrimination that hitherto found violent expression between European states.

Such pan-European institutions were critical to the seven decades of peace that followed 8 May 1945 – Victory in Europe Day. Governments were bound by mechanisms that prevented them from manoeuvring against one another. Seventy years is a short interval in human history, but intra-European wars until that point were so frequent that it marks a significant achievement. Countries which today are viewed as bastions of progressive social democracy were anything but, historically speaking.

EU influence

The EU is best described as a team. Its members are peers, not necessarily in terms of their size or wealth, but in the sense that there are no ruling or subordinate races. It is a union of equal citizens. In North America, Hispanics are often depicted as a struggling ethnic minority, fighting for acceptance. Europe's Hispanic nations of Spain and Portugal suffer no equivalent stigma in the EU.

The team grows by consent and consensus-building, and by using the power of its example to attract new members. Enshrined Democracy, the first and foremost of our 10 mechanisms, is the only political system the EU tolerates.

EU member states score highly on international measures of respect for human rights[4] and legal due-process[5], corruption[6], and the protection of workers[7] and the environment.[8] Again, these are all attributable to the primacy of the 10 mechanisms. Beyond its borders, the EU's influence spreads via standardization and formalization, by setting benchmarks the rest of the world eventually accepts through sheer public demand for brands as strong as IKEA, Rolls-Royce, Champagne or Lego.

The EU's critics, Russia included, have derided the EU as an imperial project. Russia viewed the EU's growth through the prism of its own imperialist history. In 2007, the chief of the European Commission, José Manuel Barroso, acknowledged the comparison with an empire, but he made a crucial distinction.[9] The EU was an empire without imperialism. Its ruling ideology was one not of imperial expansionism, but of standardization; meeting the standards set by the rest of the team was the condition of entry.

Empires expand by force of arms and operate under the direction of a central authority. The empires operated in the recent past by Britain and France, Belgium and the Netherlands, Japan and the Soviet Union, incorporated their constituents most often by brute force. They violated human rights with impunity. Their competing imperial ambitions culminated in the two World Wars.

Smaller nations looked at the EU and realized that being subsumed into a regional union did not mean being dominated by their neighbours. They saw instead an opportunity to pool some of their sovereignty, but also, if anything, to exert more regional influence, rather than less. The accession of Eastern European states expressly reflected the collective will of their inhabitants, unlike their previous membership of Comecon or the Warsaw Pact.

Of course, Eurosceptics do not accept this argument. They argue that smaller European countries are in fact being dominated by larger EU states. In November 2011, Nigel Farage, the leader of the UK Independence Party, claimed that Europeans were living in 'a German-dominated Europe', something which he noted 'this European Union was supposed to stop'. He argued that the EU had, in effect, ousted the elected governments of Greece and Italy and replaced them with 'puppets'. Germany, by his account, was playing the same role in the EU that Russia had played in the old Soviet Union and was now playing in the new Eurasian Economic Union (EEU).

Within a few months, events would demonstrate the inaccuracy of the 'German dominance' theory. Italy's 'puppet' leader was soon replaced by the elected Matteo Renzi. Greece's 'puppet' leader was replaced by the elected Antonis Samaras and then by the far-Left Syriza party, which actively sought confrontation with Germany over Greek debts. Syriza went so far as to demand hundreds of billions of Euros in reparations for the German occupation of Greece during World War Two.

Germany does not loom over its neighbours. In terms of its physical size, even the reunified Germany is only 56 per cent the area of France. It is physically smaller than Spain or Sweden. Germany has the largest population of any EU member state, at roughly 80 million, but as a proportion of the EU's entire headcount the Germans make up only 11 per cent. It represents about 20 per cent of the EU economy,[10] which makes it the EU's leading economic power, but in terms of military power and foreign influence it is eclipsed by France and the UK.

By contrast, Soviet Russia dwarfed all the other members of the Warsaw Pact and Comecon in its physical, industrial and human scale. Economic figures for the Soviet Union are unreliable, but those that exist support this assumption.[11] The EU does not face the challenges of incorporating into its union a country the size of Russia, or the US, China, India, Brazil or even Nigeria. Convincing smaller neighbours that they can work as equals with such giants, within the context of an EU-like regional integration, is one of the main challenges to the creation of similar entities worldwide.

Germany's relative influence within the EU tends to grow when economic problems come to the fore. In the years following the 2008 financial crisis, one politician after another denounced Germany's supposedly overbearing role in healing the economic wounds. Serious commentators put pen to paper to question whether Germany was once again the 'greatest threat to Europe'.[12]

Nevertheless, there was some confusion among Eurosceptics on this point. Before the crisis, it was common to hear accusations that the EU was, in fact, dominated by France. France's central location, its cultural *savoir-faire* and its enthusiasm for the EU project made it the leader of the pack. Critics would complain that French farmers were the greatest beneficiaries of the Common Agricultural Policy, which France managed to preserve despite the objections of other large EU members.

A third group claimed, by way of compromise, that a Franco-German 'axis' dominated the EU. They carefully overlooked the frequent disagreements between France and Germany. These included spats over who pays for the common banking union, a serious division on whether to impose sanctions against Chinese solar-panel exporters, and a failure to co-operate on industrial and defence manufacturing.[13] Energy policy is a source of fundamental division in this so-called 'axis'. France is among the world's leading exponents of nuclear-energy technology; Germany is the world's leading critic of nuclear energy and has committed to phase out all its nuclear energy by 2022.

In reality, the EU's Veto and Consensus function ensures that neither Germany nor France carries a whip-hand in Europe. Jonathan Golub of the London School of Economics studied legislation passed by the European Parliament between 1996 and 2001 to assess which countries encountered the most success in having their priorities acted upon.[14] His findings suggested that France and Germany fared poorly in this regard, even though they were both large net contributors to the EU budget. Rather, it was countries such as Finland, Sweden and Luxembourg whose arguments tended to win the day. The UK, another large net contributor, performed better than either the Germans or the French.

Golub's research suggests that the EU has championed the interests of smaller members against those of the largest and richest, as well as transferring wealth from the richer net contributors to the poorer, smaller countries. In return, all members receive access to a giant common market in which trading across borders has, according to everyone involved in business, become radically easier over the past 30 years. Far from being subjugated, smaller countries clearly had a strong incentive to sign up to the European project.

The NATO effect and relations with Russia

NATO was not the force driving this peaceful, equitable integration. The question now is whether that military alliance, far from rescuing Europe, is actually endangering it. NATO's greatest rival, the Warsaw Pact, disbanded in 1991. NATO, however, did not. On the contrary, the alliance, led by the US, continued its relentless efforts to outmatch Russia militarily, to build anti-missile systems in Eastern Europe, to isolate Russia diplomatically and to impose ruinous financial experiments.

In the 1990s, Russia and Eastern Europe lurched out of communism and into capitalism. At first, it seemed that a new era had dawned. The launch of the International Space Station in 1998 was a moving symbol of how the West and Russia could work in harmony. Communism was buried. Under the chaotic presidency of Boris Yeltsin, and at the urging of a 38-year-old US economist named Jeffrey Sachs, Russia subjected itself to free-market 'shock therapy', demolishing the communist apparatus and ignoring many who advocated a gradualist approach.[15] The result was to create a handful of murky Russian billionaires, and to plunge the rest of Russia into destitution.

NATO, far from disbanding, exploited this turmoil. It absorbed former Eastern Bloc countries such as Albania, Bulgaria, Poland and Estonia. The US lobbied the EU to expand eastwards as rapidly as possible, to suck countries from

Russia's orbit. Internally, the entry of much poorer post-Soviet countries created predictably massive surges of migration across the EU. Externally, Russia, which throughout the 1990s seemed reconciled to rejoining the West, once more viewed NATO as an existential threat. The gap between the desires of governments and peoples was widening. And, as history has often showed, it is in this gap that wars begin.

Russia began to view with suspicion and then alarm the rapid eastwards spread of NATO and the EU. By 2014, the EU had absorbed nine countries that were formerly members of the Russian-led Council for Mutual Economic Assistance, or Comecon (see Figures 1 and 2, below). Several more had signed or were negotiating accession agreements to put them on the path towards EU membership. President Vladimir Putin watched the defection, into the orbit of his former Western enemies, of countries he had grown up with as part of the

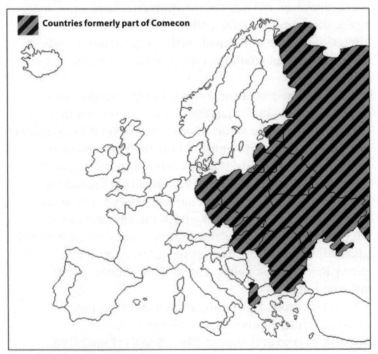

Figure 1: The strategic picture in 1987

Russian-led Soviet Empire.

The EU had an economy almost 10 times the size of Russia's, with the option of adding new countries to enlarge it still further. Although Russia committed more of its economic output to defence spending, in absolute terms the EU outspent it on defence[16] – even though many EU members were also members of NATO, and were thus fused with the giant military might of the US.

In the words of Professor Joan DeBardeleben, 'the accession of Russia's former allies to the EU contained an implicit message of Western superiority'.[17] The EU was not interested in absorbing Russia, but it had set its sights on recruiting all Russia's smaller neighbours. Experts testifying before a British parliamentary panel said that Russians viewed the West as 'using Russian weakness to achieve their goals'. They said the 'feeling of humiliation in Russia is enormous'.[18]

In this environment, the advent of Putinism was unsurprising. In the early 2000s, his aggressive new nationalism sought to protect Russia's sphere of influence. It pitched the country's democratic momentum into reverse. Putin used the new network of oligarchs and media magnates to exert personal control over the fledgling democracy, placing strict curbs on opposition and dissent.

Putin created the Eurasian Economic Union, or EEU, to challenge the EU's expansion. The EEU was conjured into force on 1 January 2015 by Russia, Belarus and the former Soviet republic of Kazakhstan, as a more integrated version of Russia's Customs Union. By then, a strategic battle was already under way in which the EU and the Customs Union were pressuring undeclared Eastern European states to swear loyalty to one side or the other.

The conflict came to a head in Ukraine in 2013. Putin was almost certainly correct when he claimed the West purposely destabilized Ukraine's pro-Russian President Viktor Yanukovych. Mass protests began after Yanukovych refused to sign an association agreement with the EU and instead signed one with Russia. They reflected what the Voice of Russia

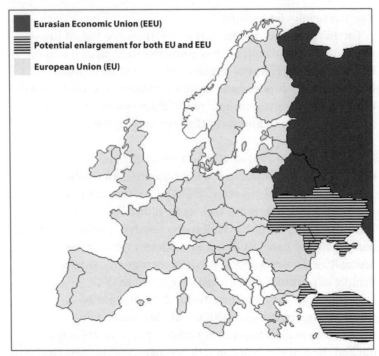

Figure 2: The strategic picture in 2014

called 'EU meddling in the sovereign affairs of Ukraine' in combination with the US.

The US government scarcely bothered to deny its role. In 2011, the US State Department allocated over $100 million to the National Endowment for Democracy (NED), a body which, according to its website, 'helps strengthen the bond between indigenous democratic movements abroad and the people of the United States'.[19] In Ukraine, the NED saw its goal as promoting the 'reforms necessary for Euro-Atlantic integration'.

The NED viewed Putin's ally Yanukovych as an obstacle to this 'integration'. It described its response as follows:

...NED strengthened regional NGOs engaging in grassroots campaigns to foster local civic activism. Support also went to traditional and new media outlets fostering freedom of the press, defending journalists, and informing citizens about the country's direction.[20]

In other words, the US government sponsored the very activists and propagandists who for months camped outside the Ukrainian parliament buildings and brought the pro-Russian government to a standstill. The EU also donated funds.[21] Neither the protesters nor their sponsors seemed to care very much about democracy. Yanukovych was elected in 2010 in polls described by international observers as an 'impressive display' of democracy.[22] The protesters were elected by no-one.

When Yanukovych finally fled to Russia, the head of the US Central Intelligence Agency, John Brennan, immediately flew to Kiev.[23] It was a gesture that seemed to say to Russia, 'you're next'. Russia had already complained about the antics of foreign NGOs within its borders. In 2006 the Russians exposed efforts by British spies to channel money to NGOs critical of Putin's government.[24]

What happened in Ukraine had been tried before. Ten years earlier, in November 2004, the European editor of the *Guardian* newspaper, Ian Traynor, reported that Ukrainian youngsters agitating against Ukraine's pro-Russian government were 'coached' by US diplomats and by NGOs specifically dedicated to removing anti-Western governments. These included the National Democratic Institute, the International Republican Institute, USAid, and Freedom House.

Working with them during that year's US-backed 'colour revolutions' were pollsters charged with discovering suitable pro-Western candidates who were capable of unifying a protest movement under a single, carefully crafted brand. The NGOs arranged the monitoring and exit-polling of the elections – potentially allowing them to frame their candidate as the winner before any official results and thus undermining any official results that suggested otherwise. The protests were not 'grassroots', as frequently reported in the Western media. They were AstroTurf.

As the Ukraine crisis unfolded, Putin's tanks rolled into Ukraine's Crimea and annexed it for Russia in February 2014, before eastern Ukraine erupted into war between Ukraine's

US-backed army and pro-Russian proxies directed from Moscow. Various foreign policy commentators, particularly on the political Right, castigated the EU and the US for their 'weakness' in failing to offer a robust response to this Russian aggression.[25]

Yet it was not US weakness that had caused the war. Rather, it was NATO's refusal to give up its Cold War mind-set and disband, as the Warsaw Pact had done. NATO cornered Russia into mirroring its hostility. The EU's intentions had become confusable with those of NATO, in Russia's eyes. Western leaders such as US President Barack Obama castigated Putin for his 'wrong-headed desire to recreate the glories of the Soviet empire'. He did not concede that Russia might have legitimate cause to doubt whether the West was actually its friend.

Humankind will never know whether a different Russia might have emerged had NATO disbanded in 1991 and the military savings been spent on a less-painful economic reconstruction in Russia. What would have happened had the EU held open the door to eventual Russian membership, on the condition that it met the bloc's democratic standards? What if it had expanded east at a more considered pace?

As far as Eastern Europe is concerned, a destabilized and isolated Russia is in no-one's interest. Russia is central, not just to a stable and prosperous Eastern Europe, but also to some of the most pressing issues we face in the Middle East and North Africa. This is evident from the success of the Iran-US nuclear deal, in which Russian diplomats played a critical role.

The fate of Ukraine demonstrated the many risks faced by European states that fell outside a regional union. Absent the Resistance to External Interference effect, foreign intelligence agencies can use so-called NGOs to sponsor political figures and protest leaders, and to spread propaganda. Without an Economic Truce, neighbours can threaten trade for political ends. And without Veto and Consensus and Permanent Dialogue, there was nothing to prevent the dispute from escalating into armed conflict.

The EU's rapid eastwards expansion was largely a product of NATO's anti-Russian strategy. While alarming Russia, it also created serious internal division within the EU. Mass immigration was one by-product of the EU's dash towards the Russian border. Now with the right to work where they pleased, Eastern Europeans flowed towards the wealthier economies in large numbers. This influx of workers into Western Europe stoked political resistance. Low-skilled workers in the wealthier countries argued that their wages were depressed by competition from these new arrivals. The only people who benefited from the influx, they argued, were the well-heeled managerial class who could spend less on their payrolls and more on their own bonuses.

Labour and migration

Statistical data showed some evidence for this. A study of income inequality in the EU found that:

in general the 10 per cent highest income recipients have seen their incomes grow much more rapidly than the rest of the population over the past 25 years.[26]

Wisely, the paper did not hazard a theory as to why this was. There were many possible explanations; the causes and effects of income inequality are hotly disputed and heavily politicized. Greater automation of industrial and clerical processes, coupled with the computerization of communications, has eliminated many professions, and new ones have risen to replace them. The advent of the World Trade Organization in 1995 and the shift in manufacturing to Asia reduced the work for blue-collar workers in Western Europe, and diminished the powers of trade unions. All this benefited the owners of capital rather than labour, as the inequality figures suggest, leading to a huge income disparity between rich and poor.

Nevertheless, economic theory dictates that increasing the supply of a commodity reduces its price. Logically, increasing the labour supply in Western Europe should therefore suppress wage growth, and it takes a certain amount of special pleading to argue otherwise. Some claim that immigration has positive effects on GDP growth and in reducing inequality, by bringing in new employers and consumers.[27] But it is notable that they never take this argument to its logical conclusion – to end all border controls and actively court multi-billion-strong immigration from the developing world, as a panacea to inequality and recession. Presumably, this is because only *moderate* immigration delivers such benefits. How one defines 'moderate' is the nub of the political dispute.

The rightwing, pro-business case is not entirely convincing, either. Typically, it takes the role of an employer who claims that Western European workers are not willing to do the jobs he has to offer. A more accurate rendering of that sentence, however, would be: not willing to do the jobs he has to offer *at the wages he is willing to pay*. The second, more accurate version does little to reassure workers in Western Europe that employers are not deliberately undercutting their wage demands through recourse to cheaper eastern-EU labour.

Pro-Europeans have a tendency to dismiss the anecdotal evidence of ordinary workers, without themselves having shared their experiences. French lorry drivers and builders, for instance, know exactly by how much they are being undercut by Eastern European hauliers and construction workers.[28] These are precisely the voters who handed Marine Le Pen's anti-immigrant Front National a nationwide victory in the May 2014 European elections, taking a quarter of all ballots cast in France. Such voters are unreceptive to the pro-immigration arguments advanced above – particularly when those making the arguments are members of an elite that benefits from cheap manual labour, without personally ever participating in it.

The May 2014 European elections not only delivered great victories to Le Pen and to the UK Independence Party, but saw gains for anti-immigration parties in Germany, Austria, Greece, Denmark, Sweden and Finland. Evidently, pro-Europeans need a more convincing case for how expanding the EU benefits everyone.

A better case would be to admit that the circulation of labour around the EU has disrupted patterns of employment. At the same time, it has served to enrich Eastern European countries, which only 20 years ago were mired in the economic collapse of Comecon and the Soviet Union. So Team Europe is not only expanding, but it is creating new, wealthy teammates whose presence enriches the whole. Research released in March 2014 found that parts of the Czech Republic, Slovakia, Lithuania, Latvia and Estonia were now richer than the EU average.[29] The wealthier parts of Poland are now better off than the poorest parts of the United Kingdom and Germany.

Poland provides an example of a poor economy which has become dramatically richer as a result of its relationship with the EU. Poland entered the bloc in 2004, and since then its economy has consistently outgrown those of Western Europe, albeit from a lower base. As of 2012, it was the world's 24th-largest economy, according to the World Bank. Poland imports more and more goods from overseas, and more and more of those goods are from the richer countries within the EU.[30]

Poland is buying ever more of the goods produced in Germany, the UK and France, allowing exporters in those countries to expand and hire new workers. This not only benefits those countries, but it undermines the argument that the eastward expansion of the EU is absorbing only poor countries. Rather, the EU is expanding to incorporate countries that may be poor now, relatively speaking, but that will soon be as wealthy as many of those already within the bloc. The Open Borders and Human Ties function is spreading prosperity.

Were Norway to join the EU, its entry would not attract the same resistance as the accession of Romania. Norway is already a rich country. Rather than allowing Romania simply to be perceived as a 'poor country', proponents of EU expansion must make the case that Romania's relative poverty is a temporary phase, and one that will improve the prosperity of all EU citizens in the longer term.

It is possible to envision a future in which the EU has absorbed all the countries along Russia's western border. By then it would have fully integrated the former republics of Yugoslavia, and perhaps even Muslim Albania. At that point, it is vital the EU has friendly relations with Moscow. This extends to the possibility of Russia itself becoming a member of the bloc.

Were Russia to reverse Putin's anti-federal approach, and instead to become a true federation along the lines of Canada, this prospect would become much more realistic. By distributing political power more evenly across Russia, the country would appear less threatening to the former Comecon states now part of the EU, who fear any return of Russian domination.

The result would be a vast continental team, almost a billion strong, a global byword for excellence and high living standards, with no external enemies and therefore no need to expend precious resources on weaponry. Like the US, and indeed the EU itself, Russia is a major arms exporter. The arms these countries produce often find their way directly into the hands of insurgent groups and brutal regimes operating in the southern hemisphere. If Russia did not perceive NATO to be a threat, it would reduce its arms production and instead concentrate on the very serious economic challenges it faces domestically. Disarmament and friendship go hand in hand.

The benefits of EU membership are obvious to many states outside Europe. They realize that small- and medium-sized nations must club together to defend themselves against the diktats of major powers (including the regional unions). Independence, paradoxically, cannot be preserved alone, but only in partnership with others who wish to preserve their own autonomy. Resistance to External Interference is one of the 10 peace-promoting factors that stabilized Europe, and it is a theme of most of the regional unions now being attempted. The EU's model is spreading.

The multi-polar world of the 21st century will see the emergence of a Team Africa, a Team Asia, a Team South America, a Team North America and a Team Oceania. Withdrawing from such regional unions will become entirely self-defeating. Even now, for a European country to exit the EU would be unthinkable. Those countries that remain formally outside, such as Switzerland and Norway, cannot escape the EU's gravity in terms of trade, regulation, interest rates and freedom of movement. Nevertheless, the continental blocs must continually make the case for their own existence. The EU has been remiss in this regard. Too often, it has allowed its opponents to frame the debate, allowing them to denigrate and dismiss the bloc's achievements – the cause of peace high among them – while exaggerating the union's flaws. Moreover, its decision to become NATO's 'political wing' has damaged its credibility and soft-power appeal.

It is time for pro-Europeans to rally, and to promote the uptake of the EU model elsewhere, particularly in those regions where peace is most elusive. Violent radicals often create their own 'open borders', and so uniting countries against asymmetric military threats is important, particularly in Africa and the Middle East. The African Union has played a major part in defusing hostilities on a continent once mired in wars and military takeovers. Rather than every state maintaining its own standing army, by combining their forces states can reduce their military expenditure while at the same time creating a force better able to tackle cross-border threats.

Most vital of all is to stress the common humanity and common cultural values that unite humans across vast territories. In Europe, the mechanism of Human Ties and Open Borders ensures that nations that once viewed each other as mortal enemies now live side by side, street by street, in cosmopolitan cities such as London, Amsterdam and Berlin. This is the true triumph of regionalism: it brings the world to one's doorstep, and reminds individuals that truly, there is no such thing as a foreigner.

1 Kneezle, Sarah, 2012, 'EU's Nobel Peace Prize: Does NATO Deserve It More?', *TIME*, 12 October.
2 Kesternich et al, working paper, 'The Effects of World War II on Economic and Health Outcomes across Europe', RAND, January 2012. **3** Lunak, Petr, 2001, 'Reassessing the Cold War alliances', *The NATO Review*, Vol. 49 - No 4. **4** See UN Human Rights Index.
5 See World Bank, Strength of Legal Rights index. **6** See Transparency International, 2015 Corruption Perceptions Index. **7** See OECD Indicators of Employment Protection. **8** See Environmental Performance Index, the Yale Center for Environmental Law & Policy. **9** Mahony, Honor, 2007, 'Barroso says EU is an 'empire'', *EU Observer*, 11 July. **10** See OECD GDP figures.
11 Socio-Economic Data Division, International Economics Department Development Economics, World Bank, 'Measuring the Incomes of Economies of the Former Soviet Union', December 1992. **12** Kaletsky, Anatole, 2012, 'Can the rest of Europe stand up to Germany?', Reuters blog, 20 June. **13** Guérot, Ulrike, 2008, 'French-German disputes are tearing the EU apart', Commentary, European Council on Foreign Relations, 11 December. **14** p. 1294-1315, Golub, Jonathan, 'How the European Union does not work: national bargaining success in the Council of Ministers', *Journal of European Public Policy*, Volume 19, Issue 9, 2012. **15** See Passell, Peter, 1993, 'Dr Jeffrey Sachs, Shock Therapist', *New York Times*, 27 June. **16** de France, Olivier, 2014, 'Defence budgets: Europe's Maginot moment?', briefing paper, European Union Institute for Security Studies, March. **17** p93-112, DeBardeleben, Joan, 'The Impact of EU Enlargement on the EU-Russian Relationship,' in *A Resurgent Russia and the West: The European Union, NATO, and Beyond*, ed. Roger E Kanet, Dordrecht, Netherlands: Republic of Letters Publishing, 2009.
18 Chapter 3, 'The EU and Russia: before and beyond the crisis in Ukraine', European Union Committee – Sixth Report, House of Lords, published 20 February 2015. **19** Text of the Department of State, Foreign Operations, and Related Programs Appropriations Act, 2012.
20 NED website, original URL: www.ned.org/where-we-work/central-and-eastern-europe
21 See 'EU assistance to Civil Society Organisation in Ukraine', a written response from the European Commission to Peter Hitchens. **22** Harding, Luke, 2010, 'Yanukovych set to become president as observers say Ukraine election was fair', *The Guardian*, 8 February. **23** Kaylan, Melik, 2014, 'Why CIA Director Brennan Visited Kiev: In Ukraine The Covert War Has Begun', Forbes, 16 April. **24** Unnamed author, 2012, 'UK spied on Russians with fake rock', BBC News, 19 January. **25** Thiessen, Marc A. 2014, 'Marc Thiessen: Obama's weakness emboldens Putin', *Washington Post*, 3 March. **26** Fredriksen, Kaja Bonesmo, 2012, 'Income Inequality in the European Union', OECD, Economics Department Working Papers no. 952. **27** W.W., 2010, 'Immigration reduces inequality', *The Economist*, 28 December. **28** Astier, Henri, 2014, 'French National Front: Far right or hard left?', BBC News, 16 May. **29** 'GDP at regional level', Eurostat.
30 See Poland country report, ING International Trade Study, 2011.

Chapter 3 – The United States of Africa (African Union)

An analysis of how the African Union, by emulating the structures of the EU, has already begun to reduce the risk of conflict in Africa, for instance over Ethiopia's Grand Renaissance Dam. This chapter questions the traditional explanations for Africans' alleged propensity for warfare, such as tribalism and botched state-creation, and instead argues that the continent's bloody 20th century was attributable to its inability to resist external interference – one of the 10 pro-peace factors enforced by regional unions such as the EU.

'Renaissance' is an apt name for the dam rising by the headwaters of the Blue Nile. The Grand Renaissance Dam is a marvel of architecture, structural and financial. The financial marvel is that it has been funded mostly by the country building it, through special bonds. A country that until the last decade was the world's primary synonym for poverty and war: Ethiopia.

Once complete, the dam will be Africa's largest hydroelectric project, its 6,000 megawatts quadrupling the power available to 100 million Ethiopians and their rapidly growing economy. Any excess will be sold to the country's neighbours. Kenya and Djibouti, Eritrea, Sudan, even Uganda all stand to benefit.

Yet, as is often the case with dams constructed on shared rivers, the Grand Renaissance Dam has its enemies. Foremost among them is Egypt. For millennia, Egyptian farmers have relied on the waters of the Nile for irrigation. Egypt's own Aswan Dam sits downstream of the Ethiopian project. When the sluices are closed to fill the Renaissance Dam's lake, what becomes of those downstream?

As construction of the dam began, panic began to spread in Egypt. Some said that the Nile's restricted flow would desiccate two-thirds of Egypt's farmland, and cause the Aswan Dam to collapse.[1] Egypt began to rattle its sabres. In 2013, its then-president, Mohammed Morsi, said that 'all options were open' when it came to dealing with Ethiopia. 'If our share of Nile water decreases, our blood will be the alternative,' he warned.[2] What happened next offered a fascinating insight into 21st-century Africa. Morsi was ousted in a military coup, even as major powers such as the US and EU glossed over the circumstances surrounding his downfall. With democracy's traditional defenders so silent, the African Union (AU) stepped up. It expelled Egypt. Suddenly, the Egyptians were outcasts from Africa's regional body.

To those who view the AU as a pointless talking shop, Egypt's response was surprising. In the words of Africa analyst Solomon Dersso, it 'fought tooth and nail for its reinstatement to the AU.'[3] Part of Egypt's campaign was to soften its position on the Renaissance Dam, aware that Ethiopia had strong support from other major AU members such as Kenya. Officials from Ethiopia and Egypt met on the sidelines of an AU summit in June 2014 and agreed to resolve their differences peacefully.[4] Then, in March 2015, Egypt, Ethiopia and Sudan signed a deal to manage the Nile's waters peacefully and end the dispute over the dam.

A situation that could have resulted in war was defused.

In the process, Africa deployed many of those same 10 factors that brought peace to Europe. The AU used its collective power to expel Egypt and thus to support Democracy, the first and foremost of those 10 factors. Then the AU's ability to offer Permanent Discussion, Dialogue and Diplomacy brought the disputants back to the table to discuss a way forward. This supported the tenth, binding development of Mutual Trust and Peaceful Coexistence, which ensured that relations remained friendly enough for such discussions to take place.

Egypt was not the only country the AU has sanctioned for a democratic shortfall. In March 2013, the AU suspended the Central African Republic after the Seleka rebel coalition seized power, freezing the assets of Seleka leaders and banning them from travel in Africa. Similar suspensions were dealt to Guinea-Bissau and Mali after coups in 2012. The AU suspended and sanctioned Côte d'Ivoire in 2010 after defeated president Laurent Gbagbo refused to relinquish power after an election, but it was reinstated in 2011 when Gbagbo bowed to pressure and left office.

This is a huge change for many African countries. The decision to replace the Organization of African Unity in 2002 with the African Union (AU) was a watershed in pan-African collaboration. The OAU had tolerated the worst excesses of African leaders. In the immediate post-colonial period it was common for successful independence leaders to view themselves as the fathers of their nations. In many cases, they had endured imprisonment, or worse, by the colonial powers, and they felt entitled to proclaim themselves presidents-for-life. Such men, such as Kwame Nkrumah of Ghana and Hastings Banda of Malawi, created autocratic, open-ended regimes that concentrated power and wealth in their own hands.

Corruption thrived in such regimes. The only way of removing them, in most instances, was via a military coup. Military officers realized they could commandeer not only the seat of government but also the central bank vaults, with their stores of foreign currency, and thus treat themselves to foreign luxuries. Coups begat coups. The Soviet Union backed communist coups; the US backed capitalist ones. Neighbours backed coups against neighbours; Ghana's Nkrumah was a particular offender in that regard.[5]

In Nigeria, a series of coups and counter-coups for control of the country's increasingly lucrative oil revenues persuaded Colonel Odumegwu Ojukwu of the necessity for his Igbo people to separate from the rest of Nigeria in 1967. He declared the independent state of Biafra, a Christian entity no longer attached to the less educated, more aristocratic Muslim north.

The rest of Nigeria did not accept this unilateral secession. The subsequent civil war caused the deaths of somewhere between two and three million people. Disruption to food supplies and starvation claimed most of the victims. The conflict remains intensely sensitive in Nigeria. When Libya's ruler Muammar Gaddafi said in 2010 that Nigeria should break into separate states, Nigeria's foreign ministry issued a strongly worded rebuke, accusing him of irresponsible grandstanding. In a grim irony, a year later Gaddafi was deposed, captured and murdered as his country disintegrated.

The death toll from Africa's cycle of coup, corruption and counter-coup ran into the tens of millions. The new leaders would often purge not only the personal aides of the old regime, but entire ethnic groups associated with them. Dictators clung to power for dear life. The looting of central banks and treasuries crippled the sub-Saharan economy. Africa was the battleground on which some of the 20th century's deadliest wars were fought. Nine of the 10 bloodiest conflicts of the 1990s took place in the continent: in the Democratic Republic of Congo (DRC), Sudan, Rwanda, Angola, Somalia, Zaire, Burundi, Liberia and Algeria.[6]

The role played by the AU in sub-Saharan Africa's stabilization is a significant one. The AU mirrors the European Union. It has an executive council of foreign ministers – the equivalent of the EU's Council of Ministers – and a committee of permanent representatives akin to the European Commission. The AU's administrative capital is Addis Ababa, the now-booming capital of Ethiopia.

On a practical level, the AU has already achieved more, albeit often in partnership with Western agencies, than is generally known. Agriculture is an important area of its work. Throughout the 1980s the continent became synonymous with famine and food insecurity, Ethiopia in particular. The Western response – a massive influx of food aid – was subsequently blamed for forcing African farmers out of business, as they could not compete with free aid shipments.[7,8]

In 2003, the AU's assembly established the Comprehensive Africa Agricultural Development Programme (CAADP), with a mandate to improve agricultural productivity across the bloc. It worked with the UK's Department for International Development (DFID) to improve agricultural research and systems across sub-Saharan Africa. The CAADP's foundational pledge was for AU members to dedicate 10 per cent of their national budgets to agriculture by 2008. By 2013, only 10 members had reached or exceeded this total, and only one – Senegal – had both hit this target and the secondary goal of increasing year-on-year growth in agriculture to six per cent.[9]

Yet within the countries some remarkable progress was being made. Ethiopia's progress under CAADP has attracted praise from its international partners for exceeding its goals. Because the CAADP was Ethiopia's sole agricultural development plan, foreign donor agencies co-ordinated around it, ensuring their work was not duplicated and fitted into strategy. It also meant that the government needed to align its procedures against only one set of benchmarks, rather than the conditions set by dozens of governmental and private donors. In January 2011, the Ethiopian government founded the Agricultural Transformation Agency (ATA) to fulfil the CAADP targets.

This new agency set about solving the problems of Ethiopian agriculture. Its plan for 2011-15 concentrated on upping production from small farms and herds and on improving irrigation, as well as increasing the role of private enterprise. Where previously farmers had to place seed orders six months in advance, via a cumbersome bureaucratic process, the agency put in place a new distribution network so that farmers could buy seeds much closer to planting.[10] This allowed for more efficient decisions to be made about volume and variety.

The ATA overhauled credit for farmers, introducing a voucher system to ensure that loans were used productively. It began updating soil maps to understand where crops were most productively planted. Some aspects of the agricultural programme have proved contentious. Ethiopia's embassy in the UK was forced to deny claims that its 'villagization' programme was forcing small farmers from their land to make way for commercial crops. The leasing of farmland to foreign corporations has also caused concern in some quarters.[11]

One of the most radical advances was in rice and coffee production. Although touching the equator, Ethiopia's wide range of altitudes created a variety of microclimates and therefore the potential to cultivate a variety of crops. Traditionally seen as an Asian foodgrain, the production of rice has grown exponentially since the advent of CAADP. The ATA identified about 30 million hectares as being suitable for rice production and between 2005 and 2010 the land being used to cultivate rice increased from 6,000 to 222,000 hectares.[12] This expansion improved the food security of Ethiopia's 100 million-strong population.

Whereas rice was only recently introduced, coffee is an ancient Ethiopian crop. The country is hailed as coffee's birthplace. The World Bank reported that in October 2014 coffee specialists from nearby Burundi and Rwanda visited Ethiopian coffee plantations to learn skills that could be transferred to their own countries.[13] Ethiopia is today one of the world's leading suppliers of Arabica coffee, but with GDP growth racing around the 10-per-cent mark in recent years, Ethiopians themselves have become consumers of their own produce, rather than just exporters. Trendy coffee shops owned by Ethiopians are becoming popular in Addis Ababa.[14]

The CAADP has produced positive effects across Africa. The 10-per-cent spending commitment is a benchmark against which governments can be held, and those that fail to meet it are criticized for this failure. Efforts to improve the supply and quality of seeds, prioritized for reform in Ethiopia, are being developed on a pan-African basis.[15] Nigeria's tactic of offering seed subsidies through mobile-phone vouchers was praised by Kenya's CAADP organizer, with Kenya working towards a similar scheme.[16]

A key role of the AU in seed development is to ensure effective communication with AU member countries.[17] Such communication and networking would be impossible without a peaceful basis for co-operation. Countries that are fighting wars against one another, or even proxy wars, find it very difficult to share expertise and resources. The AU provides an institutional basis where peaceable countries can work together, and those with military or genocidal governments can be excluded. As trading links become established, these increase the costs of inter-state war, reinforcing the Economic Truce mechanism.

This learning function is encompassed by the Rules, Rights and Multiculturalism factor. By identifying their mutual challenges and comparing notes on how to overcome them, African nations have seen each other in a new light, as companions rather than rivals. It allows for the agreement of common standards, for instance in agriculture, that improve the lot of the whole continent.

Alexander Pick, a former official in South Africa's Treasury, puts it another way. 'Africa needs sustainable institutions, and a supranational such as the AU can serve as an example and a buttress in terms of turbulence at national level.' Moreover, 'a functional AU also gives Africa greater say in multilaterals, since an African bloc can strongly influence who takes over the World Bank, for example. But to do so it needs to agree on a common position through the AU.'

It is worth noting that there remains a widespread scepticism among many commentators over whether Africa can transform itself with an EU-style union. Despite the evidence offered above, some continue to argue that African regionalism is a romantic fantasy.[18] That Africa is too vast, too tribal, too atomized, and too corrupt for such unity.

One criticism is that Africa's history is too different from that of Europe to replicate the experiment. Europe's success rested on a longstanding tradition of nation-states. Africa, on the other hand, is merely a jumble of lines on a map, lines that subdivide primitive peoples with no common notion of unity. With no 'naturally formed' countries, Africa lacks the building-blocks for regional union.

It is true that Europe's colonial withdrawal from Africa was devastating to the cause of peace in the 20th century. Most African countries were based on the old resource-extraction zones established by the Belgians, Portuguese, French, British, and even the Italians and Germans. After decolonization, the arbitrary and alien origins of the new countries became clear: the colonists had simply ruled straight lines on the map, crisscrossing tens of thousands of tribes.

Shortly after he became president of the US, Barack Obama, the son of a Kenyan, pointed to this history in a speech in Ghana. Obama spoke of Africa's 'unnatural borders' and 'a colonial map that made little sense', of the corruption and the 'tribalism and patronage' that, he said, derailed his father's career in Kenya. The Obamas hail from Kenya's Luo minority; before his election, they had a bitter joke that the US would elect a Luo before Kenya did. The joke proved accurate.

Ethiopia

Ethiopia's long independent history did not save it from the depredations of the 20th century. It suffered more, even, than the new countries ruled carelessly onto the map by departing Europeans. Just before World War Two, this time led by the fascist dictator Benito Mussolini, the Italians took revenge for Adwa. Dropping mustard gas from the air, they killed some 15,000 Ethiopians, according to one Soviet estimate.[19] This brutal campaign was enough to blunt the Ethiopians' counter-offensive and turn the tide of the war.

By 1936, Ethiopia's Emperor Haile Selassie had fled, and the Italians occupied the capital, Addis Ababa. Despite the emperor's appeals to the League of Nations, the rest of the world sat back. The British and French refused to close the Suez Canal to Italian ships resupplying Mussolini's campaign in Ethiopia. It was only after Mussolini joined the Axis cause in the Second World War, forcing the British Empire to invade Italian-held Abyssinia, that Selassie was restored as ruler.

If long-established states were the key to peace, Ethiopia should have been well placed to transform itself into a successful modern country. After all, this was a state based on an ancient kingdom, with its own autocephalous Orthodox Church, its own language and writing system, and ruled by a hereditary emperor who traced his lineage back to King Solomon and the Queen of Sheba. Ethiopia was by no means an invention of Europeans.

Moreover, Ethiopia was led by one of the world's most

esteemed statesmen. Emperor Haile Selassie's stand against the
Italians, his lineage, his international stature and his personal
gravitas raised him above the level of other African leaders.
The Jamaican religion of Rastafarianism was devoted to him as
a divinity and drew much of its theology from Marcus Garvey,
a poet who envisioned a United States of Africa in 1924:

Hail! United States of Africa-free!
Hail! Motherland most bright, divinely fair!

In his book *The Horn of Africa*, Kidane Mengisteab hinted at
why Ethiopia's ancient legacy made little difference. Nation-
building, he said, requires a 'participatory process of creating
socioeconomic institutions' that cater to the 'historically
marginalized'.[20] Ethiopia created no such institutions. The
emperor's court retained strong and arbitrary powers over,
for instance, land rights, thereby stripping poor farmers of
incentives to increase productivity and ensuring that Ethiopia
remained impoverished.

The country's wealth was commandeered by a small,
defined group, to the exclusion of the rest of society. In this
respect, Ethiopia was little different to the strongmen and
soldiers who seized power elsewhere in Africa. In Ethiopia's
case, a land-owning aristocracy exercised feudal rights over
tenant farmers that left them with no legal rights whatsoever,
fertilizing the ground for the Derg's communist revolution in
1974.

Selassie died a year later, in the Derg's captivity. He had
led his country for almost 60 years. During that time, the
world had changed dramatically. The emperor made some
attempts at modernization, but he had not addressed the
feudal structure of land ownership that imposed a crippling
burden on tenant farmers.[21] Ethiopia saw itself not as a
modern nation-state but as an empire, with the continuously
expanding borders that empire implies.

The communist complexion of the Derg regime immediately
fed Ethiopia, now led by Mengistu Haile Mariam, into the

meat-grinder dynamics of the Cold War. The Soviet Union supported Mengistu with weapons. He used these to slaughter his domestic opponents, including a patriarch of the Ethiopian Orthodox Church – the most senior clergyman in the country – in a period that became known as the Red Terror.

Rebels rose up against his oppression. The Derg oversaw a drought in 1984-85 in which hundreds of thousands of Ethiopians died. With the sides using food as a weapon of war, caught in the middle was a civilian populace that had no chance of escape. Mengistu also waged war against his neighbours. Ethiopia's Somali-majority province of Ogaden became the battleground between Ethiopia and Somalia, now supported by the US.

Here we saw the absence of several of the 10 key factors. Ethiopia's inability to Resist Foreign Interference or to maintain Permanent Discussion, Dialogue and Diplomacy with its neighbours, coupled with the absence of an Economic Truce that would prevent food being used as a weapon, resulted in a human catastrophe. The absence of the Democracy and Rules, Rights and Multiculturalism preconditions meant that the governments concerned had no need to listen to its people. Without Open Borders and Freedom of Movement, the territorial dispute over Ogaden's Somali population exploded into inter-state conflict.

Most Africans were never consulted about which nation they wished to join, nor about which state they wished to inhabit. Despite their storied history, Ethiopians were in the same position as every other African; they were born into a nationality. This is why it is too simple to ascribe Africa's troubles to the botched process of state-creation. Alone, it cannot explain why Africa endured such a painful 20th century, or why African regionalism will necessarily fail.

Tribalism is another common explanation. The concept of tribe was reinforced by invading Europeans. Around the close of the 19th century, the 'scramble for Africa' coincided with burgeoning interest in the study of anthropology and ethnography. The European impulse was to taxonomize the peoples they conquered, to attach labels and attributes to them and thus to systematize notions of racial hierarchy – placing themselves at the top, of course.

Rwanda and Burundi

In 1962, the Belgian colony of Ruanda-Urundi region split into two new countries, Rwanda and Burundi. The Hutu people had a majority in both countries but the two tribes were found throughout Africa's Great Lakes region. Exiled Tutsi soldiers, for instance, assisted Uganda's long-serving president Yoweri Museveni in overthrowing the dictator Idi Amin in 1986.

The Tutsis' support for Museveni was to exact a heavy toll on the Great Lakes neighbourhood. In return for their help, Museveni agreed to assist the Tutsi guerrillas in raising an army to invade Rwanda and retake power from the Hutus.[22] Once they had succeeded, Tutsis then looked west towards the Democratic Republic of Congo (DRC), a resource-rich but ungovernable giant. The M23 rebels were born.

The M23 were mostly Tutsi soldiers who mutinied against the Congolese army in 2012. The UN accused Rwanda's Tutsi-led government of supporting the M23 in the eastern DRC. In December 2005 the International Court of Justice had also found Uganda's government guilty of plundering the DRC's natural resources.[23] Although the UN said that Museveni's government was not directly aiding the M23, it found that virtually all the gold being mined in Congo's M23-held areas was finding its way to the Ugandan capital, Kampala. By the time the M23 renegades were defeated by a United Nations brigade in November 2013, they had displaced hundreds of thousands of Congolese civilians.

Hutu militias also operated in eastern DRC, having fled Rwanda in 1994. The largest, the FDLR, remained ostensibly committed to overthrowing the Tutsi-dominated Rwandan government. It included men who massacred Tutsis in the Rwandan genocide. Twenty years later, they today terrorize the Congolese civilian population instead. Like the M23, they prey upon the small-scale artisanal miners who tap the region's mineral resources. They also play a role in deforestation and the killing of elephants for ivory.[24]

Still too tribal?

There is a tendency outside Africa to view the continent's tribal divisions as quintessentially African, and fundamental to the continent's problems. *The Economist* magazine headlined a 2012 piece on Kenyan politics as simply 'Still too tribal'. Tribalism is a theme of the magazine's coverage of Kenya; in 2010 it wrote that tribalism is the 'motor – and the bane – of Kenyan politics'.[25] Its coverage is invariably accompanied by tables showing the exact tribal breakdown of the country.[26]

It is interesting to imagine how *The Economist* would report on its own country if it applied the same standards to Britain as it does to Kenya. Doubtless it would make much of the fact that, after decolonization by the Roman Empire in the fifth century, the island's fertile southern lowlands were overrun by seafaring Germanic tribes such as Saxons and Jutes. The hilly north and west, meanwhile, remained in the hands of Celts, a genetically diverse people whose appearance was quite distinct from the fair-haired invaders. DNA studies show that, to a large extent, these tribal groups remain embedded in the modern British population.[27]

The tribal division also remains a factor in British politics. The seven former Saxon kingdoms are today areas that vote heavily in favour of the centre-right Conservative Party. The rest of the island, including the Celtic-majority Wales and Scotland, vote for other parties, such as the left-of-centre Labour Party. Labour retains support within large cities that fall within the Saxon kingdoms, such as Liverpool and Manchester, but which have large ethnically Celtic populations.

The tribal dimension to British politics was sufficiently pronounced as to make the English nationality of former prime minister Tony Blair a factor in his becoming leader of the Labour Party in 1994, a fact emphasized in Stephen Frears' 2003 movie *The Deal*. Blair's task was to make the party palatable to Anglo-Saxons as well as to Celts. As *The Economist* itself noted, the Labour Party gives the 'impression that it concentrates on Britain's Celtic fringes' at the expense of the English.[28]

Yet to offer 'tribal' explanations for European politics is to risk accusations of over-simplification. While commentators get away with talking about tribalism as a defining feature of Africans, Europeans prefer to view themselves as more nuanced. They do not care to be lumped into regional 'tribes' or ethnicities, in a way that ignores their individuality and their often ambivalent personal relationships with those wider communities.

The same, of course, is true of Africans. In Africa there is no clear dividing line between tribe and class. The Hutus and Tutsis were a classic illustration of this confusion. A great scholarly literature has exposed the extent to which the concepts of 'Tutsi' and 'Hutu' were largely created by Belgian colonists.

In reality, the Hutus and Tutsis were scarcely able to tell each other apart, so similar were they in appearance, habits and language.[29] The colonial powers turned the two tribes into a class system, enforced by often arbitrary assignations of 'Hutu' or 'Tutsi' status to individuals depending on whether they tilled the land or raised cattle. In the 1920s and 1930s, Belgians decreed that only Tutsis could become officials or receive higher education. They also decided that every Rwandan had to be apportioned to a tribe for official purposes. The Belgians had no means by which to decide this accurately, however, so many Hutus simply declared themselves Tutsi in order to access the associated privileges.[30]

The Belgian tendency to view the Tutsis as racially superior to the Hutus was unscientific. It had more to do with divide-and-rule. By demarcating tribal blocs that might hitherto have connected together communities whose only solidarity lay along loose linguistic lines, the European empires encouraged Africans and other subjugated peoples to be more fixated with their own internal dynamics than with overthrowing foreign rule. The effect was to dehumanize Tutsis and Hutus in each others' eyes. This racism propelled the genocidal anti-Tutsi violence in the 1990s and Burundi's equally genocidal anti-Hutu violence in the 1970s.[31]

The class and ethnic divisions that pervade Africa are not dissimilar to those found within human populations elsewhere. Until now, the difference has been the ferocity with which, especially during the 20th century, those divisions manifested themselves. Without institutions able to manage conflict at a political level, it proved all too easy for demagogues to exploit any division between Africans, no matter how imaginary.

Regarding Rwanda and its neighbours, it is useful again to return to the 10 principles of regional integration. With neither the Rules, Rights and Multiculturalism condition in place, nor Democracy, nor the Soft Power that encourages people to identify with one another, rather than against one another, the climate was set for bloodshed. Uganda's turmoil become Rwanda's, which became the DRC's, with no common institutions to prevent one group of people pillaging another.

Mandela, Mugabe and minorities

To end this cycle of violence, one must look to the example set by South Africa's Nelson Mandela. Mandela emerged from captivity seeking not revenge against the white South Africans who imprisoned him and had subordinated non-white ethnic groups, but seeking to work with them to preserve South Africa's relative wealth and living standards, and to cultivate a new racial harmony. The experiences of Zimbabwe and Uganda, where white and Asian citizens were driven out by black governments, were ones that South Africa avoided.

The world's attention settled on South Africa's apartheid system because its dominant minority was white. Across most African countries, the dominant minorities were black. The world criticized President Robert Mugabe for his treatment of white Zimbabweans, but the reality was that Mugabe persecuted non-Shona-speaking Zimbabweans, whether black or white. His treatment of the Ndebele was far harsher than his treatment of white farmers. Most estimates put the number of civilians killed in the 1980s at around 20,000.[32]

In Africa, however, there are signs that the rule of oppressive minorities is becoming less pernicious. A change in the political weather has allowed some African countries the stability needed for rapid economic growth.[33] Although this growth is from a very low base, it has been enough to improve the view of Africa as an investment destination. Foreign companies are rushing to participate in African markets. Nor is their interest solely in extractive industries of the kind that attracted European empires in the 19th century; consumer products are also taking off.[34]

There are many explanations for why Africa might finally have turned a corner. The end of the Cold War was certainly a factor, with the US and Russia no longer manipulating dictators against one another. The Resistance to External Interference factor was no longer as crucial as it was. Chinese investment was another, more tangible factor. But the most crucial development has been the willingness of African governments to view each other as permanent partners, laying the groundwork for the same 10 factors that pacified Europe.

The East African Community

The AU is not the only African multilateral making progress on intra-African trade. The East African Community (EAC) has made even more ambitious commitments to joint work. The EAC unites traditional rivals Uganda and Kenya with their Great Lakes neighbours – Tanzania, Rwanda and Burundi. Given that Uganda, Rwanda and Burundi are landlocked, a key goal of the community is to give them access to seaports.

In November 2013 the members signed a protocol to establish a single currency. This came four years after they had signed up to other EU-like innovations, to create a common market and permit the free movement of people across borders.[35] Implementation is a slow process, but now the EAC negotiates external trade agreements as a bloc. In

October 2014, for instance, its negotiators agreed an economic partnership agreement with the EU to stabilize the terms of access to European markets. The EAC runs a trade deficit with the EU, but nevertheless finds customers for its horticultural, plantation, fish and vegetable exports. 'The East African Community region stands out for its dynamism, and ambition to develop as an integrated region,' said EU Commissioner for Trade Karel De Gucht.[36]

Shared infrastructure has also made impressive gains. Since the foundation of the EAC's common market, Rwanda's cross-border truck traffic has doubled, according to its EAC minister Valentine Sendanyoye Rugwabiza.[37] She noted that the common customs territory has reduced the cost of delivering a shipping container from Kenya's port of Mombasa to Kigali by $1,000. The journey now takes five days rather than 21.

The discovery of oil in Uganda has been one propeller for the EAC's pragmatic partnership. Exporting the oil means access to the sea. That means going through Kenya, and developing new cross-border infrastructure to make it cost effective. This race for prosperity means the EAC differs from the EU in one crucial institutional aspect. Whereas the EU is highly averse to the concept of a 'two-speed Europe', and insists that its members walk in step, the bigger members of the EAC are comfortable cutting deals and allowing the smaller members to catch up.

For example, Kenya, Rwanda and Uganda agreed to slash the price of cross-border mobile phone calls by 60 per cent, by working with operators to reduce their roaming charges.[38] Although Tanzania and Burundi did not join the agreement, its existence increased pressure on them to do so at a later date. Not only does the agreement cut the cost of business communications, but Kenya's Safaricom has led the world in transforming mobile-phone credit into banking services. Given that many Africans are unbanked, the economic benefits are therefore twofold.

The EAC's plans for a currency union perhaps seem unfashionable and far-fetched when the Eurozone's early-

21st-century woes are considered. Yet two similar currency unions have existed for decades in Africa. They are the West African CFA Franc and the Central African CFA Franc. The West African version is used by Benin, Burkina Faso, Côte d'Ivoire, Guinea-Bissau, Mali, Niger, Senegal and Togo; the Central African currency by Cameroon, the Central African Republic, Chad, the Republic of the Congo, Equatorial Guinea and Gabon.

The experience of the West African countries suggests that the currency zone can promote intra-regional trade. One third of Benin's exports, for instance, go to Mali, also a user of the West African Franc.[39] Half of Senegal's exports go to the rest of the currency bloc and almost a third of Côte D'Ivoire's exports go to other West African countries, though not all within the Franc zone. This has been enough to persuade other West African countries of the desirability of building their own single currency.

In 2000, other countries in West Africa – Gambia, Ghana, Guinea, Nigeria and Sierra Leone – formed the West African Monetary Zone to prepare for the launch of their own single currency, the Eco. However, as has often been the case with Africa's transnational endeavours, implementation was much more difficult than visualization. The deadline for the currency's introduction was delayed repeatedly. Unlike the CFA Franc, the Eco's value would not be underwritten by France, which guarantees an exchange rate to the Euro. Moreover, the huge gulf in size between Nigeria, Africa's largest economy, and the rest could severely damage the smaller economies.

Nigeria

Nevertheless, Nigeria is showing signs of throwing off its old malaise. The election victory of Muhammadu Buhari in 2015 was remarkable for being the first time the opposition had ousted the incumbents through the ballot box. Buhari, a former dictator turned democrat, based his campaign on a war against corruption. Already, though, rapid urbanization offered new opportunities to create zones of better governance in concentrated areas. This is particularly true of Lagos, the largest city in Africa, with a population of around 20 million. Long a byword for crime, violence and corruption, there are some signs the city has turned a corner.

Revenue collection is growing quickly and is now above $1 billion a year, according to the state government. The city is attracting back highly educated Nigerians who moved overseas for opportunity. An upmarket new district is to be built on land reclaimed from the Atlantic, although it immediately attracted criticism as an enclave for the rich.[40] Even so, the properties the rich vacate to move there will be sold to poorer Nigerians, creating a virtuous chain of housing upgrades.

The paradox facing Lagos is that the more it thrives, the more Nigerians flock to the city and the greater the challenge of building them homes and infrastructure. The Nigerian academic Chike Fidelis Okolocha argues that coastal cities like Lagos, founded by European colonists, are responsible for much of Africa's social dislocation. They sucked the economic life out of existing African cities such as Kano in northern Nigeria which were not connected to the new, tarmacked roads, railways and power lines that served to transport commodities from the interior to the coast and thence to Europe.[41] The social, political and trading patterns of those old African cities crumbled accordingly.

The legacy of colonialism means that African infrastructure was built to transport commodities out of the continent to Europe. The result is that in many cases trade between African countries remains extremely weak. Because extractive industry far outmatches manufacturing, neighbours have little reason to import and process each others' raw materials. Correcting this is a primary objective of the AU and is one that the regional body is well placed to address. Creating an African free trade area was targeted by the union at a major summit in Addis Ababa in January 2012.[42] As ever, though, the risk of implementation drift remains.

A profusion of regional groupings – eight economic

communities alone – has in some cases drained each one of
the attention and political capital needed for them to achieve
genuine progress. East Africa's recent successes in terms of
EAC integration were driven by powerful leaders in Uganda,
Kenya and Rwanda and the mutual necessity of preparing for
an oil boom, with the EAC simply the mechanism through
which they operated.

African leaders must realize that if their voices are to be
heard internationally, they must speak in unison. This was
demonstrated by the defeat of Nigeria's finance minister, Ngozi
Okonjo-Iweala, to the US-backed candidate Jim Yong Kim in
the 2012 race to become managing director of the World Bank.
She lost despite doubts over Kim's credentials and allegations
that the result was a 'stitch up'.[43] 'The West won't give up its
hold over these institutions until they need something from
the emerging markets,' former World Bank official Professor
Simon Evenett told a British newspaper.[44] The AU is the logical
forum to forge such a single position.

The International Criminal Court

The activities of another transnational institution have
helped to unite the AU. The International Criminal Court
is a body designed to prosecute genocide, war crimes and
other atrocities. Although 122 countries have signed up to it,
there is a perception that the ICC exclusively concentrates on
prosecuting African leaders. The ICC's decision to prosecute
Kenya's leader Uhuru Kenyatta for post-election violence
in 2007 prompted particular anger. The AU debated a mass
withdrawal from the court in protest.

By the end of 2013, all eight of the cases and all 21
defendants at the ICC were African. Given the extensive
violence committed by governments against civilians in Asia,
the Middle East and Latin America, this seemed odd and
discriminatory to many Africans. In reality, the reason was
more that many countries had failed to sign up for the court.

Sri Lanka, for instance, whose former government stood
accused of massacring Tamil civilians in 2008, is not a

signatory. Nor is Burma, whose government stands accused of ethnic cleansing of Muslims. Big countries such as the US, China and India have also failed to ratify the statute. Kenya, on the other hand, has ratified it, ensuring that its leaders, although accused of lesser crimes than the governments of Sri Lanka and Burma, are subject to the court's decisions.

In this respect, Africa is already setting a better example than many wealthier parts of the world. By embracing regionalism and multilateralism, the continent is reaping the benefits of the 10 factors that foster peace and its natural counterpart, prosperity. Softening borders and spreading the fruits of economic growth, creating regional rules and institutions, maintaining a perpetual dialogue and setting common goals: all these unpick the bloody conundrums that set African against African in the 20th century. Strengthening the new bonds will ensure that the continent finally secures its independence, in all senses of the word.

1 Hussein, Walaa, 2014, 'Egypt fears Ethiopia Renaissance Dam threatens water supply', Al Monitor, 13 January, translated by Kamal Fayad. **2** El-Behairy, Nouran, 2013, 'Morsi: If our share of Nile water decreases, our blood will be the alternative', *Daily News Egypt,* 11 June. **3** Dersso, Solomon, 2014, 'Egypt vs African Union: A mutually unhappy ending?', Al Jazeera, 14 July. **4** Al Sherbini, Ramadan, 2014, 'Egypt, Ethiopia agree on "new chapter" in ties', Gulf News, 27 June. **5** See Willoughby, Syerramia, 2013, 'Remembering sub-Saharan Africa's first military coup d'état fifty years on', blog post, London School of Economics, 19 August. **6** See Hawkins, Virgil, 'Measuring UN Security Council Action and Inaction in the 1990s: Lessons for Africa', *African Security Review* Vol 12 No 2, 2003. The only other war to make it into the top 10 was Bosnia, in 8th place. **7** Moya, Dambisa, 2009, 'Why Foreign Aid is Hurting Africa', *Wall St Journal,* 21 March. **8** Melamed, Claire and Kraev, Egor, 2005, 'The economics of failure', Christian Aid. **9** Jobson, Elissa, 2014, 'Has Africa's focus on farming borne fruit?', *The Guardian,* 14 February. **10** Ethiopian ATA, 2014, Quarterly Update, March, Volume 3. **11** Davison, William, 2011, 'Saudi Billionaire's Company Will Invest $2.5 Billion in Ethiopia Rice Farm', Bloomberg, 23 March. **12** p.26, Mohapatra, Savitri, 2012, 'Rice: Ethiopia's millennium crop', *Rice Today,* January-March edition **13** Staff, 2014, 'In Kaldi's Footsteps: A Journey to the Birthplace of Coffee', World Bank, 7 October. **14** Jeffrey, James, 2014, 'Boom times for Ethiopia's coffee shops', BBC News, 16 October. **15** Staff, 2014, 'Africa's Seed Sector To Receive Boost', spyghana, 22 October. **16** NAN newswire, 2014, 'Kenya Commends Nigeria For Boosting Its Agric Policies', *Leadership,*

28 September. **17** www.abcic.org **18** Wonacott, Peter, 2014, 'A United States of Africa? Not Yet', *Wall St Journal*, 18 July. **19** Grip, Lina and Hart, John, 'The use of chemical weapons in the 1935-36 Italo-Ethiopian War', SIPRI Arms Control and Non-proliferation Programme, October 2009. **20** p.93 Mengisteab, Kidane, *The Horn of Africa*, Polity, 2014. **21** p.207, Meredith, Martin, 2005, *The State of Africa*, Simon & Schuster. **22** Schmidt, William E. 1994, 'Rwanda Puzzle: Is Uganda Taking Sides?', *New York Times*, 16 April. **23** Bauer, Isabella, 2013, 'Uganda's hidden role in Congo's conflict', Deutsche Welle, 4 January. **24** Unnamed author, 2014, 'Will FDLR rebels ever leave Congo and return to Rwanda?', BBC News, 11 February. **25** Unnamed author, 2010, 'The politicians just don't seem to get it', *The Economist*, 18 February. **26** Unnamed author, 2014, 'Trotting Ahead', *The Economist*, 13 March. **27** Leslie S et al. 'The fine-scale genetic structure of the British population', *Nature*, 2015. **28** J.C. 2014, 'Land of hope and Tories', *The Economist*, 19 September. **29** Gwin, Peter, 2014, 'Revisiting the Rwandan Genocide: Hutu or Tutsi?', *National Geographic*, 5 April. **30** See Human Rights Watch, www.hrw.org/reports/1999/rwanda/Geno1-3-09.htm **31** Lemarchand, René, 1999, 'Ethnicity as Myth: The View from the Central Africa', presented at Centre of African Studies, University of Copenhagen. **32** Dube, Pindai, 2014, 'Zimbabwe: Commemorating Gukurahundi', allfrica.com, 17 January, **33** Kawa, Lucas, 2013, 'The 20 Fastest-Growing Countries In The World', *International Business Times*, 29 January.

34 Press release, 2014, 'Foreign direct investment in Sub Saharan Africa on the rise', Ernst & Young, 15 May. **35** www.eac.int **36** Press release, 2014, 'EU strikes a comprehensive trade deal with East African Community', European Commisson, 16 October. **37** Kabeera, Eric, 2014, 'Rwanda deserves equal access to EAC markets', *Uganda Independent*, 20 October. **38** Padmore, Russell, 2014, 'Cheaper cross-border phone charges in East Africa', BBC World Service, 8 October. **39** MIT Observatory of Economic Complexity, 2010 figures. **40** Lukacs, Martin, 2014, 'New, privatized African city heralds climate apartheid', *The Guardian*, 14 January. **41** Okolocha, Chike Fidelis, 2014, 'Nigeria: The Afropolis and the African Urban Revolution', allafrica.com, 8 October.

42 AU Assembly, 'Boosting Intra-African Trade', 'Issues Affecting Intra-African Trade', Proposed Action Plan for boosting Intra-African Trade and Framework for the fast tracking of a Continental Free Trade Area, 29-30 January 2012. **43** Staf and agencies, 2012, 'US choice named World Bank chief', Al Jazeera, 17 April. **44** Rushe, Dominic, Stewart, Heather and Mark, Monica, 2012, 'World Bank names US-nominated Jim Yong Kim as president', *The Guardian*, 16 April.

Chapter 4 – The Trouble with Giants (Asian Union)

Integrating Asia, the world's most populous and diverse continent, is a challenge far beyond that of uniting Europe. Nevertheless, regional unions are already in place. The most successful, the Association of South-East Asian Nations (ASEAN), set 2015 as the deadline to put in place its own economic common market, a hugely significant shift that has gone mostly ignored by the outside world. ASEAN does not face the challenge of uniting a country as large as India or China, however. This chapter assesses ways in which even such giants can be brought within the ambit of a unified Asia.

'Pathan popular dances are singularly like Russian Cossack dancing.'

India's founding prime minister made this observation while sitting in prison in 1943. With time on his hands, Jawaharlal Nehru was writing a book, one in which he tried to describe the country he sought to lead. The Pathan people of the northwest frontier were causing him difficulties because, as he noted, they took their cultural cues from Russia and Central Asia.

Nehru admitted that 'there is little in common, to outward seeming' between the Pathans and, as an extreme example, the dark-skinned Tamils of the far south.[1]

Their racial stocks are not the same, though there may be common strands running through them; they differ in face and figure, food and clothing, and, of course, language. Nevertheless, Nehru believed that the Pathans bore the 'impress of India'. In the end, the point was never tested. The lands of the Pathans, or Pashtun, fell within what became Pakistan and Afghanistan. Today, they are the group from which the Taliban recruits. How they would have responded to being governed from New Delhi is imponderable.

To introduce India into a book about continental unions may at first seem curious. The wider world looks on India simply as another country. A very large one, yes, with a population three times that of the European Union, but nonetheless a nation-state, in the same way that the People's Republic of China is a nation-state. India has one flag, one cricket team, one army, one prime minister. It is a country.

The view from within is not quite so simple. India is a young state, in terms of its unification and independence. It is far more complex than many outsiders realize. Its population is not only far larger than that of the EU and US combined, but it is also far more diverse in terms of language, religion and economy. Were its constituent states to be independent countries, their unification would undoubtedly pose an even more daunting task than Europe's ever-closer union.

Consider the following. Residents of India's most populated state, Uttar Pradesh (UP), earn on average just $541 a year.[2] Most work in agriculture. There are over 200 million people in the province, meaning its population is 25 per cent larger than Russia's. The language they speak is Hindustani, which, when written in the Devanagari script, is known as Hindi, but when written in the Persian-Arabic script is known as Urdu, the language of India's 200 million or so Muslims. Only Indonesia has more followers of the Prophet.

The northern province of Sikkim, by contrast, has only 600,000 inhabitants – a population similar to that of Luxembourg. The province is wedged between Nepal, Bhutan and China, with only its southern border open to the rest of India. Its climate is foggy and cool, quite unlike that of the Indo-Gangetic Plain to the south. Sikkim has a Hindu majority, but a third of the population is Buddhist or Christian. Most residents are ethnically Nepali, and they therefore look quite different from people in southern India. The economy is sustained by plantation agriculture and tourism and people in Sikkim earn $2,300 a year, on average – quadruple the average income in UP.[3]

Sikkim and UP are as different from one another as Iceland and Spain. The union binding them together is in some ways surprisingly weak. India does not have a single market.

Provinces stop trucks from other states at their border and demand state taxes. Rajasthan, for example, charges an entry permit of 500 rupees per ton for vehicles under 5,000 kilograms, and 800 rupees for each ton above that weight.[4] These stops often elicit demands for bribes. The World Bank has said the elimination of such obstacles could cut freight times by as much as one third.[5]

It is understandable why many observers in the mid-20th century were so pessimistic about the survival of the newly independent India. As the scholar Sunil Khilnani noted, such 'discordant material was not the stuff of which nation states are made'.[6] He points out that before the 19th century, no residents of the subcontinent would have described themselves as 'Indian'[7] Nehru's optimism was not widely shared by those who knew India less well than he did.

Visiting in 1896, the US author Mark Twain declared: 'If there had been but one India and one language – but there were 80 of them!' The English writer Malcolm Muggeridge, on becoming assistant editor of the *Calcutta Statesman*, admitted to pouring 'scorn and ridicule' on the idea that India could become a self-governing democracy. A favourite saying of the British at the time was that if they left, 'within six months the Indians would be down on their knees begging them to come back'.[8]

Seventy years later, India has become a successful model of a federal structure that minimizes the conflicts of diversity. That is not to say there is no conflict or violence. But India, with a population larger than sub-Saharan Africa, has not experienced the hellish conditions of a Congo, a Rwanda, a Central African Republic or a Derg-era Ethiopia at any point in its independent history, despite that history coinciding with the decolonization of Africa.

In this regard, India was fortunate to have been colonized by a single European power. Although other Europeans had small footholds, for instance at Pondicherry and Goa, the subcontinent was overwhelmingly controlled by the British Raj. Had a single power achieved such a grip over Africa, rather than it being carved up by half-a-dozen European countries, it is possible that pan-African political parties would have emerged to create a single African nation-state.

At independence, India had just 17 provinces. Today, it has 29, as well as seven union territories that represent islands and the old French and Portuguese holdings. Understanding why the number of provinces has mushroomed is a useful key to how India's federation has prevented civil war. The creation of new states allows India to accommodate distinct identities without bowing to outright separatism. Its federation binds the states with the 10 crucial factors for peace, but affords them enough latitude to reflect distinct regional identities.

In 1956, Nehru's government decided to split the provinces along linguistic lines. India's southern states have languages and scripts that are unrelated to those spoken in the north. A similarly dramatic linguistic split was introduced into the EU after 1995, with the accession of Finland, Estonia and then Hungary; their languages are from the Finno-Ugric group and are very different from the Indo-European tongues of the rest of the EU.

Nehru's decision to re-cast India's states by language followed one of the earliest crises he faced as prime minister. The Nizam of Hyderabad, a Muslim monarch in the south, had refused incorporation into the new Indian union. In turn, the Nizam faced rebellion by peasant speakers of the local language, Telugu, who rose in arms against their overlord with the support of communist radicals.

The Nizam's troops, the Razakars, were famous for their brutality, but they were not alone in this. Conservative estimates suggest that 50,000 Muslims in Telangana were killed in reprisals by their Hindu neighbours.[9] India's first response was military: it launched Operation Polo first to crush the Nizam, then against the communist-backed revolt.

The military's campaign against the communists was bloody, but once victorious the newfound Indian state adopted many of the anti-feudal reforms demanded by the insurgents. Nehru's government decided to reorganize south-central

India entirely. The Telugu-speaking part of the Nizam's old domain merged with another Telugu-speaking state called Andhra. Other parts of his kingdom were likewise hived off to neighbouring states on linguistic grounds.

Ultimately, however, a shared language was not enough to hold the new state of Andhra Pradesh together, any more than a single language could unite Britain and Ireland, or the Slovaks and the Czechs. The marriage was not a happy one. Some leaders in prosperous Telangana, centred on the city of Hyderabad, felt they were subsidizing the poorer but better-educated and coastal Andhra. The issue lingered for decades, but became more pressing once the initial dominance of Nehru's Congress Party gave way to a surge of regional parties in the 1990s, which began to win more and more seats with each general election.

As the 21st century dawned, the state's Telugu-speaking party faced a split. One faction created the TRS, a party committed to the creation of a new Telangana state. By first lending its support to the weak Congress-led coalition in Delhi, and then by threatening to withdraw this backing were its demands not met, the TRS effectively blackmailed India's national government into creating Telangana as a new province.[10] In other words, the TRS used the same kind of Veto and Consensus lever that is found in the EU.

The result was that in June 2014, after almost 70 years of agitation, Telangana became India's 29th state. It is possible to view this process as somewhat unsatisfactory. Both the national Congress Party and the regional TRS saw electoral advantage in the split. Parties associated with the creation of new states often become their longstanding political incumbents. For decades Congress, credited with winning India's independence from the British, faced little electoral opposition nationwide, and it was not until the 21st century that a non-Congress national government completed a full term in office.

Given the many perks of holding office in India, carving out new states also meant carving out new sinecures for politicians. As a result, statist movements are common in India; three new states were created in the year 2000 alone, and with every success more movements emerge to demand more new provinces. In a country where corruption and poverty are deadly issues, the creation of new layers of salaried politicians and state bureaucrats is a problem.

Yet, when compared to the convulsions endured by Africa, the process of state formation and dissolution in federal India can only be seen as peaceful and preferable. In Africa, the separation of South Sudan from Sudan in 2011 came only after decades of civil war. Namibia won independence in 1990 from South Africa after three decades of guerrilla fighting against the apartheid government in Pretoria. Eritrea spent the same three decades fighting for independence from Ethiopia.

Nor was Asia immune. Timor-Leste became independent of Indonesia in 2002 only after massacres by Indonesian forces and 'pro-integration' militias. In just a few days in August 1999, the UN Food and Agriculture Organization estimated that 7,000 Timorese were killed and at least 300,000 forced to flee their homes.[11] Order was only restored after external military intervention by Australia.

When set against such crises, India's framework for managing its conflicts begins to look quite effective. Imagine, for a moment, that the former Yugoslavia was contained within a democratic EU-like structure when it collapsed in the 1990s. The existence of an over-arching institutional framework would have identified the conflicts before they ignited, and would have arranged regular discussions between the parties. The Permanent Discussion, Dialogue and Diplomacy function would have worked its magic.

Yugoslavia was a form of transnational structure, uniting the socialist republics of Bosnia-Herzegovina, Serbia, Croatia, Slovenia, Montenegro and Macedonia. However, without the first and most critical of the 10 mechanisms, Democracy, all the union bred was mutual animosity with no outlet and no scope to renegotiate terms. The result was war, with no Permanent Discussion, Dialogue, and Diplomacy to forestall it.

The monopoly of force held by the Indian armed forces, on the other hand, meant that individual states had no option but to negotiate with words rather than weapons. In her engaging book *Punjabi Parmesan*, Pallavi Aiyar describes India as 'in some ways a proto-EU', in its ability to knit together a multitude of social and cultural norms in difficult circumstances.[12] She notes that despite the EU's failings, if Asia is to have any hope of building institutions across borders then it must hope for the EU's success.[13]

Yet she also notes that although Europe could learn from India how to create a strong, common identity out of seemingly fractured multiplicity, it seems to have no capacity to learn:

...with characteristic arrogance, the EU does not care to look elsewhere for inspiration, and certainly not towards dirty, poor, teeming India.[14]

It remains easy to critique India's model. The kind of communist militants who backed the original Telangana revolt continue to rampage across eastern India, waging Maoist guerrilla war for increasingly inscrutable purposes. Their violence is more a manifestation of economic inequality than of differences between ethnic or linguistic groups, although the two issues are intertwined. Much of India remains very poor, although that is changing rapidly.

In terms of pan-Asian regional union, India's size poses a difficulty. How can its federal system ever be incorporated into a larger regional body? If mishandled, the process could undermine the security that the Indian state has achieved, while further complicating its neighbourly relations. Nor is India the only giant that an Asian union must accommodate.

China

Like India, the People's Republic of China has harnessed the peace-making power of the 10 factors within a national context. It emphasizes some more than others. China, for instance, lacks the Democracy function, although that does not mean it lacks feedback mechanisms between the rulers and the ruled. The Chinese Communist Party (CCP) has a membership of more than 85 million, and the growth of social media has given ordinary Chinese scope to voice their opinions.

Unlike India, China does not have a federal system of government. It does not devolve specific legal powers to its provinces. It is a unitary state.[15] However, as Zheng Yongnian notes, there exists a *de facto* federalism generated by the internal dynamic of the one-party state. Successfully leading a province is a crucial yardstick for ambitious members of the CCP who want to make it all the way to the politburo. Provincial leadership has become a 'beauty contest' in which different styles of leaders compete for the party's affection.

During his years as the party chief of Guangzhou province, for instance, Wang Yang cultivated an image as a progressive liberal. From this platform, he was elevated to become one of China's four vice-premiers in 2013, although he missed out on a place on the all-powerful politburo standing committee. Nevertheless, Wang is perhaps China's most powerful reformist. By contrast, Bo Xilai took a very different approach in Chongqing, stoking nostalgia for Maoism and urging patriotism. Bo eventually fell foul of the CCP's internal politics and was imprisoned for life for corruption.

The *de facto* nature of this federal dynamic is sometimes expressed by the Chinese proverb *shan gao, Huangdi yuan* – 'the mountains are high and the emperor is far away'. No matter how devoted Beijing might be to the concept of a unitary state, the tyranny of distance imposed by China's sheer size means that a degree of regional autonomy is inevitable. This epigram is also sometimes cited to note the intensity of corruption in far-flung provinces.

The CCP derives its political legitimacy from its ability to deliver economic development, and this dynamic is present at the provincial level. Chinese provinces compete against one another to see which can attract the most investment, foster the most rapid growth, and develop the most advanced industries. This competition has been a significant driver of China's economic transformation since the late 1970s.[16]

Chinese provincial governments are permitted to negotiate directly with other countries. A delegation from the southern province of Yunnan, for instance, can visit Nepal and discuss bilateral economic co-operation, or go to Bangladesh and lobby for Yunnanese companies, or travel to Delhi to suggest greater tourism co-operation between India and their province. A delegation from Sichuan provincial government can visit the US Pacific North-West and sign a memorandum of understanding to promote trade and investment with the state of Washington. The government of Shandong can invite Californian businesses to help develop Shandong's IT industry. Inner Mongolia can forge its own distinctive relationship with the Seychelles.[17]

Here lies a clue for how Asia's giants can be integrated into a regional union. In one, extraordinary instance, Beijing allowed a single Chinese province to join a transnational grouping. The Greater Mekong Subregion (GMS) initiative was created by the Asian Development Bank in 1992 to promote integration in mainland South-East Asia. It brought together Vietnam, Laos, Cambodia, Thailand and Burma with the Chinese province of Yunnan and, from 2005, one of China's autonomous areas, Guangxi Zhuang.

China's central government maintains a guiding role in the provinces' interaction with the GMS, and Beijing sends its head of government to summits, but it has devolved practical negotiating power to the provinces. China's 2011 report on its provinces' role in the GMS acknowledges the benefits for stability that such initiatives offer, particularly in relation to minority groups that overlap borders.[18]

By allowing individual provinces to operate in this way, governments can ease any sense of national confusion felt by cross-border minorities. Fifteen such minorities exist in China's Yunnan province alone. Time and again, such overlapping groups are drawn into violent confrontation by governments suspicious of their national loyalties: the Pashtun

and Baluch of western Pakistan, eastern Afghanistan and
Iran; the Basques of Spain and France; the Kurds of Turkey,
Syria, Iraq and Iran.

China's central government therefore has good reason to
be enthusiastic about its provinces' local outreach. It trusts
its provincial leaders not to engage in separatism, because all
are members of the ruling CCP. There is little concern that
allowing them to negotiate with foreign governments poses a
threat to Chinese territorial cohesion. Every Chinese province
and major city has its own foreign affairs office, and the
contribution of the provinces to China's foreign policy is now
well documented.[19]

Bengal and Pakistan

Unfortunately, India's position is not quite the same.
Although the chief ministers of states sometimes meet visiting
dignitaries, foreign policy is heavily centralized in Delhi. This
may change: in 2014, India's newly elected prime minister
Narendra Modi promised greater consultation with chief
ministers on foreign affairs. He even suggested that each state
might be allowed to partner with foreign countries.[20] Such an
initiative would much improve India's ability to integrate into
a wider Asian union.

For this to happen, however, India needs to become much
more confident in itself. Allowing the government of West
Bengal to negotiate directly with Bangladesh over their
extensive mutual interests, for instance, would cause great
nervousness in Delhi. Both West Bengal and Bangladesh are
ethnically Bengali, and the Bengalis are arguably a nation in
their own right, with their own distinct arts and literature.
They were split along confessional lines first by the British,
who created East and West Bengal in 1905, and then again by
the creation of Pakistan, of which Bangladesh was initially the
eastern wing.

A close relationship between the Bengali capitals of Kolkata
and Dhaka might raise questions of why the two Bengals
are politically separate. Such questions would also be raised

by political propinquity between Indian and Sri Lankan Tamils, or between Mizo speakers in northeast India and in Burma. Any dialogue between the Pakistani and Indian Punjabs would be regarded with great suspicion in Delhi, given Pakistan's sponsorship of Punjabi Sikh separatists in the 1980s. As for Kashmir and Indian Muslims in general, India's security establishment would be alarmed by Pakistan speaking directly to them.

To change this mind-set, one must understand that the centralization of India's diplomacy is itself a driver of conflict. India's smaller neighbours find it difficult to negotiate with Delhi on an equal footing precisely because of India's sheer size. This breeds hostility. Devolving diplomacy to state governments would offer India a chance to improve its regional relations and to build the kind of enduring people-to-people relationships on which peace is based (Open Borders and Human Ties).

Currently, India is trapped in a halfway house. Were it a traditional nation-state, its borders would not be so messy and contested. Were it a transnational union, it would be open to admitting new members. As strange as this may seem, given India's history of conflict with Pakistan, there are those on both the Left and Right of the Indian political spectrum who believe that India should never have been partitioned in the first instance, and that the divide between the Hindus and Muslims of British India was not so great as to prevent them coexisting in the same polity. In the realms of cinema, music and sport, for instance, there is extensive crossover to the point where the two cultures can be considered as one.

Nor should it be assumed that all Pakistanis are resistant to this kind of transnational Greater India. The inhabitants of Pakistan's southwestern province of Baluchistan, for instance, are viewed with suspicion within Pakistan because some Baluch tribes appear to prefer India to Pakistan. And in the northwest, as Nehru noted, the Pashtun are culturally distinct. Many do not view themselves as Pakistani at all.

China's incorporation into any kind of pan-Asian union

presents the opposite problem. Whereas India's political centralization is a paranoid response to the staggering diversity of its population, it is difficult to disguise the fact that China is overwhelmingly Han Chinese. For a country so large, it is surprisingly uniform. A variety of dialects exists, but there is no dispute over the supremacy of Mandarin as standard Chinese speech. And no matter how much it devolves power, its neighbours (with the exception of India) know that they will be hopelessly overmatched, in terms of scale, should they pool sovereignty with Beijing.

Two trends have eventuated from this. The first is the BRICS. China, India, Russia, Brazil and (latterly) South Africa have formed a 'giants' club' to promote their claims to regional and global leadership. In retrospect, South Africa's inclusion at the expense of Nigeria looks erroneous, given that Nigeria is Africa's largest economy and most populous state. Groups that have tried to combine both giants and minnows have struggled to produce concrete policies: Apec, ACD, Bimstec, SAARC, the East Asia Summit spring to mind in this respect.

ASEAN

The second trend is that China's size incentivizes its smaller neighbours to band together. When the giants are excluded, progress is easier to come by. In particular, the Association of South-East Asian Nations (ASEAN) has become a model for transnational co-operation, with an ever-strengthening record of promoting peace and democracy within its membership.

ASEAN views the promotion of peace as one of its core objectives. It was founded in 1967, during the Vietnam War, by Indonesia, Malaysia, the Philippines, Singapore and Thailand, who despite their vast internal differences saw regional co-operation as essential to a stable future. Later, the other countries of South-East Asia joined them: those caught up in the Vietnam War, including Cambodia, Laos and Vietnam itself; the small but wealthy oil sultanate of Brunei; and even isolated Burma, renamed Myanmar by its military regime.

It was in Myanmar that ASEAN's beneficial influence

became clearest. Until internal reforms that brought civilian government to Burma in March 2011, ASEAN refused to allow the country to chair the group, and other leaders have frequently spoken out against the military government's repression. Thailand and the Philippines initially opposed Burma's accession completely, only yielding in 1997.

Some sceptics had written off ASEAN as a 'talking shop' similar to most other multilateral groups, but they were forced to re-examine this claim following the surprisingly all-embracing nature of Burma's political transformation, which included the release from house arrest of democracy leader Aung Sang Suu Kyi, although one which left the military with significant political power.

Democracy is present only patchily in South-East Asia. Of ASEAN's membership, only a minority of states boast true electoral competition between parties, unmediated by the military or a ruling establishment. Nevertheless, Burma's shift meant that after 2011 there was a brief period when all ASEAN's member governments were led by a civilian, a record that was ended abruptly by Thailand's coup in May 2014.

ASEAN's naysayers must also confront another powerful truth. Since the bloc's creation, no ASEAN member has ever declared war on another member state. Given the region's historical propensity for conflict, this achievement is an important one, although the end of the Cold War's ideological competition in the theatre was another important factor.

ASEAN has some unique advantages over other Asian multilateral groups. The bloc contains every single country in South-East Asia, which is a well-defined sub-region. The only exception is south-eastern China but, as already noted, the GMS bridges this gap. ASEAN has only 10 members, and they face many of the same challenges in terms of their peripheral geography, transitional economies and reliance on trade. Indonesia and Malaysia speak what is essentially the same language; so do Thailand and Laos, though using different alphasyllabaries.

In 2008, ASEAN enacted a charter which committed the

bloc to respect for human rights, to work in each others'
mutual defence but without nuclear weapons, and co-
operation and integration in all spheres. It also pledged non-
interference in each others' affairs, although in Burma's case
that rule proved to be flexible. Most importantly, however, the
charter committed the group to the creation of the ASEAN
Community by 2015.

That deadline lent special significance to Malaysia's chairing
of the group in November 2014. The Malaysian government
was tasked with overseeing the transition from a loose, albeit
effective, group of nation-states to a transnational organization
akin to the European Union. The Community was intended
to have three pillars: Political-Security, Economic, and Socio-
Cultural.

As of late 2014, the group had achieved 80 per cent of its
benchmarks towards economic integration,[21] but with the
hardest still to be implemented. An editorial in the *Jakarta
Post* pointed out that despite the scepticism, 187 of the
community's 277 measures had been in place by the end of
2011, and that the process was therefore 'right on track'.[22] The
ASEAN summit of April 2015 was devoted to drafting the final
blueprint for the Community before the year-end deadline.
All this went largely unnoticed outside the sub-region, even
among professional Asia watchers.

What was most striking was the unanimity among ASEAN
leaders over the importance of making the Community work,
hurdles notwithstanding. National leaders warned of the
challenges of achieving the organization's goals on time, but
it was also clear that they took their responsibility towards
unity with due seriousness. 'Indonesia will not allow itself to
become merely a market,' Indonesia's President Joko Widodo
warned his fellow ASEAN members, in a sign that he would
not allow his country's relative size to work against it within
the new system. Thailand's military leader urged the bloc
onwards, even though his junta was a potential loser from
ASEAN's preference for democracy.[23]

One outside force has added impetus to ASEAN's drive for

unity. China's claims to own disputed islands in the South China Sea have focused minds along the Ring of Fire, even as ASEAN members disputed the islands' ownership between themselves. With every passing year, China becomes richer and more technologically advanced, and its military forces have followed suit.

The governments of ASEAN have co-ordinated their responses to China's territorial claims, to the point where some governments now speak of their being only 'two sides' to the dispute,[24] a binary division reinforced by the wording of the draft ASEAN-China joint declaration of conduct in the South China Sea.[25] China, by contrast, is displeased by the unified ASEAN front it now faces. It has demanded to negotiate only with individual members of ASEAN, not with the bloc as a whole.[26]

By distributing aid and investment around the bloc, China's government has ensured that some ASEAN members take a much softer line on the dispute than others, again demonstrating the importance of the Resistance to External Interference factor. The US has sought to offset China's influence with support of its own. That the giants take ASEAN so seriously now demonstrates how powerful it could become if it achieved EU-like levels of unity.

Regional unity

Asia is not a continent in the same way that Europe is a continent, or that North America is a continent. Rather, it is a group of subcontinents, each of which carries fractures and fault lines that must be addressed if regional unity is to be found. Dreams of a single pan-Asian structure are distant ones. Sub-regionally, the picture is brighter. There is a realistic chance that ASEAN will surprise the world with the effectiveness of its EU-style community.

The same result could be achieved in South Asia by a looser, decentralized Indian federation, one which permitted closer ties between its provinces and neighbouring countries. It is now certain that any peace in Kashmir will be the result of a 'people-centric' solution, rather than any transfer of territory. Were all Kashmiris to be granted automatic dual nationality of India and Pakistan, and able to cross between the two as they pleased, much of the bilateral tension would dissipate. Just as importantly, the Kashmiris would be able to craft their own distinct identity, as the Northern Irish have done, without alienating either Delhi or Islamabad.

In the longer term, such improved relations would pave the way for a shared rupee and a free-trade zone that would unlock vast new wealth for the Indian subcontinent. A South Asia Free Trade Area already exists, under the umbrella of the SAARC regional body, but Indo-Pakistani animosity renders it dysfunctional. If that enmity can be overcome, however, the eastern and western extremities of the old British India, Burma and Afghanistan would become transit states between the South Asian bloc, ASEAN and Central Asia. Most importantly of all, the scope for armed conflict between the nuclear-armed forces of India and Pakistan would diminish dramatically.

A slightly different model is required for northeast Asia. China remains an irreducible giant, though one with profound cultural connections to Japan and the Koreas. The latitude China affords provinces to speak to other countries is key to unlocking the regional door. China could allow Manchurian provinces such as Jilin the opportunity to participate in a GMS-style combination with Japan and the Koreas, one that does not overmatch its neighbours with the sheer size of China's unitary whole. The homogeneity of China's population, and the rigidity of its one-party system, should ease any concerns in Beijing over political fragmentation arising from such initiatives.

Such a decentralized approach would serve China's internal stability. Civil unrest in Hong Kong showed the limits of the one-size-fits-all attitude to Chinese national identity. Hong Kong's educated and liberal workforce demanded greater freedoms than those available to the impoverished peasantry of the mainland interior. Governed by Beijing as a 'special autonomous region', Hong Kong was an obvious crucible in which the CCP could experiment with a democratic franchise, but its fear of a domino effect spilling into mainland cities prevented it from being attempted.

With tens of millions of Chinese nationals graduating with advanced degrees from Western universities, however, China must establish a mechanism to reflect their aspirations, without overturning a successful development model that, despite its repressive nature, has erased extreme poverty in most of the country. The only obvious means of accommodating both is to allow prosperous areas such as Hong Kong a more democratic form of government.

Such latitude is more likely to bind Hong Kong to China than to push it away from it. Foreign elections are already covered by Chinese state media in some detail. Taiwan, which China views as a renegade province, has become more welcoming to mainland investment and cultural ties just as Beijing has become less insistent on achieving direct political control of the island in the immediate future. Drawing Taiwan's ruling Kuomintang Party into mainland Chinese politics is a more productive means of reunifying China than any kind of military adventure on the part of the People's Liberation Army and Navy.

Suggesting that Tibet should be allowed to participate in the South Asian bloc is likely to be a step too far for Beijing, at least for now. China invaded India in 1962 to recapture areas of what it considers to be Tibet (and therefore China) and it still lays claims to tens of thousands of square miles of Indian territory. India retaliated by permitting the US Central Intelligence Agency to support separatists fighting Chinese rule in Tibet.[27]

Nevertheless, there is a precedent for India and China coming to terms. In 1954 they signed the Panchsheel ('Five Values') agreement, which committed them to peaceful coexistence and mutual recognition of each other's territory. The civilizations have an ancient history of tolerance and peaceful coexistence that can be traced back as far as

Confucius, Gautam Buddha and Mahavir, and enlightened rulers such as Ashoka, Akbar the Great and the second Qing dynasty emperor, Kangxi.

In the very long term, these cultural traditions have the potential to underpin a pan-Asian government that unites South and South-East Asia with China and its northern neighbours. Such a regional structure is the only sure way to manage disputes, such as those over Tibet and the South China Sea, that pit the subcontinents against one another.

Without effective sub-regional unions, Asia is likely to repeat the mistakes of the 20th century. Already, India and China are locked in an arms race. This has been encouraged by those Western powers with an interest in selling weapons (in other words, most of them). This is not in the interests of either country, whose citizens expect their quality of life to improve in proportion to the taxes they pay. Asia's newfound wealth should instead be devoted to Financial Incentives and Support, the factor targeted at impoverished zones of conflict.

Alongside a beggar-thy-neighbour arms race, the giants are seeking out smaller nations, literally to render them thorns in their opponents' sides. The US has rebalanced its military-industrial focus to the Asia-Pacific, ostensibly to respond to the alleged 'threat' posed by China but in reality to sell more armaments to a group of increasingly wealthy Asian buyers. India and the US are tightening their military co-operation with Japan, as a means of encircling China.

This strategy means unpicking Japan's highly successful post-war policy of pacifism. Japan's ruling party has announced plans to change the constitution so that the country may once again fight foreign wars.[28] Its shift has attracted no criticism from the West, even though many families in the US, UK and South-East Asia retain painful memories of Japanese militarism in the Second World War.

Instead of remilitarizing, Japan should proclaim the tremendous example that its demilitarized economy set the world in the latter 20th century, when for a time it was the world's second-biggest economy. Japan should be leading the construction of institutions that foster permanent Discussion, Dialogue and Diplomacy across Asia; a far better means of settling minor territorial spats over uninhabited islands than stocking up on imported weapons systems.

Japan is not the only Asian power being used instrumentally against its neighbours. The US, China and Saudi Arabia have cultivated Pakistan as a militaristic client state, using it as a weapon against the Taliban, India and Iran respectively. Afghanistan in particular has become an open-ended quagmire. It serves to remind the world that even after 1945, Asia endured a devastating 20th century, with wars rampaging across not only Afghanistan but Indochina, Korea, Kashmir and Bangladesh, to name but a few. Only the complacent would see modern Asia as being permanently stable.

Given that nuclear weapons form part of the arsenals of China, India, Pakistan, North Korea and Russia (which stretches into the Asia-Pacific), pooling their sovereignty should be seen as a matter of urgent priority. The likelihood of nuclear warfare between North Korea and its many adversaries, and between India and Pakistan, is greater than it is anywhere else in the world.

It is for this reason that the sometimes tortuous and hesitant moves towards sub-regional integration are so important in Asia. And it is for this reason that it is vital that the EU itself is measured as a success, and as a model for collectives such as ASEAN. As the originator of the peace-through-union approach, the EU remains the template for continents far removed from Europe, and where the humanitarian stakes are higher.

---

1 p.61, Nehru, Jawaharlal, *The Discovery of India*, OUP, 6th edition, 1994. 2 Government of India, State-wise Per Capita Income and Gross Domestic Product at current prices. 3 This difference is still much less than between the richest and poorest members of the European Union, Luxembourg and Romania. 4 Transport Dept, Government of Rajasthan, 'Tax on Vehicles of Other States'. 5 World Bank, India Development Update (English), October 2014. 6 p.152, Khilnani, Sunil, *The Idea of India*, Penguin, 1997. 7 p.154, ibid. 8 p.297-99, Muggeridge, Malcolm,

Chronicles of Wasted Time, Regent College Publishing, 2006. **9** p11, Sherman, Taylor C, 2007, 'The integration of the princely state of Hyderabad and the making of the postcolonial state in India, 1948-5', Indian Economic & Social History Review, 44 (4). **10** Sekhar, A Saye, 2014, 'Telangana: Why TRS snubbed Congress, flirted with BJP', *First Post,* 4 March. **11** Lachica, Alan A, 'Humanitarian intervention in East Timor: An analysis of Australia's leadership role', *The Peace and Conflict Review,* University for Peace. **12** p.xxiv, Aiyar, Pallavi, *Punjabi Parmesan,* Penguin, 2013. **13** p.311, Pallavi, ibid. **14** p.306, Pallavi, ibid **15** See 'China's de facto federalism', Zheng, Yongnian, in *Federalism in Asia,* eds: He Baogang, Brian Galligan, Takashi Inoguchi, Edward Elgar Publishing, 2007. **16** Gordon, Roger H. and Wei Li, 2011. 'Provincial and Local Governments in China: Fiscal Institutions and Government Behavior.' Working Paper 16694, National Bureau of Economic Research. **17** See 'Inner Mongolia: Memorandum Of Understanding Signed With Seychelles', 11 June 2013, unpo.org/article/16040 **18** Official report, 'China's Participation in Greater Mekong Subregion Cooperation', 2011, released by China's National Development and Reform Commission, Ministry of Foreign Affairs, Ministry of Finance, and the Ministry of Science and Technology, 17 December. **19** See Chen Zhimin, Jian, Junbo and Chen, Diyu, 'The Provinces and China's Multi-Layered Diplomacy: The Cases of GMS and Africa', *The Hague Journal of Diplomacy,* 5 (2010) pp331-356. **20** Nanda, Prakash, 'Federalisation Of Indian Foreign Policy', occasional paper for the Forum of Federations, www.forumfed.org/en/pubs/OPS13_Federalisation_Indian_Foreign_Policy.pdf **21** Lim, Yan Liang, 2014, 'Asean Summit: Integrated Asean economic community will help improve citizens' lives, says PM Lee', *Straits Times,* 12 November. **22** Benny Hutabarat, 2014, 'ASEAN Economic Community 2015: Will it happen?', *Jakarta Post,* 24 November. **23** Staff, 2014, 'Prayut calls for tighter Asean ahead of union', *Bangkok Post,* 13 November. **24** Ng, Eileen, 2015, 'ASEAN wants China to stop work in disputed sea: official', Associated Press, 4 August. **25** 'Declaration on the conduct of parties in the South China Sea,' ASEAN. **26** Webb, Simon. 2014, 'China offers ASEAN friendship, loans as South China Sea tension bubbles', Reuters, 13 November. **27** See Conboy, Kenneth and Morrison, James, *The CIA's Secret War in Tibet,* University Press of Kansas, 2002. **28** Sieg, Linda, 2015, 'PM Abe's party eyes revision of Japan pacifist constitution by late 2018', Reuters, 27 April.

Chapter 5 – The Quiet Continent (South American Union)

South America has made greater strides towards an EU-like regional union than any continent bar Europe. Under the ambit of UNASUR, the continent is moving rapidly towards the kind of unity envisioned by the EU, and has reaped the benefits in terms of the ebbing of serious inter-state conflict. Just as importantly, UNASUR has helped to bury South America's tradition of military dictatorship.

In late 2014, the body known as UNASUR opened its headquarters in Quito, the capital of Ecuador. Its new building was extraordinary. From one angle, the modernist architecture suggested a handgun laid to rest on its side. From another, it looked more like a series of steps. Set against the backdrop of the Andes, the headquarters were built next to the Mitad del Mundo monument marking zero degrees latitude, the equatorial line that gives Ecuador its name.

There is a certain irony to Mitad del Mundo, the 'Middle of the World'. It is decidedly not how the rest of the planet views South America. The grand opening attracted the leaders of a dozen nations and made headlines across the continent. Further afield, few paid attention. The world's eyes were fixed on the rising powers of China and India, the violence of the Middle East, and the antics of Vladimir Putin's Russia. There was little space left for opening ceremonies in Ecuador.

Yet the revolution represented by UNASUR was so profound that, soon, the rest of the world would have little option but to take heed. UNASUR is a contraction of *Unión de Naciones Suramericanas,* the Union of South American Nations. It has a second meaning: 'One South'. In 2011, at the moment the foundation stone of the new headquarters was laid, UNASUR united two customs unions, the Andean Community and Mercosur,[1] representing the upper and lower halves of South America. Twelve countries were brought into a single mechanism, stretching from Colombia in the north to Argentina in the south, with a combined population roughly equal to that of the United States.

The US provided a model and a counterpoint to UNASUR's ambitions. Although it is simplistic to lay all the continent's woes at the feet of the US, South America has long desired a more symmetrical relationship with North America, based on equality rather than patronage. In the 20th century, the white-skinned leaders of South America were the reliable partners of Washington, for the most part. By the turn of the millennium, South America's pure-blooded European elites were dwindling, however, and the rise of national leaders closely linked to South America's multicultural poor shifted the ground beneath intra-American relations.

To achieve the change it sought, the continent needed a way of speaking with one voice, rather than split endlessly between squabbling pro- and anti-US governments. Time and again, Latin American voters were offered a choice between revolutionaries and radicals on the far-Left of the political spectrum, and US-trained technocrats with policy prescriptions drafted by the US Chamber of Commerce. Finding a middle path between outright opposition to Washington on one hand, and fawning acceptance on the other, was one that only a strong and united continent could plot. It was the same path being charted by China, Russia, India and the European Union.

South America's pendulous swings between radical free markets and radical governments led to political instability and its usual corollary, political violence. It also generated a mishmash of extreme economic doctrines. Among the most dogmatic was the 1989 'Washington Consensus', a 10-point plan that boiled down to South American governments letting foreign companies do whatever they liked.

The anti-state dogma of the 'Consensus' was not justified. As China has shown, state-led economic development can be extremely rapid. Yet China's approach was only effective because it was large enough to shrug off foreign complaints about its protectionism, its currency peg (which made Chinese exports artificially cheap), its state subsidies, its industrial-scale industrial espionage, its politically controlled judiciary and the chronic pollution that accompanied its rapid development.

Cuba

Smaller countries cannot get away with China's approach. The US and Europe use the size of their markets, and their ability to bar access to them, to bring minnows into line. The Caribbean island of Cuba is a quintessential example of this big-small divergence. Like China, the island remains, in theory, a communist state. Like China, its government has sought to open the economy in some sectors, for instance tourism. Like China, Cuba's government operates a one-party state that is guilty of serious human rights abuses, but which is nevertheless accepted worldwide as the legitimate representation of its people.

There, the resemblance ends. Whereas China and the US are trading partners extraordinaire, the US maintains a trade embargo against Cuba. Whereas Beijing is a genuine strategic rival to Washington, the government in Havana could not be viewed in the same light. And whereas China and the US have broad and dense diplomatic relations, it was only in December 2014, at the instigation of Pope Francis, that the US and Cuban leaders conducted their first phone conversation since Fidel Castro's coup of 1959 against the US-backed dictator Fulgencio Batista. The following year, the countries restored their embassies in Havana and Washington DC.

Cuba's isolation arose from a combination of miscalculation and misfortune. In early 1961, the US supported the failed Bay of Pigs invasion by armed Cuban exiles. Castro then successfully persuaded the Soviet Union to position ballistic missiles on the island, bringing the world to the brink of nuclear war in 1962 as the US blockaded Cuban ports to prevent the Russian ships from docking. It continued its economic embargo even after the crisis was resolved by Moscow withdrawing its weapons, and even as Cuba not only preserved one of the best social-care networks in the region but also exported doctors to neighbouring countries.

In 1980, under intense economic pressure, Castro's government announced that Cubans who wished to leave the island could do so. Cubans in Miami organized the Mariel Boatlift to bring some 120,000 Cubans across the Straits of Florida. The exercise soon ground to a halt after the *New York Times* reported that 'retarded people and criminals' were among those making the crossing.[2] Nevertheless, the boatlift bolstered a virulently anti-Castro voting bloc in Florida. US politicians who even contemplated visiting the island paid an electoral price.[3] And with Florida notorious as the swing-state that brought President George W Bush to power in 2000, Democrats and Republicans vied to be tough on Cuba.

Some US commentators said that it was Cuba's proximity to the US that explained its harsh treatment. They argued that were China, or indeed a Vietnam or Angola, just a few miles from Key West then US policy towards them would be very different. Many observers, however, found this explanation unsatisfactory. They instead saw a clear double-standard between how Washington treats large countries such as China and those it can easily isolate.

Trade treaties

Cuba is an extreme example. Nevertheless, other regional countries have experienced US coercion when it comes to trade and sovereignty. By definition, sovereign governments are those capable of acting in a way that foreign countries dislike. If a government can only act in ways endorsed by larger powers such as the US, it is no more than a vassal state.

When negotiating trade treaties, for instance, the US and EU tend to encroach on the sovereignty of their counterparties by insisting that they open their legal environment to a process known as international arbitration. This means that disputes with foreign companies are not settled by domestic courts but by tribunals in the US and Europe operated by entities such as ICSID, the International Centre for Settlement of Investment

Disputes.

The idea is that foreign investors can be confident of a fair hearing in any dispute with the authorities, confident that the judges are not susceptible to political pressure. Yet the system is undemocratic, secretive, and vests huge power in unaccountable lawyers.[4,5] Although corporations can use ICSID to sue governments, the reverse is not true: governments cannot use it to protect the interests of their citizens. And of the 57 cases brought in 2013, 45 were lodged by companies from the wealthiest nations.[6]

These shortcomings began to attract attention in the West after the US and European Union began negotiating their TTIP trade treaty in 2013. For Latin America, however, arbitration was for years a totemic example of the hemispheric power imbalance. In 2009 a Canadian-Australian mining company sued the government of El Salvador after it was refused permission to mine for gold in the country. El Salvador had cancelled the practice of giving out new mining permits due to the widespread contamination of surface water, a ban that was popular in El Salvador. However, the terms of the country's 1999 investment law allowed foreign companies to take the government to arbitration. In this case, the mining company claimed damages of $301 million – almost 10 per cent of the country's economy.[7]

In 2007 Bolivia became the first state to repudiate ICSID entirely. Explaining his decision, President Evo Morales, the first indigenous Aymara to lead Bolivia, said that multinational corporations used ICSID to violate the sovereignty of poor nations. 'The governments of Latin America, and I think the world, never win the cases,' Morales complained. 'The multinationals always win.'[8]

Withdrawing two years later, Rafael Correa, the president of Ecuador, used stronger language. ICSID, said the president, 'signifies colonialism, slavery with respect to transnationals, with respect to Washington, with respect to the World Bank and we cannot tolerate this'.[9] According to diplomatic cables obtained by Wikileaks (its founder Julian Assange later sought asylum in Ecuador's London embassy), Ecuador was at the time facing some $10 billion in claims lodged against it with ICSID, mostly by foreign energy companies.[10] This was equivalent to $700 for every man, woman and child in a country where average incomes are less than $6,000 a year.

One factor behind many of the claims against Ecuador was a windfall tax Correa imposed on corporate profits. It should be noted that Western multinationals were not the only losers from Ecuador's radical state intervention in the economy. Brazilian and Argentine firms had major stakes in Ecuador's natural gas sector, and its re-nationalization presented a serious setback to regional economic harmony and integration.

Surprisingly, it was not until 2012 that Hugo Chávez, Venezuela's flamboyantly anti-US president, followed the lead of Correa and Morales. His decision to leave ICSID was prompted by a demand for $12 billion from the US energy major Exxon, after Chávez's government expropriated Exxon's assets in the Orinoco tar belt. Chávez called the attempted suit 'arrogant' – an accusation that even ICSID seemed to endorse. In October 2014, it awarded Exxon just $1.6 billion.[11]

Although there are other arbitral bodies, ICSID is best known because it was created under the auspices of the World Bank, a US-dominated institution that, as its former president Robert Zoellick admitted, was the main delivery mechanism for the loathed 'Washington Consensus'.[12] Such supposedly impartial bodies came to be seen in Latin America as the agents of foreign corporations, pretending to recommend fair and objective solutions while acting exclusively in the interests of their corporate and political masters.

Forging a single polity

Given this context, it is no surprise that South American nations are enthusiastic about combining to resist such pressure. The very existence of UNASUR's new HQ was a stride forward. Inside, 20,000 square metres of office space were allocated to the officials tasked with forging South America into a single polity. It is such officials, brought into a single ecosystem, who create what we mean by 'institutions': those regular, sustainable processes that outlive their creators to become a permanent system of government. In their drab, creeping way, these officials prepare the legal documents that, when signed by elected leaders, bring nation-states into ever closer union. 'UNASUR rises as a power, but as a power for peace,' said Ecuador's President Rafael Correa at the building's opening.

The nature of transnational institutions, and the complexity of their task, often draws scepticism from commentators. With so many moving parts, and such dependence on national leaders to agree, pundits flee to the safety of stock phrases such as 'talking shop' and 'opaque bureaucracy'. In UNASUR's case, critics have also tended instead to question its ideology.

They were swift to identify an anti-US slant. The Heritage Foundation, a conservative think-tank in the US, suspected UNASUR of 'camaraderie' with Venezuela's radical government. It berated US President Barack Obama for what he called his 'blind support for the new bloc'.[13] Although most US politicians are indifferent to UNASUR, or supportive of it, it was easy to see why the Right wing of the US political spectrum were suspicious. UNASUR includes among its objectives the elimination of economic inequality and reducing 'asymmetries.[14] The first objective is closely associated with leftwing politics; the second, a code word for challenging the preponderance of US power globally and in the western hemisphere in particular. UNASUR's secretary-general, Enresto Samper, has called for a review of the 'prohibitionist' approach to illegal narcotics, an approach unpalatable to many US lawmakers.[15]

When compared to the difficulties facing Europe's integration, those facing South America are easily resolved. There is a commonality of historical experience across the continent, and the vast majority of South Americans speak one of two closely related languages, Spanish and Portuguese. Many UNASUR members face the similar challenges of accommodating the rights of indigenous peoples who in some cases, such as in Bolivia, now again constitute the majority. In others, such as Peru and Ecuador, majorities are mixed raced, having both Amerindian and European heritage but a worldview not easily reconciled with either. The economic inequality facing UNASUR is more manageable than that elsewhere. Its richest country is Uruguay, with a per capita GDP of $16,810; the poorest is Bolivia at $3,150.[16] In proportional terms, this gap is smaller than those between the richest and poorest states in Europe, Asia and Africa. Within the US, Alaskans – the richest per head – earn just over twice as much on average as those in the poorest state, Mississippi, but in absolute terms the dollar gap, at around $30,000, is much wider than that between Bolivians and Uruguayans.[17] There is inequality between the countries of South America, but not of the kind that prompts the mass movement of workers across the EU.

South America is also blessed with a political culture that spawns some inspirational leaders. The former president of Brazil, Lula da Silva, received international acclaim. Chile's President Michelle Bachelet, a single mother who speaks five languages, achieved the rare feat of becoming considerably more popular in the years after she took office, largely as a result of her investment in education. José Mujica, until 2015 the president of Uruguay, was a former guerrilla and prison escapee who even in office lived a humble lifestyle and donated 90 per cent of his salary to charity.

Such is their credibility and mandate that the leaders can meet and agree real changes in an atmosphere of mutual respect. UNASUR's internal goals are comparable to those of the European Union three decades ago. In December 2014, Secretary-General Samper announced joint approval for a concept of South American citizenship.[18] Ultimately, UNASUR hopes that this will result in the free movement of people.

Bruce Douglas, a former BBC journalist based in Rio, points out that ever since Simón Bolívar's letter from Jamaica, the dream of Latin American unity has been championed by the continent's most charismatic – and occasionally demagogic –

statesmen. UNASUR was inspired by Venezuela's Chávez and brought into being by Brazil's Lula da Silva. But while previous organizations have foundered following economic crises or violent coups, Latin America's increasingly robust democracies provide a solid basis for the hope that UNASUR will be able to deliver on some of its promises.

Douglas notes that although some regional leaders, notably Ecuador's Rafael Correa, chafe at the slowness of its proceedings, during its short history UNASUR has quietly made some significant achievements. It intervened deftly in crises in Bolivia, Honduras, Ecuador and Paraguay and, in 2014, it played a key role in defusing tensions between the government and the opposition in Venezuela. With Chávez dead and Lula out of office, UNASUR is steadily developing into the kind of democratic, progressive institution that does not depend on outsize personalities to thrive.

Here we see three of the 10 preconditions for Europe's peace established: Permanent Discussion, Dialogue and Diplomacy; Resistance to External Interference; and Peaceful Coexistence and Mutual Trust. But UNASUR is not neglecting the other seven. Freedom of movement, freedom of trade, and rules and rights are all UNASUR ambitions.

One of its plans is to create three east-west trade corridors connecting the South Atlantic and South Pacific.[19] These rail and transit corridors would allow South American countries to export their goods both east and west: on the Atlantic side, to Europe or up the coast to the major demand centres on the US eastern seaboard; on the Pacific, up to Los Angeles or Vancouver or, more promisingly, across the ocean to the fast-growing economies of Asia.

At the moment, South America feels acutely the consequences of trade inflexibility. Despite the atrocious relations between Hugo Chávez's government and Washington, which were scarcely improved by Chávez's death and the transfer of power to his protégé Nicolas Maduro, Venezuela's oil exports continued to flow overwhelmingly towards refineries on the Texas coastline. As of 2013, the year of Chávez's death, Venezuela remained the fourth-largest oil exporter to the US.[20]

This reliance was due to the heaviness of Orinoco bitumen, which requires pre-processing before it can be refined – Texas has the plants needed to do this – but it also showed South America's difficulty in diversifying away from its reliance on US consumers. To take advantage of the multi-polar 21st century – indeed, to become one of the poles – South America must overcome such obstacles.

Diversification is especially important given South America's potential to become an energy superpower. Exxon has invested heavily in shale oil in Argentina, estimating there to be an astonishing 23 billion barrels in the Vaca Muerta formation. Given Argentina's rocky public finances and multiple sovereign defaults, exploiting the shale, although questionable from an environmental perspective, would ease the country's reliance on foreign bondholders. In July 2014 such 'vulture funds' used the US legal system to push Argentina back into debt default.

Brazil has staged its own energy revolution. It is the only country to have created a sustainable bioethanol industry, manufactured from waste generated by its large and efficient sugarcane industry. (Although the US biofuel sector is larger, this is because it diverts food crops into fuel production.) Between 2005 and 2011, Brazil's industry built 100 new mills and it is still growing.[21] Cars are powered by flex-fuel engines and, by law, fuel needs to be mixed with one-quarter bioethanol. Moreover, Brazil also become an energy superpower in the old-fashioned sense, after the discovery of huge offshore oil deposits known as the 'pre-salt'.

By creating a shared infrastructure, South America is moving towards a common energy market that will erode the colonial patterns of trade by which raw materials are exported from its shores rather than being traded internally. In their assessment of UNASUR, Stefano Palestini Céspedes and Giovanni Agostinis noted that only 23 per cent of the bloc's exports remain on the continent, far below the North American Free Trade Agreement (50 per cent) or the EU

(70 per cent).[22] Indeed, the genesis of UNASUR was a failed attempted by Brazil in 1993 to champion a South American Free Trade Area in response to NAFTA.

Connectivity

UNASUR now has its own infrastructure planning body, COSIPLAN, which provides a regular breakdown of the schemes underway. The projects are divided into eight hubs which skirt the Amazon rainforest; unsurprisingly, given its location, Brazil is involved in more schemes than any of its neighbours. As of September 2014, the total cost of the 579 projects was $163 billion, of which 106 were fully complete.[23] A further 179 were under construction. Two-thirds of the investment was directed towards road, rail and waterway projects, with the rest aimed at energy generation and interconnectivity.

There are no reasons for scepticism here. These new physical connections are real bridges, real roads and real border crossings. They will make it quicker, and therefore cheaper, for UNASUR members to trade with one another and for their citizens to travel around the continent. The result will be a continent that, quietly, is catching up with the US and the EU in terms of its internal coherence and connectivity.

In some regards, the lessons of the EU have prompted UNASUR to tread cautiously. In 2011, it abandoned a project to create a single currency and central bank, as a result of the Eurozone's woes. Learning from Europe's experience, a single currency will now be the final keystone in the superstructure of integration, rather than a transitional one as it was envisaged in Europe.

Financial unity is nevertheless an objective. In an attempt to wean itself away from reliance on the US-led World Bank and EU-led International Monetary Fund, and the free-market prescriptions for 'reform' they tend to impose, in 2009 seven members of UNASUR founded Bancosur, the 'bank of the south'. In the years that followed, this entity struggled to materialize in anything other than a purely notional form, in part due to the legal wrangles that its founders were having at ICSID and elsewhere.

In this case, it was not so much the IMF and World Bank against which Bancosur needed to compete, but against other 'south-south' innovations such as the New Development Bank (NDB) announced by the BRICS countries in 2014. With Chinese support, the NDB looked to be a more credible project than Bancosur, and it also had the support of Brazil, UNASUR's largest member. Attempting to discover some kind of *modus vivendi* with the NDB became Bancosur's best hope of functionality. This entails learning to live with the BRICS themselves, whose giantist approach to multipolarity could distract from efforts to build regional transnational structures.

Céspedes and Agostinis argued that Brazil has emerged as the regional leader driving the process of integration. Brasilia saw the process initially as a means of heading off any possibility, mooted in the 1990s, of Chile joining NAFTA as a 'fourth *amigo*', one that would fragment any hope of South American regional integration. They also noted that it was Brazil behind the disciplined notion of South American integration, rather than widening it to the less-coherent concept of Latin America; some Brazilian diplomats argued that 'Latin America' was a French colonial concept, and that including Mexico, another large economy, would complicate matters.

Brazil's size in comparison to its neighbours has not been a serious impediment. This can be attributed to the respect with which recent Brazilian leaders have been held internationally, particularly Lula de Silva, but also to Brazil's 'soft power' as a non-militaristic, multicultural and multiethnic society.

Brazil's moral example explains why, unlike India or China, its size is positive rather than negative for UNASUR. In the 1990s it voluntarily abandoned a nuclear weapons programme developed by its former military government, and since then it has used the Non-Proliferation Treaty (NPT) process to pressure states such as the US and China into relinquishing their own nuclear weapons.[24]

Brazil's history has been remarkably free of wars with its neighbours, and as a result there is no reason for other UNASUR members to view it as a threat. Its defence spending as a proportion of its economy (1.4 per cent of GDP) is far below that of India, China, Russia or the US, and is on a par with that of Norway and Denmark. Brazil's leadership heavily influences UNASUR as a whole. The bloc has committed to being free of weapons of mass destruction. Each member has agreed not to threaten another's territory, and all members have signed the NPT, the Comprehensive Test Ban Treaty, and the Biological Weapons Convention. Promoting peace is a core objective of UNASUR.

So too is the promotion of democracy. Of the 10 factors that pacified Europe, this is the most important factor. Although South America has avoided war more than have most continents, militarism has cast a long shadow nonetheless. Throughout the 20th century, military dictatorships were a common form of government across what is now UNASUR. The frightening confrontation with the Soviet Union over Cuba inspired the US to support anti-communist strongmen throughout the states to its south.

Their abuses were appalling. Operation Condor alone, a purge conducted by the generals who ran Argentina, Bolivia, Brazil, Chile, Paraguay and Uruguay from the mid-1970s, involved the murder of tens of thousands of suspected communists and the imprisonment of many more. Officials connected with that era continue to be investigated and prosecuted.[25]

The pall of dictatorship began to lift towards the end of the Cold War. Argentina's US-backed military junta invaded the British-held Falkland Islands/Malvinas in 1982, and its humiliating defeat was the death knell of military government in Argentina. The subsequent civilian governments prosecuted and imprisoned officers responsible for the crimes of Operation Condor.

The fall of Soviet communism in 1991 ended the binary ideological struggle for Latin America, and the US and its allies, such as France, withdrew their support for military despots. Democracy began to take root. The promotion of peace, and the refusal to allow dictatorship to creep back onto the continent, are defining features of the UNASUR mission.

The organization helped broker the release of hostages by Colombia's FARC militants in 2008, and after Paraguay's military coup in 2012 it suspended the country's membership, reinstating it a year later after the country held elections. As with the African Union, the zero-tolerance approach to the ouster of elected governments is just one of many ways that transnational unions promote peace and democracy. UNASUR offered to monitor the FARC's 2014 ceasefire, an offer that was, however, rejected.

In the impenetrable terrain of the Andes, groups such as the FARC have found that operating across borders is the safest way to evade national security forces. Opening those borders and presenting a united front is in itself an important means of limiting the scope for prolonged conflict. It is also vital to interdict or otherwise manage the source of much of the group's income: cocaine.

In May 2010 UNASUR agreed the creation of a council to co-ordinate the bloc's anti-narcotics strategy.[26] The group has some obvious advantages when it comes to tackling the problem. Unlike the Organization of American States, it excludes the US, thereby reducing some of the internal tension between the major suppliers of cocaine – Colombia, Bolivia, and Peru (since 2013 the world's largest coca producer) – and the main consumption market. UNASUR allows the countries of South America to negotiate a common position as peers, addressing difficult issues such as the traditional use of unrefined coca by indigenous peoples and the variability of enforcement across the region.

Quietly and steadily, beyond the gaze of the world's media, South America is putting in place the same 10 factors that build a peaceful and prosperous Europe. Like many gradual processes, it will come as a shock to the outside world when, one day, it realizes that it is no longer dealing with a dozen nations, but with one entity speaking with one voice. Moreover, a voice that consistently opposes militarism and war, and which has a political profile that challenges the agenda of the US and EU. At that point, the greatest challenge will be to ensure constructive relations between the UNASUR headquarters in Quito, and the White House in Washington DC.

There are reasons to believe that these relations will be better than they currently are. US engagement with South America is complicated by the sometimes subservient, sometimes rebellious posture taken by the nations to its south. Being able to negotiate with South America as a whole would permit the US the kind of peer-to-peer relationship it already enjoys with the EU, India, or even China, cancelling accusations that the US bullies smaller countries and allowing it to work with an equal partner – one with a $4 trillion economy – to achieve common goals. The result would almost certainly be a more prosperous, more stable South America that has increasingly more in common with the US, rather than less so.

1 Mercosur or Mercosul (Spanish: Mercado Común del Sur, Portuguese: Mercado Comum do Sul, Guaraní: Ñemby Ñemuha, Southern Common Market) is a trading bloc comprising Argentina, Brazil, Paraguay, Uruguay and Venezuela. Its associate members are Chile, Bolivia, Peru, Colombia and Ecuador. 2 Ojito, Mirta, 2005, 'The Long Voyage from Mariel Ends', *New York Times*, 16 January. 3 Caputo, Marc and Tamayo, Juan, 2014, 'Herald poll: Cuba, Cuban voters weigh Crist down in Miami-Dade', *Miami Herald*, 8 June. 4 Monbiot, George, 2013, 'The lies behind this transatlantic trade deal', *The Guardian*, 2 December. 5 See *The Backlash Against Investment Arbitration: Perceptions and Reality*, ed. Waibel, Michael, 2010, Kluwer Law International. 6 'Recent Development in Investor-State Dispute Settlement', IIA Issues Note, UNCTAD, April 2014. http://unctad.org/en/PublicationsLibrary/webdiaepcb2014d3_en.pdf 7 Pérez-Rocha, Manuel, 2014, 'When Corporations Sue Governments', *New York Times*, 3 December. 8 Unnamed author, 2007, 'Latin leftists mull quitting World Bank arbitrator, Reuters, 29 April. 9 Carbrera Diaz, Fernando, 2009, 'Ecuador continues exit from ICSID', *Investment Treaty News*, International Institute for Sustainable Development, 8 June. 10 Cable 09QUITO579, 'Ecuador withdraws from World Bank's ICSID', https://wikileaks.org/cable/2009/07/09QUITO579. html 11 Schipani, Andres, 2014, 'Venezuela ordered to pay ExxonMobil a further $1bn',

Financial Times, 10 October. **12** Elliott, Larry, 2010, 'A cautious welcome to the World Bank's rejection of old orthodoxies', *The Guardian,* 30 September. **13** Quintana, Ana, 2014, 'Crisis in Venezuela: UNASUR and U.S. Foreign Policy', Issue Brief #4205 on Latin America, Heritage Foundation, 23 April. **14** 'Nuestro desafío es eliminar la desigualdad socio económica, lograr la inclusión social y la participación ciudadana, fortalecer la democracia y reducir las asimetrías, considerando la soberanía e independencia de los Estados.' See www.unasursg.org. **15** UNASUR press office, 2014, 'Secretary General discusses new proposals to develop a drug policy in the region', unasursg.org, 10 July. **16** Word Bank data, 2010-14 in current USD. **17** US Bureau of Business & Economic Research, 2012, real per capita Gross Domestic Product by state. **18** AFP, 2014, 'Unasur camina hacia libre movimiento de gente en su territorio', *La Nación,* 5 December. **19** Quispe, Aline, 2014, 'Gobierno: Corredor bioceánico es una prioridad para Bolivia y Perú', *La Razón,* 15 December. **20** US Energy Information Administration (EIA) **21** Phillips, Leticia, 2014, 'Brazilian Biofuels Policy Under a Second Rousseff Term', *Ethanol producer Magazine,* 20 November. **22** Palestini-Céspedes, Stefano and Agostinis, Giovanni, 2014, 'Constructing regionalism in South America: the cases of transport infrastructure and energy within UNASUR', Robert Schuman Centre for Advanced Studies (RSCAS) Working Papers, European University Institute. **23** Activity Report 2014, IIRSA Technical Forum, XXV Meeting of IIRSA National Coordinators 2 December, Montevideo, Uruguay. **24** Statement By H. E. Ambassador Maria Luiza Ribeiro Viotti, Permanent Representative Of Brazil To The United Nations, at the General Debate of the First Committee, 9 October 2012. **25** Romig, Shane, 2013, 'An Exhumation Reopens South America's Historical Scars', *Wall Street Journal,* 14 November. **26** CNNMéxico, 2010, 'Bolivia, Colombia, Perú y Ecuador tendrán Consejo contra el narcotráfico', CNN, 17 February.

Chapter 6 – Lands of the Free (North American Union)

Perhaps surprisingly, North America remains an incubator and testing ground for forms of federalism and regionalism. This chapter draws a contrast between the federal systems of the US and Canada, noting that whereas the latter has maintained true federalism, the former has slipped towards a unitary super-state – with alarming consequences for civil unrest, criminal violence and militarization.

When considering the North American continent, there is one country that springs inexorably to mind. A physical and economic giant with an expansive military industrial complex, it has become known for its ruthless attitude towards trade and for pursuing a rightwing, free-market agenda. Yet this country offers lessons in federalism and the management of trans-continental diversity from which the rest of the world can learn a great deal.

That country is, of course, Canada.

To understand why Canada bears comparison with the European Union, it is important to dispense with two popular myths. The first is that Canada is a kindly, herbivorous antidote to the rapaciousness of United States. This, as we shall see, is untrue. On the contrary, Canada ruthlessly defends its own interests, sometimes at the expense of the rest of the planet.

The second myth is that Canada is an easy country to govern. In fact, the opposite is true, which is why Canada's federal model is so instructive.

In 2008, when the liberal Democrat Barack Obama became president of the US, Canada elected the vigorously conservative Stephen Harper for a second minority term. Harper went on to win an outright majority three years later on promises of cutting back the government and reducing taxes for corporations. Under his rule, Canada's corporation tax rate fell from 34 to 26 per cent.

Harper built a political coalition that united the western

prairie provinces, which specialize in resource extraction, and the industrialized, urbanized Ontarians to the east. The economics of this inter-provincial base were complicated. The exploitation of national resources in the west, particularly Alberta's oil sands, revolutionized Canada's economy, while turning the banks of the Athabasca River into a poisonous black swamp.

Oil exports rapidly inflated the value of the Canadian dollar, making Ontario's manufactured goods more expensive in foreign markets, and therefore less competitive. This led Harper's opponents to accuse of him of overseeing 'Dutch disease', whereby one industry – oil, in Canada's case – destroyed the rest of the economy. Rebutting this accusation became crucial to Harper's political survival.

Much hope was pinned on the Keystone XL pipeline, which would funnel Alberta's dark, sticky bitumen down to processors in the US that could refine it into petroleum. This project was opposed by US environmentalists – one of Obama's key constituencies – because of the ecological damage associated with the oil sands. When Obama delayed approval, Harper accused him of playing politics with the pipeline.[1] If Obama failed to sign off, Harper threatened instead to export the oil east through the province of British Columbia, and then onwards on to China.

Put another way, Canada cared less about climate change than did the famously polluting US; indeed, in 2011 it became the first country to withdraw from the Kyoto climate change protocol. Nor was this the only way in which Canada can be 'more American than the Americans'. It is an enthusiastic member of NATO that works hand-in-glove with the US military, dispatching troops to Afghanistan and the first (though not the second) Iraq war. It is also a major participant in the militarization of the Arctic Circle.

Canada lays claim to much of the Arctic and regularly conducts military exercises in its frozen northern territories. The country has stockpiled munitions in the region in case of any escalation, for instance with Russia, over the competing territorial claims to hydrocarbon resources.[2] It has wasted billions of dollars on US-made F-35 fighter jets to prepare for such a conflict. The jet has only a single jet engine, which makes it prone to failure in the extreme cold and thus dangerous to fly in the Arctic.[3] Nevertheless, its arms race with Canada has prompted Russia to increase its own military presence in the north.[4]

Canada's Arctic territory is largely inhabited by its indigenous peoples, the First Nations, and it is they who are most at risk from the militarization and exploitation of natural resources in the region. James Aniya, the UN special rapporteur, said that the human rights deficit afflicting the First Nations in Canada had reached 'crisis proportions in many respects'.[5] He noted that despite the vast economic inequality between First Nations and other Canadians, 'it does not appear that Canada has dedicated greater resources to social services for indigenous peoples'.

As a result, indigenous Canadians lag far behind educationally and in terms of life outcomes, and are far more likely to be victims of crime. One case provides a particularly horrifying example. Since 1969, at least 18 women have been murdered or disappeared along Highway 16 in northern British Columbia. Many of the victims were First Nations women forced to hitchhike because of the region's sparse transportation options.[6] The perpetrator, or perpetrators, remain at large. The road has come to be known as the Highway of Tears.

The First Nations have separate constitutional rights, which protect their traditional lifestyles but often bring them into conflict with major development and industrial projects.[7] Harper's efforts to develop British Columbia's coastline as an oil gateway to China accentuated the incompatibility of the tribal and Canadian economies. Plans to build infrastructure on the salmon fisheries of the Skeena River prompted alarm from First Nations concerned by the effect on their livelihoods. First Nations also combined to oppose the traffic of oil tankers and the associated risk of oil spills in their fisheries,[8] and have worked to prevent the building of pipelines (also prone to leaks) across their ancestral lands.

These observations serve not to denigrate Canada but to demonstrate that, contrary to perceptions overseas, there is nothing inevitable about its peace and stability. It is not an 'easy' country to govern, any more than is a Mexico or a Sudan. Canada is extremely large in proportion to its 35 million citizens. At almost one million square kilometres, it is physically bigger than the US. Only Russia covers more land, but there are four times as many Russians as there are Canadians, and they are governed in a highly centralized and autocratic manner.

All this is before one even considers Quebec, a province of six million French speakers who almost voted for independence in 1995, when the No vote prevailed by a mere 58,000 ballots. Like the EU, Canada must accommodate large, regionally defined blocs of people, such as the Quebecois and the First Nations, who might reasonably consider themselves to be distinct nations in their own right.

So Canada's success was by no means preordained. That the country is unique in the western hemisphere for preserving a liberal democracy throughout its history while avoiding civil war; that it has created a strong social-security net; that it has earned the respect and even admiration of the world at large; and that its cities are regularly voted the world's best places to live, are achievements that required overcoming some very serious human and geographical challenges within a short space of time. The year 2017 marks the 150th anniversary of Canada's foundation.

Strong provincial governments were a crucial ingredient to this success. Martha A Field, a Harvard law professor, notes that Canada's federal government has no 'effective power to impose economic plans and solutions without the participation and assent of the provinces'.[9] Provincial law covers all labour legislation, from the minimum wage to health and safety. (Exceptions are made for national financial and transport infrastructure.) The provinces' strength has been reinforced by the courts, which interpreted the powers of the provinces as covering a very wide field.[10]

In the US, by contrast, labour regulation is the responsibility of the federal government. US federalism became even weaker after the Great Depression, which required massive federal intervention under the New Deal, and then again in the civil rights era, when the concept of 'states' rights' became associated with segregation in the south. Today, many US citizens complain about the overweening power of the federal government, but there is little sign of any significant return of powers to the states.

Professor Field questions whether the US can be considered a federation at all. She notes that the US and Canada diverged in the way their constitutions were drafted. The US constitution defined the powers of the federal government, leaving the residue to the states. Canada did the reverse, defining the mandates of the provinces with residual powers falling to Ottawa. In both cases, the effect was contrary to the framers' intention. Those in the US failed to foresee how the US Congress would encroach on the powers left to the states, while those in Canada did not anticipate how narrowly the courts would interpret the powers of the federal government.

The result was that Canada's provinces are able to do things their US counterparts cannot. Take Harper's plan to funnel Alberta's oil to China. This entailed building a dual pipeline from Bruderheim, Alberta, to Kitimat on the British Columbia coastline. The project was heavily opposed by First Nations groups, but Harper's government saw it as a vital lifeline to ensure that the oil was exported.

The government of British Columbia took a different view. Its premier, Christy Clark, announced that her province's tax-take from the pipeline was insufficient, given the environmental risks and the opposition by First Nations. She set down five conditions, one of which was that her own province must have more money from the pipeline. Unless her conditions were met, British Columbia would not allow the pipeline to be built. When another pipeline was mooted between Alberta and the east coast, the provinces of Ontario and Quebec took a similar approach.[11]

Quebec's feisty French-speaking government was extremely sensitive to diktats from Harper's mostly English-speaking federal government. Although Quebec's 1995 referendum failed to deliver independence, 'sovereigntist' sentiments persisted. At the ballot box, however, the appeal of the separatist movement dwindled in the decades afterwards. This was even though, in theory, a Roman Catholic Francophone enclave in a mostly Protestant Anglophone country should be ripe for secession.

That this is no longer the case is attributable to Canada's aptitude for devolution and for its respect for provincial autonomy. To a great extent, Quebec can already consider itself a nation within Canada. So can the other provinces, which frequently defy the central government on all manner of issues.[12] Often, a Canadian prime minister's real opposition lies not in the Ottawa parliament, but in provincial capitals held by opposition parties.

Canada is thus an example of true federalism. It is North America's closest equivalent to the European Union. Its member provinces have broad latitude to define their own internal affairs, while keeping intact the 10 peace-promoting factors that pacified Europe. The autonomy enjoyed by the provinces does not undermine mutual trust across Canada, nor the central government's ability to concentrate finances on areas of need, nor the perpetual dialogue between the provinces and central government in Ottawa. Hence, Canada is as peaceful as the modern EU.

United States

By contrast, the US offers an example of federalism in reverse. Its once-devolved state structure has given way to a unitary super-state. Vast powers lie with the president and his advisers, while the states have become ever weaker. This difference between the two political systems explains a great deal about the violence and militarism of US society.

Budgetary figures illustrate the extent of the US federal-state mismatch. In 2013, the US federal government budgeted to spend $3.5 trillion. That year, California, the biggest and richest US state, budgeted just $96.3 billion – less than 3 per cent of the federal total.[13] By contrast Ontario, Canada's most populous province, budgeted to spend $126 billion. Not only was its budget greater than California's, which has three times Ontario's population, but it was equivalent to fully 46 per cent of Canada's entire federal outlay.[14]

The relative independence of Canadian provinces means they are free to pursue a far broader range of policies than their US equivalents. According to a 2014 report by the Fraser Institute, Canada contains both the freest economy in North America (Alberta's) and the least free (Prince Edward Island).[15] Not only do the provinces set their own minimum wages, but they can set individual minimums for particular professions.[16]

It is true that US states are able to set some taxes, and can hand out subsidies and tax breaks to lure businesses from other states. But this has created a race to the bottom, whereby companies relocate to states that tax them least and offer the most generous handouts. It actually reduces the amount of money available to state governments, weakening them further in relation to Washington DC. It should be noted that such a 'race to the bottom' also exists in the EU, where countries such as Ireland have undercut their neighbours' corporation tax rates. Unlike US states, however, the Irish have faced intense pressure to raise their rate, and not only from their EU neighbours – the US has also complained.[17]

In Canada, responsibility for keeping unemployment in check falls on provincial governments; as noted, they control labour legislation and many other levers crucial for tackling joblessness. Provinces are also responsible for providing health services, with the federal government setting benchmarks.[18]

In the US, however, the president and Congress in Washington DC are held primarily responsible for the economy. The Commerce Clause of the US constitution gives the central government powers to 'regulate nearly everything', in the words of one scholar.[19] As a result, the president and Congress are scrutinized relentlessly by the media over the state of the economy and national unemployment. Their electoral prospects hinge on them.

The federal government therefore tries to 'create jobs'. One department in particular takes a lead on this. According to the website of the US Department of Defense:

With over 1.4 million men and women on active duty, and 718,000 civilian personnel, we are the nation's largest employer. Another 1.1 million serve in the National Guard and Reserve forces. More than 2 million military retirees and their family members receive benefits.[20]

Among its other purposes, the US military serves as a giant job-creation scheme. In 2010, as the world recovered from financial crisis, Berkeley professor Robert Reich noted that without 'this giant military jobs programme, the US unemployment rate would be over 11.5 per cent today instead of 9.5 per cent'.[21]

Reich did not see this as a good thing. His view was that this was an 'insane way of keeping Americans employed' because it 'creates jobs we don't need'. For Reich, it explained why the Pentagon could not end even its most wasteful weapons programmes: 'because they're covert jobs programmes that employ thousands'. Many other studies, both for and against military spending, have noted the US military's role as a jobs scheme.[22]

Republican politicians often claim they want to reduce government spending, but they offer lavish spending for the military. Running for president in 2012, the Republican candidate Mitt Romney said he would increase defence spending by a third, to almost $1 trillion a year.[23] This was far more than the Department of Defense had requested. In the words of one leftwing commentator, such 'rightwing socialism' was a jobs-creation plan designed to buy Romney votes.[24] US military personnel vote heavily Republican.[25] Hiring more of them meant more voters for Romney.

The US military is a soak for some of the least employable members of society. Entry requirements are far laxer than in other Western countries. The British army, for instance, does not accept recruits who have served prison sentences.[26] Many US service personnel have not graduated from high school; by 2007, the total was more than 20 per cent.[27] The military recruits heavily from the poorest states in the union, particularly in the south.[28]

With armed forces so large and so expensive, it is no surprise that politicians have sought reasons to use them. There is a 'use it or lose it' mentality endemic across US budgetary planning: if resources are idle, they are shrunk. So, to maintain the military jobs programme, wars must be fought. Every US president in living memory has ordered his forces to subdue some foreign threat through force of arms.

Using the military as a welfare system is highly counterproductive. The men and women who fight overseas often come home with serious physical and psychological injuries. A study published in the British medical journal *The Lancet* found that more than a fifth of British military men under the age of 30 had a conviction for violent crime, compared to just 6.7 per cent of the same age-group generally.[29] Those who had served in Iraq and Afghanistan were 53 per cent more likely to be a violent criminal. Research in the US found a similar correlation.[30]

Due to the fragmented nature of the US prison system, there is no reliable data for how many US veterans are incarcerated. Estimates range from 140,000 up to one million (a number that includes those drafted into Vietnam).[31] In 2012, the state of Georgia, a major contributor of military manpower, opened the nation's first jail dedicated exclusively to housing veterans.[32] Homelessness among veterans is an additional problem that makes them especially vulnerable to crime – both as perpetrators and victims – and to physical and psychological maladies.[33]

Suicide rates among US veterans are 50 per cent higher than the population at large.[34] Two-thirds of all US citizens who die from a gunshot inflict the wound upon themselves.[35] Somewhat confusingly, these deaths are often included in the statistics for gun violence in the US. Whereas murders committed with firearms have fallen, this decline has been offset by the rising numbers committing suicide.[36] Suicides trended upwards during the war-torn years of the early 2000s. By the end of the decade, the US suicide rate was 12.5 per 100,000, against Canada's 10.8.[37,38]

The epidemic of suicide among soldiers returning from Iraq and Afghanistan was a major contributor. By 2012, at least 22 veterans were committing suicide in the US every single day, according to official figures.[39] Among those under the age of 30, the rates were 'astronomically high and climbing', according to the director for suicide prevention at the department of Veterans' Affairs.[40]

Health provision for US veterans is poor. In May 2014 the Secretary for Veterans' Affairs Eric Shinseki resigned after it emerged that his officials conspired to disguise the chronic inadequacy of veterans' care.[41] US health services are a mishmash of federal and private schemes, which means that it is easy for the vulnerable to fall through the cracks of psychiatric supervision. The shambolic state of the Veterans' Affairs department exacerbated the problem. One returning Marine compared the scenes at his VA hospital in Wyoming to *One Flew Over the Cuckoo's Nest*.[42]

Canadian soldiers served in Afghanistan for a decade, but the situation they faced on their homecoming was not so severe.[43] Canada has provincially administered, tax-funded healthcare for its whole population, eliminating the cracks apparent in the US system. Also, there were far fewer people affected by the wars. Canada does not view the military as a jobs-creation scheme and it spends only one per cent of its GDP on defence, compared to the US's 3.8 per cent.[44]

This situation begins to demonstrate how over-centralization contributes to violence. Ironically, one federal body that understands this all too well is the US military. Providing civilian work and economic policies tailored to regions was a tactic the US used to reduce violence in Iraq and Afghanistan.[45] As one official put it:

The security progress we've made in Iraq is because of our realization that everything in Iraq is local... Coalition officials made a mistake in 2003 by thinking that macroeconomic policies [that] work in Qaim, in the west, would also work in Basra, in the south.[46]

It took the US military billions of dollars and countless lives to learn this lesson.

The over-centralization of political power in Washington has caused some of the 10 pro-peace factors to unravel within the US. In terms of Veto and Consensus, state governments that oppose national policy have little ability to veto it. Permanent Dialogue between states has degenerated into legislators often trying simply to bring federal funding – 'pork' – back to their home state. These insiders spend vastly more time in Washington than they do among the people they represent, also eroding the Enshrined Democracy factor.

The growth of state-level parties that could rival the Democrats or Republicans is constricted by a two-party system entrenched by outrageous gerrymandering.[47,48] Without a democratic outlet, this sense of alienation from national politics has arguably promoted extreme ethno-nationalist ideologies that manifest themselves among neo-Nazi prison gangs such as the Aryan Brotherhood, which is now among the most powerful criminal organizations in the US.[49]

The US response to such organized crime is, again, militarized and centralized. Whereas Open Borders are another pre-condition for peace, the very hard border between the US and Mexico is a driver of violence. Because Mexico is a conduit for cocaine from South America, and because its drugs cartels are so powerful, this creates a channel of violence into the US inner cities.

Narcotics and weapons

Mexico has become notorious for the brutality of its cartels. Among the worst are Los Zetas, originally a US-trained special forces unit before they decided it was more profitable to become traffickers. The Zetas murder journalists and bloggers who report on their activities, in 2001 decapitating a woman called Marisol Macías Castañeda and leaving a note on her body to warn other web users that they face the same fate.[50]

The contrast with the 'softer' northern border is instructive. Like Mexico, Canada is also a massive exporter of illegal narcotics to the US. In August 2014, a Canadian man named Jimmy Cournoyer was sentenced to 27 years in a US federal prison for running a billion-dollar cannabis ring. Cournoyer's operation hired the Hell's Angels motorcycle club to move the drugs over the border, aided by members of the Mohawk tribe whose reservation overlapped the province of Ontario and upstate New York. Cournoyer's Montreal-based gang worked with New York's Rizutto and Bonnano crime families, and Mexico's Sinaloa cartel.[51]

Why, given the scale of such operations, is Canada not victim to the same level of violence as Mexico? The answer in Canada's case is border-management. Unlike the militarized border between the US and Mexico, the US border with Canada is relatively open. Cannabis plantations are considered a police matter and are dealt with accordingly, and the government has worked to divert cannabis production towards lawful medical uses. Canada also takes an easy-going attitude towards drug use: when the federal government tried to stop medically qualified Canadians from growing their own marijuana, the courts ruled against it.[52]

The US, on the other hand, declared a 'war' on drugs and adopted a militarized approach to stopping drugs production and trafficking. The agents of the Bureau of Alcohol, Tobacco, Firearms and Explosives (ATF), a federal law-enforcement body, are equipped like soldiers and they adopt military techniques. The results sometimes backfire. Between 2006 and 2011, the ATF smuggled guns to Mexican cartels in what was known as Operation Fast and Furious, in the hope of using them to track down the cartel leaders. In the process, it lost 1,400 powerful firearms. Two of these weapons were used in the murder of a US Border Patrol guard.[53]

The militarization of the ATF is part of a broader trend across US law-enforcement agencies. Police forces across the country snapped up the surplus military vehicles and equipment created by the wasteful military-industrial complex for the wars of the first decade of the 21st century, despite opposition from both sides of the political spectrum. Republican Senator Rand Paul described the police militarization and the war on drugs as 'out of control'.[54] According to an investigation by the *New York Times*, from 2006 to 2014 the US police bought up over 93,000 machine guns, 44,000 pairs of night-vision goggles, 533 aircraft and 435 armoured vehicles.[55] The paper reported that masked heavily armed police were raiding business for trivial offences such as 'barbering without a licence'.

Some police officers claim they are locked in an 'arms race' with criminal gangs to see who can carry the most powerful weaponry.[56] Yet by purchasing military-grade equipment, they feed this arms race. Stephen Downing, a former deputy chief of the Los Angeles Police Department, drew the following distinction: 'The military mission is to confront and kill a defined enemy,' he said. 'The police officer has no enemies.' As battle armaments have flooded into police precincts, Downing argued that this distinction has been lost.[57]

There are now 24 federal agencies with at least 250 armed men and women on their payroll. These include the Veterans Health Administration, the US Postal Inspection Service, the Bureau of Indian Affairs, and the Bureau of Land Management.[58] Those with fewer than 250 armed personnel – but still with some – include the Environmental Protection Agency, the Food and Drug Administration, the National Institutes of Health, the Government Printing Office and the Library of Congress. Why librarians need guns is a difficult question to answer.

Whichever way one reads the statistics, the US is a much more violent society than Canada or the EU. Most explanations for why this is the case, such as the rate of gun ownership, fail to account for the extent of the problem. Many Canadians own firearms, but gun-related murder rates are far below those of the US, which are the highest in the rich world.[59,60]

A better answer lies in the difference between the two federal models. The US tackles social problems by creating paramilitary federal agencies to deal with them, even when those problems are regulatory, administrative or local in nature. With the workforce needing to absorb so many veterans, and with so much surplus military equipment, vast swathes of the federal government have become hammers in search of a nail.

Many US citizens are concerned about the demise of their once-federal system of government, and the rise of militarized federal agencies. Whereas Canada, like the European Union, affords the bulk of decision-making powers to its provinces, the US central government hoards ever more power centrally. It enforces this power with military tactics, even when federal solutions to local problems are usually inefficient or worse.

Ending this militaristic cycle requires a return to federalism. The historical connection between states' rights and racism is a barrier to this objective, but breaking the association between the two is by no means impossible. Some commentators point to the increased influence of city mayors as a sign that, perhaps, localism is making a comeback, at least at the municipal level.[61]

The US must learn from Canada and entrust state governments with greater financial resources and autonomy. Such flexibility would allow local problems to be solved with local knowledge. Their weakness and lack of resources mean that US state governments cannot provide the services necessary to counter the localized social desperation that forms the context to violence and suicide, even though it is they, not officials in Washington DC, that have the necessary knowledge to understand the situation. Nor are they able to address local pockets of high unemployment. Such areas tend to have high gun-murder rates.[62]

As a corollary to re-federation, the US needs to dismantle much of the military-industrial complex that acts as a multi-trillion-dollar draw on national resources. This complex has not made the US more secure. Despite its vast military spending, the US has not won a full-scale war conclusively since 1945. Korea, Vietnam, Afghanistan and Iraq cost millions of lives only to leave in place a dictatorship, an ongoing civil war, or both.

Nor does the US need its military contractors to be a world leader in technology. Japan demonstrated during the latter 20th century that it was possible to transform military-focused companies such as Mitsubishi and Kawasaki, which produced military aircraft during World War Two, into peaceful and successful conglomerates. Dismantling the US military-industrial complex need not mean the end of companies such as Lockheed Martin and Boeing, but instead repurposing them for peaceful output.

For such a reconstruction, the US will require better leadership than it has lately exhibited. In 2008, President Barack Obama came to office promising 'nation-building at home', but his presidency corresponded with overt CIA chicanery overseas and by a Middle East even more violent than when he took office. His country still awaits the leader that can fulfil his promise of nation-building in the US itself.

Regional unions

Until the US returns to federalism, it is hard to see how it could participate in any North American regional union. Canada's provincial autonomy, by contrast, means that other countries have actively sought to become provinces. It is a near-forgotten historical footnote that, at various points, Caribbean islands contemplated becoming part of Canada. As the *Chicago Tribune* reported in February 1919:

The council of Montego Bay, Jamaica, the second town of the island, has unanimously resolved to approach the government with a request that confederation of Jamaica with Canada be brought about.[63]

Jamaica was not the only applicant. In 1911, the Canadian government received word that the Bahamas' parliament had voted for inclusion in Canada's federation. During the short-lived Federation of the West Indies, when Caribbean islands in the late 1950s and early 1960s tried to unite, there was some talk of the entire region confederating with Canada.

Interestingly, such initiatives have never gone away. In 2014 the premier of the Canadian province of Saskatchewan, Brad Wall, said his province would welcome the accession of the Turks & Caicos Islands. The federal government took this sufficiently seriously to respond. Canada is 'not in the business of annexing islands in the Caribbean,' said Foreign Affairs Minister John Baird, in a tone described by one newspaper as 'exasperated'.[64]

Supporters point to the example of Hawaii, which was annexed by the US in 1898 despite fierce opposition from Japan, and which gained statehood in 1959. Canada and the former British colonies of the Caribbean share a constitutional history and, for the most part, have the British monarch as their head of state. Their economies are complementary, with the Caribbean producing very different goods and services from those produced in Canada.

Another model is offered by Puerto Rico, one of the Caribbean's larger islands. The Spanish ceded it to the US in 1898 and Puerto Ricans were granted US citizenship in 1917. Since then, the island has held four referendums on whether to become a full US state. Each time it has voted no – Puerto Ricans can move to any of the other US states if they wish to, and staying outside the union means avoiding a hefty tax bill and the overbearing force of the federal government.[65]

Relations between the Caribbean and Canada are already extremely close. Most black Canadians have Caribbean heritage.[66] In English-speaking Ontario, most hail from

Jamaica, but in Quebec it is Haitians who form the majority, drawn by the French-speaking culture. In 2005 Michaëlle Jean, a member of the Haitian community, became the first black governor-general, a post representing Queen Elizabeth II in Canada.

The countries of the Caribbean have experimented with their own regional unions. The Organization of Eastern Caribbean States (OECS) incorporates nine small states and British territories, eight of which share the same currency and the same supreme court. Since 2011, they have also enjoyed the right to free movement throughout the OECS.

It should be noted that the members of the OECS are tiny. They have a combined population of around 600,000 people and are dwarfed by Caribbean states such as Cuba, Haiti and the Dominican Republic, each of which have a population of about 10 million. Moreover, these larger countries speak Spanish and French, rather than English, and they have very different political systems and heritages. Building a regional organization across the Caribbean requires managing these differences.

Although the Caribbean is understood as a geographical region, there is no reason why individual islands should not join whichever transnational union most fits their cultural context and political system. Cuba might find itself most comfortable within the pan-South American organization that is UNASUR, whereas Haiti could see an institutional accommodation with Quebec as a more logical and advantageous pattern of transnational association. Likewise, the English-speaking countries of the Caribbean might build their own transnational institution entirely separate from either the Canadian federation, the United States or the countries of South America.

Then again, they might look to Central America. Since 1991 the countries of the Central American isthmus have operated within the framework of the Central American Integration System (Sistema de la Integración Centroamericana, SICA). In 2013 they were joined by their first island state from the Caribbean, with the accession of the Dominican Republic – another example of a state choosing its transnational membership not according to precise geography, but with reference to historical ties. SICA's members are not exclusively Hispanophone; Belize is an English-speaking country, as attested by the first two lines of its national anthem, 'The Land of the Free, By the Carib Sea' – a reminder that the US is not the only land of the free in the Americas.

Central America faces its own severe problems with violence; it has some of the highest murder rates in the world. Yet the region also includes Costa Rica, a country that has abolished its military altogether. Operating within SICA's Democratic Security council, it may be the case that Costa Rica can promote its policy of disarmament regionally, while working with its partners to address their common security threats.[67]

That Hawaii and Puerto Rico are governed by the US demonstrates that there is no particular reason why geographical proximity should dictate the membership of a regional union. Hawaii is almost as far from the US mainland as Caribbean nations such as Guyana are from West Africa. Alaska is closer to Russia than it is to US, from which it is separated by Canada.

North America is a continent where perceptions of a settled international system are at odds with reality. Rather, what is emerging is a shifting pattern of ever-stronger regional affiliations. So long as these institutions adhere to the Canadian model, with defined powers vested in their constituent members, then there is no reason for this process of agglomeration to falter.

The process must overcome the old-fashioned variety of exclusionary nationalism. The way that Canada has addressed the threat posed by Quebec's separatists demonstrates the extent to which traditional notions of unitary nationalism are today discredited. As Justin Trudeau, the 23rd Prime Minister of Canada and leader of the Liberal Party, put it:

Nationalism is based on a smallness of thought that closes in, that builds up barriers between people, and has nothing to do with the Canada we should be building.[68]

This mind-set unites the Canadian political spectrum. Canadians, many of whom are of Scottish and English heritage, watched in bafflement as millions of Scots flocked to vote in favour of independence from the UK in that country's September 2014 referendum. Scots and English Canadians 'are so completely integrated in Canada that the idea of separating English people from Scottish people in Canada is almost inconceivable,' then-Prime Minister Harper said before the vote.[69]

Alas, Canada is not the world's most renowned federation. That honour falls to the US which, as we have seen, is now a federation in name only. The modern US is better understood as a unitary super-state with excessive powers vested in its central government, and with state governments more akin to weak French *régions* than to strong Canadian provinces. Unfortunately, given that the US is the world's most famous federation, this toothlessness has much wider consequences.

In Europe, the idea of a 'federal EU' has become a rallying cry for Eurosceptics, a counterpoint to Churchill's foundational 'United States of Europe' concept. In their minds, Brussels is set to become a domineering Washington DC, rendering the statehouses in London, Paris and Madrid as parochial as those of Albany, Sacramento and Tallahassee.

The idea that the US is the exemplar of federalism has become, ironically, an impediment to the global spread of federalism. To justify the existence of a military-industrial complex that doubles as a massive welfare scheme, the US government continually seeks out new enemies. It is thus not only US citizens who suffer from its failure of federalism, but the world at large.

The Canadian model is a far better guide for the rest of the planet. A union that actually understands and celebrates the importance of local autonomy, and accepts that central authority must be relatively weak in domestic areas, is one that can unite even the most difficult and expansive terrain, and peoples of vastly varying cultural heritage. Canada, not the US, is the model which applies to Europe, and it should also guide the movement towards North American unity as a whole.

1 Hughes, Brian, 2011, 'Obama Defends Keystone Pipeline Delay', *Washington Examiner*, 7 December. 2 Pugliese, David, 2014, 'Canadian Forces to stockpile military equipment in Arctic 'hubs' for faster response in case of emergency', *National Post*, 21 August. 3 Byers, Michael, 2014, 'Single-engine F-35 a poor choice for Canada's Arctic', *Toronto Star*, 12 June. 4 Jennings, Gareth, 2015, 'Russia to build more Arctic Airfields', *IHS Jane's 360*, 12 January. 5 Anaya, James, 2014, 'Report of the Special Rapporteur on the rights of indigenous people, *United Nations General Assembly, Human Rights Council*, 4 July. 6 Unnamed Author, 2014, 'B.C. Highway of Tears study polls hitchhikers' habits', *CBC News*, 25 May. 7 See Fishing, Hunting and Gathering, The Rights and Responsibilities of First Nations People in Manitoba, www.gov.mb.ca/conservation/ firstnations/hunting_fishing_oct_09.pdf 8 Unnamed author, Save the Fraser Declaration, available here http://savethefraser.ca/fraser_declaration.pdf 9 p108, Field, Martha, A. 1992, 'The Differing Federalisms of Canada and the United States', *Law and Contemporary Problems*, Duke University, Winter, pp1-6-120. 10 Forsey, Eugene A., 2012 'Powers of the National and Provincial Governments', Parliament of Canada. 11 McCarthy, Shawn, 2014, 'Ontario, Quebec to craft united stand on Energy East pipeline project', *The Globe and Mail*, 21 November. 12 Hebert, Chantal, 2014, 'Provinces, not PM, speak for Canada now', *Guelph Mercury*, 12 December. 13 Christie, Jim, 2013, 'California ends decade of deficits as governor signs a new budget', Reuters, 27 June. 14 There are differences between the accounting standards of US states and Canadian provinces, although they do not significantly alter the vast gap in per capita expenditure. See the interesting comparison of California and Ontario's public finances by Clemens, Jason and Veldhiis, Niels, 'The State of Ontario's Indebtedness', Fraser Institute. 15 This excludes Mexico, which had the least free state economies overall. See 2014, 'Economic Freedom of North America', 2014, Fraser Institute. 16 Minimum Wage by Province, Retail Council of Canada. 17 Unnamed Author, 2012, '12.5% corporate tax rate under pressure', *Irish Examiner*, 13 December. 18 Government of Canada, 'Provincial/territorial role in health'. 19 McGimsey, Diane, 'The Commerce Clause and Federalism after Lopez and Morrison: The Case for Closing the Jurisdictional-Element Loophole', *California Law Review,* (90) 1675. 20 www.defense.gov/about/ 21 Reich, Robert, 2010, 'America's Biggest Jobs Program – the U.S. Military', robertreich.org, 11 August. 22 Waldman, Paul, 2014, 'Defense Spending Is the Most Expensive Way to Create Jobs', *The American Prospect*, 22 January. 23 Giacomo, Carol, 2012, 'How Mitt Romney Would Force-Feed the Pentagon', *New York Times*, 25 August. 24 Lawrence, John, 2012, 'Romney's Job Creation Plan That No One Is Talking About', *San Diego Free Press*, 27 October. 25 Clement, Scott, 2014, 'Veterans are voting Republican. And that's not likely to change', *Washington Post*, 11 November. 26 Unnamed Author, 2008, 'US military recruits more ex-cons', *BBC News*, 22 April. 27 Jordan, Miriam, 2014, 'Recruits Ineligibility Tests the Military', *Wall Street Journal*, 27 June. 28 Burgess, Rebecca, 2014, 'US military enlistment rates by state: A Texas-sized difference', American Enterprise Institute, 22 June. 29 Suchet,

Richard, 2013, 'Soldiers More Likely To Commit Violent Crime', Sky News, 15 March. **30** Wood, David, 2012, 'Combat Veterans with PTSD, Anger Issues More Likely To Commit Crimes: New Report', *Huffington Post*, 9 October. **31** Johnson, Robert, 2011, 'One Million US Veterans Are In Prison, And 18 Commit Suicide Every Day', *Business Insider*, 18 July. **32** Prann, Elizabeth, 2012, 'First Veteran Exclusive Jail Dorm Opens', Fox News, 5 May. **33** Meghan, Alvaro, Sean, & Abt, 2013, 'The 2013 Annual Homeless Assessment Report (AHAR) to Congress', The U.S. Department of Housing and Urban Development. **34** Zarembo, Alan, 2015, 'Detailed study confirms high suicide rate among recent veterans', *Los Angeles Times*, 14 January. **35** Drexler, Madeline, 2013, 'Guns & Suicide: The Hidden Toll', Harvard T.H. Chan School of Public Health. **36** Millman, Jason, 2015, 'Many more people are dying from gun suicides than gun-related homicides', *Washington Post*, 14 January. **37** Facts and Figures, American Foundation for Suicide Prevention, Permanant URL: https://www.afsp.org/understanding-suicide/facts-and-figures **38** Table 102-0551, 'Suicides and suicide rate, by sex and by age group (both sexes rate)', Statistics Canada, permanent URL: www.statcan.gc.ca/tables-tableaux/sum-som/l01/cst01/hlth66d-eng.htm **39** Table 2, Kemp and Bossarte, 2012, 'Suicide Data Report, 2012', Department of Veterans Affairs Permanent URL: www.va.gov/opa/docs/Suicide-Data-Report-2012-final.pdf **40** Shane III, Leo, 2014, 'Report: Suicide rate spikes among young veterans', *Stars and Stripes*, 9 January. **41** Jaffe and O'Keefe, 2014, 'Obama accepts resignation of VA Secretary Shinseki', *Washington Post*, 30 May. **42** 2014, Testimony of Vincent Vanata and Jona Vanata, Mental Health Care and Suicide Prevention. **43** Unnamed Author, 2015, 'Suicide and suicide prevention in the Canadian Armed Forces', National Defence and the Canadian Armed Forces, 25 February. **44** Military Expediture (% of GDP), World Bank, Permanent link: http://data.worldbank.org/indicator/MS.MIL.XPND.GD.ZS **45** Comeaux, Monika, 2008, 'Contracting Office Fights Poverty by Keeping Afghans Employed', US Department of Defense, 8 February. **46** Garamone, Jim, 2007, 'Security, Economy in Iraq Improving From Local Level Up', US Department of Defense, 6 December. **47** Wang, Sam, 2013, 'The Great Gerrymander of 2012', *New York Times*, 2 February. **48** Unnamed Author, 2013, 'How can Republicans be both safer and numerous?', *The Economist*, 3 October. **49** Miller, Michael E., 'Meth torture and the grip of the Aryan Brotherhood', *The Washington Post*. **50** Unnamed Author, 2011, 'Woman's decapitation linked to web posts about Mexican Drug cartel', *The Guardian*, 25 September. **51** Press Release, 2014, 'Canadian Drug Kingpin With Ties To The Rizutto And Bonanno Crime Families, The Hells Angels, And The Mexican Sinaloa Cartel Sentenced to 27 Years For Leading A Billion Dollar Narcotics Trafficking Enterprise', U.S. Department of Justice, 20 August. **52** Keller, James, 2014, 'Federal government loses appeal to stop medical marijuana patients from growing pot at home', CBC News, 15 December. **53** Unnamed Author, 2015, 'Operation Fast and Furious Fast Facts', CNN, 21 April. **54** Killough, Ashley, 2014, 'Rand Paul: Police militarization, war on drugs is 'out of control'', CNN, 19 September. **55** Apuzzo, Matt, 2014, 'War Gear Flows to Police Departments', *New York Times*,

8 June. **56** Candiotti, Susan, 2007, 'Cops find themselves in arms race with criminals', *CNN*, 6 November. **57** Downing, Stephen, 2014, 'The Militarization of American Policing', *Huffington Post*, 28 August. **58** Reaves, Brian A., 2012, 'Federal Law Enforcement Officers, 2008', U.S. Department of Justice Bulletin. **59** Grant, Deanna, 2014, 'Fact-checking Michael Moore: Does Canada have more guns per capita than the US?', *Global News*, 26 May. **60** Table 3, 'Homicides involving firearms, by types of firearm, Canada, 2001 to 2011', Statistics Canada. **61** Luce, Edward, 2014, 'The rise of a new US federalism', *Financial Times*, 19 January. **62** Florida, Richard, 2012, 'The Geography of U.S. Gun Violence', *The Atlantic CityLab*, 14 December **63** Unnamed Author, 1919, 'Jamaica Confederation with Canada is favored', *Chicago Tribune*, 18 February. **64** Fekete, Jason, 2014, ''Canada needs a Hawaii': Conservative MP pushing for Turks and Caicos to become 11th Province as island's premier visits Ottawa', *National Post*, 26 May. **65** Fiscal Effects of Puerto Rico Statehood, US Government Accountability Office, Permanent link: http://recend.apextech.netdna-cdn.com/docs/editor/GAO%202.pdf **66** Archived, The Caribbean Community in Canada, Statistics Canada, Permanent link: www.statcan.gc.ca/pub/89-621-x/89-621-x2007007-eng.htm **67** Central American Security Commission, Permanent link: www.sica.int/consulta/entidad.aspx?IdEnt=330&Idm=1 **68** pesoliv, Justin Trudeau on Nationalism, 1:12, Permanent Link: www.youtube.com/watch?v=rMssx2SvTDc **69** Chase, Steven, 2014, 'Harper speaks out in favour of Scotland remaining part of U.K.', *The Globe and Mail*, 3 September.

Chapter 7 – Beyond the Oceans (Australia and Oceania Union)

Oceania presents some of the starkest differences between neighbours. Australia is vastly larger and more developed than some of the nearby islands, a fact that has generated friction with the rest of the region. Now, however, the Pacific Islands Forum is working with the explicit aim of building the same kind of regional institutions that brought peace and prosperity to Europe.

Successful genocides are mercifully rare. Millions of Jews survived even the Holocaust to preserve the culture and traditions of Judaism. Attempted genocides are remembered, because there are people left to remember. Successful genocides, on the other hand, tend to be forgotten.

In 1830, 2,000 British soldiers fanned out in a line across Tasmania, a large island off Australia's southern coast. Their mission was to drive the native Tasmanians onto two peninsulas on the far southeast of the island. The intention of the so-called 'Black Line' was to end any resistance by the native islanders, permanently. Their treatment by the British had made such resistance inevitable.

In fewer than 30 years, when the British first started using it as a penal colony, the aboriginal population of Tasmania had halved. Riven by imported diseases, they were terrorized by convicts and soldiers.[1] The kidnapping of their children was common practice. Some settlers hunted the aborigines for sport. Roaming convicts known as 'bush rangers' slaughtered women and children in the most barbaric ways imaginable.[2]

The Line operation was a fiasco. Only two Tasmanians were captured, and hundreds slipped through it to attack unprotected homesteads in the north of the island. In a shift of tactics, intended as a humane measure to avoid conflict between the peoples, the British transplanted hundreds of aborigines to other islands. But without shelter or means of survival, they perished in their droves. Their children were forcibly removed and put in the care of the Australian state. By 1944, Tasmania determined that it had no aboriginal people left. The genocide was complete.

Why did the British feel entitled to behave in this way? For affluent Westerners, it is an article of faith that the world desires to be like them. That humanity aspires to electrify urban and suburban housing, to die not from malaria or malnutrition but from the ailments of the West: cancer, strokes, heart disease, and the other ailments of a long, sedentary life. It is self-evident, so the theory goes, that staring at a screen in London is better than growing rice in Asia.

Doubters are pointed towards the migration numbers. The poor move to wealthy countries, but few Westerners make the reverse journey. Why would Bangladeshis and Peruvians emigrate if they did not prefer life in the wealthy world? What more proof is needed of the superiority of Western civilization and, indeed, of the urgent need to Westernize the world as a whole?

There are contradictions in this logic. Mexicans migrate to the US far more frequently than vice-versa, but recent reports by the UN and the Global Happiness Index have suggested that citizens of Mexico are happier, by and large, than citizens of the United States.[3,4] A similar survey, by the polling firm Gallup, ranked the US slightly above Mexico, but it found that the world's happiest people were Paraguayans, for the third consecutive year.

The Paraguayans were followed by Panamanians, Nicaraguans, Ecuadorians and Costa Ricans.[5] Peace seems to be an important factor in happiness. Many of the unhappiest nations were those with a recent history of conflict. Syria, Bosnia, Serbia, Nepal and Yemen were all in Gallup's bottom 10. Costa Rica, a country with no military, performed the best across all three surveys.

When considered more closely, it is hard to see why migration flows should be regarded as evidence of cultural superiority. When US engineers are employed in Saudi Arabia's oil fields; or when Europeans work in the service industries of Dubai or Abu Dhabi; or when Indian builders travel to Qatar, there is no suggestion that any of them desire to be 'Arabized'. They are simply moving for the money.

On the contrary, in many cases these economic migrants have severe reservations about Arab cultural practices. Few Westerners approve of the Saudi attitude towards capital and corporal punishment, or women's rights, or foreign policy, or religion. And yet, when the money is right, they move there anyway. Saudi Arabia's Dhahran camp has a population of 10,000, most of them US oil workers.[6]

There is a double-standard at play. Westerners rarely assimilate into those cultures they colonize, thinking of themselves instead as 'expatriates', but they nevertheless expect immigrants to the US and Europe to relinquish their own cultural practices. The French *pieds-noirs* who colonized Algeria made little effort to adopt the local way of life, but Algerians who live in France are expected to become entirely French. This attitude complicates Europe's relations with its Muslim minority.

Once the hypocrisy is stripped away, the West's attitude boils down to the view that rich countries are better than poor ones. China's conversion to this way of thinking was articulated by Deng Xiaoping in 1980: 'To be rich is to be glorious.' It is a view that persists regardless of how wealth is accumulated – how much damage it inflicts on the environment, or how many wars are launched to capture resources, or how many despotic regimes are protected to access those resources.

Like the poor Tasmanians a century ago, the inhabitants of pre-industrial economies are demonized as 'impoverished'. Subsistence farming, a process that sustained humanity for millennia, is viewed as a problem to be fixed. This goes for any lifestyle that Westerners deem to be precarious or uncomfortable. It rarely occurs to them that outsiders could view their own society as unpleasant, even dystopian: massed ranks of workers sitting at glowing screens in congested and polluted cities, working frenetically to competing deadlines, their incomes absorbed by the cost of simply living in those cities.

The Organization for Economic Co-operation and Development (OECD) forecasts that by 2050 urban air pollution will be the main environmental cause of death, overtaking poor sanitation.[7] Already, one in 17 deaths in New York is linked to polluted air;[8] in London, the figure is one in 12.[9] Cases of rickets, caused by sunlight deprivation, have soared.[10,11] The psychological toll of a Western lifestyle is a heavy one: occupational stress costs the US economy alone $300 billion a year, according to the World Health Organization.[12]

In exchange for full bellies and endless electronic amusements, many Westerners have sacrificed parenthood, clean air, an extended family life, physical activity, mental wellbeing, the beauty of natural surroundings and the knowledge required to live from the land or construct their own shelter. It becomes readily apparent why polls suggest that poor but peaceful countries such as Costa Rica are happier than wealthier ones such as the UK.

And yet despite this, the assumption that the world must inevitably move towards the Western model is heavily ingrained in development policy. The very word 'development' implies transforming traditional lifestyles into urban and sub-urban ones. This unthinking assault on pre-industrial lifestyles coincides neatly with the objectives of multinational corporations, constantly in search for cheaper workforces and exploitable resource deposits.

Bougainville

There is no better case study than the Panguna copper mine.

Owned by a subsidiary of the giant Rio Tinto corporation, the mine was once the largest of its kind in the world. Its operations led directly to a civil war that raged throughout the 1990s. The local population was aghast at the social and economic disruption caused by the open-cast pit, and viewed with suspicion the influx of outsiders who overturned not only the land but the islanders' customary systems of land ownership. Such conflicts are common across the Global South. This one took place in Bougainville.

Bougainville is the easternmost island of Papua New Guinea, though geographically it is part of the Solomon Islands archipelago. Like Solomon Islanders, whose country covers most of the archipelago to the south, Bougainvilleans are ethnically Melanesian. Germany was the colonial master for many years, but its defeat in the First World War saw Bougainville's transfer to Australia. This ensured that it became a bitter battleground during the Second World War, albeit a less famous one than Guadalcanal in the Solomon Islands. Some 40,000 Japanese soldiers died of starvation and disease in Bougainville's rainforests.

When Papua New Guinea (PNG) won its independence from Australia in 1975, the new government's most important source of revenue was the Panguna mine. Production had begun three years earlier on a billion-tonne deposit of copper. Under Australian law, the islanders owned the land's surface. What lay beneath, however, belonged to the Crown, in the form of the Australian state. As the UN noted many years later, this was a concept the islanders found very difficult to understand or accept, then and now.[13]

The mine shattered the social equilibrium on Bougainville. Some clans benefited financially, others did not; but most of the revenue went to Rio Tinto and to the PNG government. In 1988 a former mineworker, Francis Ona, led a group of disaffected Bougainvilleans in disrupting its operations as a means of renegotiating the royalties. The PNG government responded with force. Ona founded the Bougainville Revolutionary Army.

At first, the rebels fought against the mine using bows and arrows. Later, when the government sent in the army, they adapted to using rifles. The government resorted to hiring British and South African mercenaries to restore control. After at least 10,000 deaths, a truce signed in 1998 brought an uneasy peace. It could collapse at any time, especially if the company tries to reopen the mine. The rebels still control much territory, and they retain their arms.

In 1989 the guerrillas succeeded in closing the Panguna mine. PNG's armed forces failed in their efforts to retake it and instead, they blockaded the island, denying its inhabitants fuel, food and medicine. Thousands died on Bougainville as a result of the blockade. An Australian-led peacekeeping intervention in 1994 failed to resolve the conflict and in 1997 the PNG government hired Sandline, a private military contractor, to find and kill Ona and his closest associates.[14] In return, PNG, one of the world's poorest countries, would pay Sandline $36 million.

The PNG army refused to co-operate. Its commanding general, incensed at the importation of a foreign, for-profit military force, broke the news of Sandline's contract and demanded that the prime minister, Sir Julius Chan, resign. Under heavy international pressure, Chan quit. The Sandline mercenaries, many of them South Africans subcontracted from the Pretoria-based Executive Outcomes, were rounded up and deported. Nevertheless, and almost unbelievably, in 1998 a three-man arbitration tribunal in London demanded that PNG pay Sandline another $18 million, plus interest, on top of the $18 million it had already received from PNG's taxpayers.[15]

Decades later, Bougainvilleans near the Panguna mine remain opposed to its reopening, according to a study conducted by an Australian NGO in late 2013.[16] Bougainville's autonomous government supports the reopening if it could be done in a way that limits environmental and social damage, and it took issue with the report's findings, which were based on a small sample.[17] Nevertheless, in August 2014 the autonomous government stripped Rio Tinto of its operating rights, prompting the company to consider selling the site.[18] Should it try to sell Panguna to another developer, the risk of war will escalate once again.

Panguna showed the hazards of forcing Western priorities on a society with a different worldview. That it was even possible to impose the Panguna mine demonstrated the deficiencies of the political model that allowed the project to proceed. Had

Bougainville won its autonomy in 1975, located in the context of a developing regional union akin to the EU, the interests of the islanders would not have been subsumed into the interests of Papua New Guineans and Australian mining executives. The island's distinct culture would have been recognized and preserved at an institutional level by its own representatives.

Timor-Leste

Bougainville is not the only dispute in Oceania that would benefit from regional integration. To its west, the Christian-majority country of Timor-Leste (East Timor) sits on Oceania's boundary with South-East Asia. It won its independence from Muslim-majority Indonesia in 2002, with Australian support. Over the course of its independence struggle, a quarter of a million Timorese fled their homes. Some 100,000 died.[19]

Timor-Leste's troubles did not end at independence, however. In 2006 veterans of the struggle against Indonesia revolted over their pay and conditions, leading Australia and other nations to send in troops to protect the Timorese government. The crisis ended two years later when the rebel leader was killed as he attempted to assassinate the president and prime minister; the latter almost lost his life in the raid.

Australia's help came with a price. Its government attempted to intimidate and undermine Timor-Leste over their maritime boundary, which cuts across huge undersea gas deposits – deposits that Australia plans to develop. Timor-Leste's government discovered that Australian agents had spied on its officials to secure an advantage in the 2002 boundary negotiations. It started a legal process to have the agreement overturned.

In response, Australian spies raided the home of the former agent who blew the whistle on the bugging. They also raided the offices and home of Bernard Collaery, Timor-Leste's lawyer in Canberra, seizing documents. This prompted Timor-Leste to bring in the International Court of Justice (ICJ) which, embarrassingly for Australia, demanded that it seal the seized documents and 'not interfere in any way in communications' between Timor-Leste and its legal counsel, or indeed to spy on the maritime border discussions.[20]

Even that was not enough to dissuade Australia from its bullying behaviour. It used diplomatic channels to warn Timor-Leste not to be 'naïve' when it came to their relationship.[21] This warning seemed to suggest that, should the Timorese government face any more security emergencies, it might not be able to count on Australian troops.

Spying and threats are a poor basis for co-operation. In this case, the imbalance in size, power and wealth made equitable negotiations impossible. Timor-Leste's weakness relative to Australia, which by some counts is the world's wealthiest nation,[22] meant that its only hope of justice was to rely on external bodies such as the ICJ. That Timor-Leste resorted to such channels was also deeply embarrassing for Australia, its close neighbour, erstwhile benefactor and in many respects the regional leader of Oceania.

Regional union

An EU-like regional union would have provided a less-confrontational resolution, counterbalancing Australia's regional dominance with the collective needs of Oceania's smaller governments. Not all of these are as tiny as their international obscurity suggests. The Solomon Islands cover 11,000 square miles (28,000 square kilometres) and has half a million inhabitants. Fiji, with over 800,000 inhabitants, is even more populous. Together, the combined population of Oceania's other countries, including PNG, New Zealand and Timor-Leste, is roughly equal to that of Australia itself.

Integrating Australia into a regional union should be made easier by Australia's federal structure. As elsewhere on the planet, when the local giant devolves powers, this reassures smaller members of a regional union that the giant will not seek to dominate them. Australia is divided into six states, each with its own parliament, and two territories. If the states were able to interact with other members of an Oceanic regional union in a meaningful way, Australia could shift towards a Canadian federal model of genuine provincial autonomy.

As things stand, however, Australia has work to do if it is to remain a true federation. As with the US, its central government has sapped the provinces of much of their power. A series of court decisions from the 1920s onwards reduced the powers of state governments relative to Canberra. There is a risk that Australia, like the US, is losing the benefits of political devolution.

This erosion of provincial power runs against the aspirations of those who framed the constitution. In the words of Sir Samuel Griffith, who prepared the first draft:

It is not intended to transfer to the Executive Government anything which could be as well done by the separate governments of the colonies.[23]

Returning to this original concept might mean, for example, that Timor-Leste would have been negotiating with Australia's Northern Territory over its maritime boundary, rather than with Australia as a whole. This would 'level the playing field' in terms of the sides' diplomatic and intelligence resources and improve the chances of a fair deal.

At the moment, the Pacific Islands Forum (PIF; originally the South Pacific Forum) is the closest Oceania has to the European Union. PIF's 16 members unite Australia with most of Polynesia, Melanesia and Micronesia. In recent years, US and French territories such as American Samoa and New Caledonia have joined as associate members and observers. PIF has set Oceania on the road to achieving many of the 10 factors that support peace in the European Union.

PIF has already recognized the need to move beyond mere co-operation to embrace regional integration.[24] In June 2014, its leaders endorsed the Framework for Pacific Regionalism. Its definition of 'regionalism' could usefully serve on any continent:

The expression of a common sense of identity and purpose, leading progressively to the sharing of institutions, resources and markets, with the purpose of complementing national efforts, overcoming

*common constraints, and enhancing sustainable and inclusive
development within Pacific countries and territories and for the
Pacific region as a whole.*[25]

The agreement committed PIF members to co-ordinating
their regional and sub-regional policies. Most public services
would be funded and delivered nationally, but some would
be delivered on a regional basis to tap economies of scale;
one bulk buyer can secure a better price for goods than can
small purchasers negotiating individually. Governments
would legally commit to setting aside a share of their national
resources to fund such joint services. They would also
harmonize their business and environmental legislation, and
reduce barriers to the free movement of goods and people.

These requirements fulfil the Economic Truce; Financial
Incentives and Support; Soft Power and Shared Values and
Veto and Consensus Building factors. They also put Oceania
on the road towards Mutual Trust and Peaceful Coexistence
and Resistance to External Interference. It is possible that
freedom of movement, in the form of Open Borders and
Human Ties, might have alleviated some of the tensions in
Fiji by demonstrating that it was not only Indian-Fijians who
were mobile. Should a Fijian student wish to be a mining
engineer, she is more likely to find relevant education and
work in Australia than in her own country. Likewise, when
smaller countries need particular technical skills, a regional
union provides a much wider pool of graduates to choose
from.

Given the threat posed by climate change to many of the
islands, regional freedom of movement could also provide a
last means of escape. In 2013, the president of the Republic
of Marshall Islands, a PIF member, warned that the Pacific
is 'fighting for its survival' against rising seas and erosion.[26]
Kiribati's president said that his country was likely to become
uninhabitable in the next 30 to 60 years.

In March 2015, a Category 5 cyclone named Pam devastated
Vanuatu, forcing islanders to drink saltwater. Baldwin

Lonsdale, the country's president, said that climate change was making such storms more intense. This being the case, regional contingency planning would seem a far better way of managing these potential disasters than disaster relief efforts when they finally occur.

Working together on shared infrastructure is another important task, although the PIF's insular geography presents a different challenge than other continents. PIF has described Oceania as a 'Maritime Silk Road' and has sought investment from China as part of its One Belt, One Road initiative.[27] The potential for a safe and swift network of ferry and flight crossings would consolidate the regional tourism market, with Chinese visitors already representing a major new market. Since 1995, China's travel departures have increased at an annual rate of over 15 per cent a year.[28] India may also become a major source of tourists, given its strong human links to the Pacific.

As elsewhere, building a regional union in Oceania will allow countries with similar challenges to pool their resources in search of common solutions. And, like other regional unions, it will also establish the 10 factors that create a lasting continental peace. The first and foundational mechanism is Democracy and Rule of Law. Maintaining democracy in Fiji has been a particular challenge, given its unusual social make-up.

Fiji

Fiji's 2006 coup was its fourth in two decades. The cycle began in 1987 when an election brought to power a government dominated by Indian-Fijians. The British Empire brought Indians to the islands as plantation workers, but by the mid-1940s the number of Indian-Fijians exceeded that of Melanesian islanders.[29] After the 1987 election, Indians formed the majority in parliament and in the cabinet.

Alarmed by the demographic change, Lieutenant-Colonel Sitiveni Rabuka led two coups in 1987, demanding that native Fijians be granted permanent structural control of the government. Knowing that the Commonwealth would expel

Fiji for his actions, he declared Fiji a republic and began a process of drafting a new constitution.[30]

New elections were held in 1999, after which Fiji's Commonwealth membership was restored. These polls delivered a landslide victory to Mahendra Chaudhry, Fiji's first ethnically Indian prime minister. He had powerful enemies, including Rupert Murdoch's *Fiji Times* newspaper.[31] The following year a man named George Speight led a gang of protesters into the parliament and took hostage the prime minister and 35 other legislators. Speight was aided by Fiji's special forces chief Colonel Ilisoni Ligairi, a veteran of the UK's Special Air Service who had fought in dozens of conflicts across the globe.[32]

However, the rebels had not reckoned on an even tougher soldier. The man in charge of Fiji's military was the charismatic Commodore Frank Bainimarama. Acting unconstitutionally, he dismissed the president and created an interim government to negotiate with the hostage-takers. Within a few weeks, all hostages were released and Speight's gang were arrested. The commodore was hailed as a national hero for ending the crisis without bloodshed. Bainimarama restored civilian rule, narrowly avoiding assassination himself by climbing out of a window at his officers' mess when nationalist mutineers attacked the building.

Democracy was not to last. In December 2006, after falling out with the increasingly nationalist government, Bainimarama staged a coup. Although ethnically Melanesian himself, he justified his coup in defence of Fiji's Indian community, thousands of whom had fled the country in the years beforehand.[33] As the commodore said in late 2013:

Tens of thousands of Fijians suffered and many made the decision to leave their home forever, to leave Fiji... This is one of the most shameful episodes of our history and I determined that this must never, never happen again. We must never allow a fellow citizen to be second class, to be less than an equal of his neighbour.[34]

The commodore's humanity towards Indian-Fijians was commendable. His dictatorship was less so. The media dubbed Fiji a 'Bainimarama Republic' and, indeed, it did have aspects of a banana republic. In 2009 the junta unilaterally abolished the constitution and assumed untrammelled power. It expelled the Australian and New Zealand envoys and attempted to replace Fiji's chief justices with lawyers imported from overseas.[35]

Thankfully, Bainimarama was genuinely popular in Fiji. After years of international pressure, in 2014 he relinquished his military command and held elections. His subsequent victory was deemed credible by foreign observers, despite complaints by opposition parties.[36] Fiji was reinstated to the Commonwealth, and the US and Australia lifted their sanctions against the country.[37,38]

Bainimarama's coup was a symptom of the interlocking problems posed by nationalism. From one perspective, it was possible to understand why Melanesian Fijians were concerned at becoming a minority. Similar anxieties propel violence and unrest across India itself, particularly in the northeastern provinces and among Hindus who fear the growth of the Muslim population.

The military coups unsettled Fiji's traditional pattern of alliances at a time of rising geopolitical competition in the South Pacific. In 2014 Fiji was visited both by India's Prime Minister Narendra Modi and by China's President Xi Jinping[39] – two guests that very few Western countries could hope to attract in a single year. Bainimarama played them against each other to secure their investment in Fiji.

China and India are battling for influence in the Pacific islands, some of which still recognize Taiwan as the 'official China', much to Beijing's irritation. Although Fiji and the other islands gain economically from this courtship, geopolitical competition has a habit of exploding into war. Such competition between the EU and Russia looked to be in Ukraine's interest for a few years, until it descended into a devastating conflict between pro-Russian and pro-EU forces.

Regional alignment

Oceania's big countries are just as much at risk as its smaller ones of becoming the instruments of larger powers. The US classifies Australia as one of its major non-NATO allies, and US President George W Bush memorably described Australia as his 'sheriff in Asia.'[40] The northern Australian city of Darwin now hosts a rotating contingent of US Marines, part of the US strategic 'pivot' to Asia. New Zealand, by contrast, has declared a nuclear-free zone and thus effectively banned US warships from its ports, given that they refuse to confirm or deny whether they carry nuclear weapons. The US retaliated by barring New Zealand's navy from its ports, although it has eased that ban in recent years.[41]

The history of islands such as Guadalcanal and Bougainville shows why, in the long term, stable systems of regional alignment are the best hope of peace and prosperity in the Pacific. As in Europe, regional blocs offer a bulwark against external interference and democratic backsliding. Although the Commonwealth's suspension of Fiji clearly had some impact, it was PIF's decision to follow suit in 2009 that proved decisive. This was the first time PIF had suspended a member. Bainimarama was clearly shocked, as became apparent when, in 2012, he tried to establish the Pacific Islands Development Forum as a rival to PIF – one that excluded Australia and New Zealand.

Its first summit was a fiasco: only 14 of the 23 invited nations sent anyone, and only three sent their leaders (the Solomon Islands, Kiribati and Timor-Leste, the latter relishing a chance to avenge its bullying by Canberra).[42] After PIF lifted its suspension of Fiji, Bainimarama said his country would only participate if Australia and New Zealand were expelled. Eventually he backed down, saying only that he would not personally attend the meeting. In doing so, he voiced the kind of complaints that must be managed if such regional blocs are to succeed.

'Rather than side with us, Australia in particular is siding with what I call the coalition of the selfish,' the commodore

said in May 2015.[43] 'Those industrialized nations which
are putting the welfare of their carbon-polluting industries
and their workers before our welfare and survival as Pacific
Islanders... This is not me "mouthing off", as the New Zealand
prime minister so condescendingly put it.'

Such complaints would make sense to people in
Bougainville. Nevertheless, those are the people who are
also likely to benefit from a stronger PIF. If it is to thrive,
Bougainville needs the assistance of its neighbours. PIF, which
includes PNG, Australia and the Solomon Islands, can work to
reassure Bougainvilleans that those cultures closest to them,
whether culturally or geographically, are working in the
collective interest, rather than trying to exploit each other. The
Mutual Trust factor is especially important in a post-conflict
environment such as Bougainville's. Indeed, PIF has used its
collective weight to lobby the UN over the need to manage
more carefully conflicts between resource extraction and
communities.[44]

The challenges of Oceania's regional integration are as
daunting as those anywhere in the world. Its dazzling expanse
of cultures, economies, history and languages eclipses that
of the other continents. So too does the logistical challenge
of uniting thousands of islands across vast tracts of water.
Oceania combines some of the world's poorest people and
some of its wealthiest.

Bridging the differences between them requires the building
of new, regional institutions. Trying to impose a Western
developmental template without such a regional mechanism
will inevitably create conflict. To have Soft Power and Shared
Values, it is first necessary to discuss what those shared values
actually are. A compromise needs to be reached between
the Western extractive, industrial mind-set and other, less
materialistic worldviews.

There are plenty of grounds for optimism. A glance at
the national rugby teams of Australia and New Zealand
demonstrates the extent to which islanders already circulate
around their continent. Australia's troubling hostility towards

immigrants is directed largely at Asian asylum-seekers, rather than against migrants from Oceania; indeed, Nauru and PNG have assisted Australia in its attempts to prevent the asylum-seekers reaching its shores.

Australian dollars already serve as a *de facto* single currency across the continent, and Fiji's return to democracy allowed the renewal of institutional regionalism. If Oceania can resist the temptation to become entangled in the multipolar competition of the 21st century, and instead become a peaceful pole of its own, it will spare itself the worst effects of war, disaster and climate change, and become instead the paradise islands that many outsiders already perceive them to be.

1 Part 6, 'Report of the National Inquiry into the Separation of Aboriginal and Torres Strait Islander Children from Their Families', Commonwealth of Australia 1997. **2** p278-79, Hernon, Ian, *Britain's Forgotten Wars,* Sutton Publishing, 2002. **3** UN World Happiness Report 2013, eds. Helliwell, John, Layard, Richard and Sachs, Jeffrey, UN Sustainable Development Solutions Network. **4** Happy Planet Index, www.happyplanetindex.org/data/ **5** Clifton, Jon, 2014, 'People Worldwide Are Reporting a Lot of Positive Emotions', Gallup, 21 May. **6** 'Living in Saudi Arabia', Saudi Aramco website. **7** Wong, Edward, 2013, 'Air Pollution Linked to 1.2 Million Premature Deaths in China', *The New York Times*, 1 April. **8** Air Pollution, NYC Environmental Protection, Permament Link, www.nyc.gov/html/dep/html/air/index.shtml **9** Cooper Charlie, 2014, 'Air pollution linked to one in 12 deaths in London – and it takes six months off the average Briton's life expectancy', *The Independent*, 10 April. **10** Unnamed Author, 2014, 'GPs taught to spot rickets in London children as cases soar', *Evening Standard*, 13 January. **11** Thacher et al., 2013 'Increasing incidence of nutritional rickets: a population based study in Olmsted County, Minnesota', US National Library of Medicine, National Institutes of Health, PubMed, February, Permanent Link: www.ncbi.nlm.nih.gov/pubmed/23374621 **12** Martin, Judy, 2012, 'Stress at Work is Bunk for Business', Forbes, 2 August. **13** UN Commission on Human Rights, 1981, 'Question of the violation of human rights and fundamental freedoms in any part of the world, with particular reference to colonial and other dependent countries and territories', Assistance to the Central African Republic, 9 March 1981. **14** Country profile/ Background, 2012 'Bougainville', Australian Army. **15** Byrne, Peter, 1998, 'Mercenary scandal continues to plague Papua New Guinea government', World Socialist Website, 5 November. **16** Survey, 2014, 'Voices of Bougainville', Jubilee Australia, 12 September. **17** Davidson, Helen, 2014, 'Bougainville landowners defend consultation over Panguna mine', *The Guardian*, 30 December. **18** Wilson, James, 2014, 'Rio Tinto puts Papua New Guinea copper mine under review', *Financial Times*, 18 August. **19** Ofstad, Olav, 2012, 'Reconciliation and Conflict Resolution in East Timor', Oxford Institute for Ethics, Law and Armed Conflict, April 2012 . **20** Allard, Tom, 2014, 'Australia ordered to cease spying on East Timor by International Court of Justice', *Sydney Morning Herald*, 4 March. **21** Cronau, Peter, 2014, 'Australia issues diplomatic warning to East Timor saying maritime boundaries case risks relationship', ABC News, 6 September. **22** Commins, Patrick, 2014, 'Property makes the Australians the world's richest, says Credit Suisse', *Sydney Morning Herald*, 14 October. **23** Bolton, Geoffrey, 1991, 'Samuel Griffith: The Great Provincial', Papers on Parliament, no. 13, November. **24** Unnamed author, 'The Framework for Pacific Regionalism', Pacific Island Forum Secretariat. **25** Unnamed Author, 2014, 'The Framework for Pacific Regionalism', Pacific Island Forum Secretariat, July 2014. **26** Vidal, John, 2013, 'We are fighting for survival,' Pacific island leader warns', *The Guardian*, 1 September. **27** Wang, Xu, 2015, 'Pacific islands welcome Belt and Road opportunities', *China Daily*, 31 July. **28** See Chen et al, 'Pacific Island Countries: In Search of a Trade Strategy', IMF Working Paper, August 2014. **29** '2007 Census of Population', Fiji Bureau of Statistics, 2007. **30** Country profile/Background, 'Fiji', The Commonwealth. **31** Field, Michael, 2010, 'Cloud coup coup land', *Sunday Star Times*, 16 May. **32** Dutter and Harnden, 2000, 'Fijian coup colonel took part in SAS blunder', *The Telegraph*, 22 June. **33** Field, Michael, 2009, 'Fiji's Indian population collapsing', Stuff.co.nz, 10 March. **34** Unnamed author, 2013, 'Fiji interim PM Frank Bainimarama defends 2006 coup in UN General Assembly address', ABC News, 26 September. **35** Marks, Kathy, 2014, 'Bula Bully?', *The Sydney Morning Herald*, 21 July. **36** Unnamed author, 2014, 'Fiji's Frank Bainimarama confirmed as election winner with outright majority', *The Guardian*, 22 September. **37** Unnamed author, 2014, 'Fiji reinstated to the Commonwealth following 'credible elections'', ABC News, 26 September. **38** Unnamed author, 2014, 'US and Australia lifts Fiji's sanctions', *The Guardian*, 31 October. **39** Veisamasama, Malakai, 2014, 'India's Modi pledges $70 million credit for Fiji sugar industry', Reuters, 19 November. **40** Unnamed author, 2003, 'Bush hails 'sheriff' Australia', BBC News, 16 October. **41** See Alexander, David, 2012, 'US lifts ban on New Zealand warships, New Zealand keeps nuclear-free stance', Reuters, 21 September. **42** Poling, Gregory B, 2013, 'Pacific Partners Outlook: The Pacific Islands Development Forum: Keep Calm and Carry On', volume 3, issue 9, Center for Strategic and International Studies, 29 August. **43** Fox, Liam, 2015, 'Fiji PM Frank Bainimarama to shun Pacific Island Forum over "under influence" of Australia, NZ', ABC News, 6 May. **44** Unnamed author, 2015, 'Pacific Forum chief sets issues for UN', Radio New Zealand News, 4 May.

Chapter 8 – What the Ottomans Knew

Nowhere is more in need of peaceful, permanent institutions than the Middle East and North Africa. Little progress has been achieved in this regard. Regional groups such as the Arab League and Gulf Co-operation Council only find strong consensus when presented with an external enemy such as Israel or Iran. This failure has promoted the success of groups such as the Islamic Caliphate (IS), which seeks to deliver a regional union at the point of a gun.

In the spring after he became president of the United States, Barack Obama flew to Europe to attend a NATO summit. The president came with a specific demand. The European Union, he said, must admit Turkey, a country poorer and more populous than any it had admitted before. He flew onwards to Ankara to convey the same message to his Turkish hosts. 'Let me be clear,' Obama said. 'The United States strongly supports Turkey's bid to become a member of the European Union.'[1]

Obama, a Democrat, was walking a familiar path. Five years earlier, his Republican predecessor George W Bush carried the same message to Europe. Bush demanded that the EU admit Turkey. The union is 'not the exclusive club of a single religion,' he argued. Although not known for his academic interests, Bush attacked the scholar Samuel Huntington. He said that the EU admitting Turkey 'would expose the "clash of civilizations" as a passing myth of history.[2]

Jacques Chirac, the president of France, became irritated by Bush's intervention. Chirac mentioned Mexico.[3] How would Americans react if he, a French president, travelled to Washington and demanded the inclusion of Mexico as the 51st state of the US?

Chirac's analogy was a fair one, in some ways. Like Turkey, Mexico has a large and relatively poor population. Some Turks, like some Mexicans, are attracted to working in the wealthier economies to the north. And, like Mexico, Turkey is often associated with another geography altogether. Just as many Europeans see Muslim-majority Turkey as a Middle-Eastern or Asian culture, so many in North America see Mexico as a Latin American state.

There is an idea, seldom expressed but often implied, that regional unions should overlay onto 'civilizations'. In 2004, leaked diplomatic cables revealed that Cardinal Joseph Ratzinger, a future pope, opposed Turkish membership because he saw the EU as a Christian entity.[4] Three years later, Nicolas Sarkozy, Chirac's successor as president of France, said that Turkey was part of Asia Minor, not Europe, though he denied that Turkey's majority Muslim culture was a factor in his opposition to its EU membership.[5]

If President Bush was correct, then Europeans were unduly susceptible to the thinking of his fellow American, Harvard scholar Samuel Huntington. Few academic works attracted as much scorn and criticism at Huntington's 1993 essay, 'The Clash of Civilizations'. In it, he argued that the 20th century's conflict between the competing dogmas of capitalism and communism would yield to a 21st-century confrontation between incompatible civilizations.

The theory offended the values of anyone who believed in the essential commonality of humankind, and the possibility of friendship between black and white, rich and poor, atheist and believer. A month after the al-Qaeda attacks on New York and Washington in 2001, Palestinian academic Edward Said published an article entitled 'The Clash of Ignorance'.[6] He assailed Huntington for his 'cartoonlike world' in which complex swathes of humanity were reduced to 'Popeye and Bluto [who] bash each other mercilessly'. Huntington, said Said, was a 'clumsy writer and inelegant thinker'. His thesis was a 'gimmick' around which the ignorant could gather.

By 2014, however, Huntington's critics were on the back foot. Violence was flaring along the lines he had suggested, particularly along the borders of his 'Muslim civilization'. Where Russia's south met the Muslim world, Chechen and Dagestani separatists waged war against Moscow, tracking the seam between Huntington's Eastern Orthodox and Islamic civilizations. Further east, the perceived threat of Muslim radicalism prompted Russia and China to form the Shanghai Co-operation Organization, a security umbrella designed to preserve the brittle Central Asian dictatorships from a tide of transnational Muslim revolt emanating from Afghanistan and Pakistan. Muslim separatists in China's western province of Xinjiang perpetrated ever bloodier attacks.[7]

Where Islamic civilization met others in southern Thailand and the southern Philippines, Muslims fought the state. The Buddhist government of Burma inflicted brutal violence against Muslims in its state of Rakhine, even as the country's other internal conflicts ebbed and its leaders shed their uniforms.[8] India's Kashmiri frontier with Muslim Pakistan remained febrile.

In Africa, violence perpetrated by Islamist militant groups such as Al-Shabaab and Boko Haram followed the line Huntington drew between his 'African' and Islamic civilizations. Sudan was partitioned into the Muslim north and Christian-majority south in an effort to end the country's internal conflict.[9] In the southern portion of Africa, however, the tribal and ideological wars that had decimated much of the region during the 20th century gave way to a newfound peace under the auspices of the African Union.

Huntington's critics countered with a straightforward argument. There was even worse violence occurring *within* the 'Islamic civilization'. They pointed to conflict between Sunni and Shi'a Muslims in Pakistan, Afghanistan, Iraq, Bahrain, Yemen and Syria. This sectarian bloodshed was often more extreme than that on the fringes of the Islamic world. How could there be a monolithic 'Muslim civilization' when so often the worst violence occurred between Muslims?

To those within the Middle East, however, it was more that Huntington simply omitted a major civilization from his list – one driving much of the violence in the Middle East. The Persian Empire once stretched from the borders of India to the islands of Greece. Its modern inheritor is Persian-speaking Iran, an 80-million-strong regional giant that is larger by population than the six members of the Gulf Co-operation Council combined.

Sunni and Shi'a

Iran is the world's largest Shi'a Muslim country, whereas most Arab states are overwhelmingly Sunni. They view Iran as an expansionist power that has used its spiritual leadership of the world's Shi'a Muslims to drive a 'Shi'a crescent' through the Middle East, extending from Damascus to Tehran.[10] Its instruments in this regard include Shi'a militias in Iraq,[11] Hezbollah in Lebanon,[12] Shi'a protesters in Bahrain[13] and Houthi insurgents in Yemen.[14]

Increasingly, this Iranosphere is not dependent on a shared religion. Scratch beneath the surface of the Shi'a theocracy and Iran's Persian legacy is not hard to find. Iran's most popular festival is not the religious Eid or Ashura, but Nowruz, Persian New Year. Lately, even the most outwardly pious of Iran's leaders have taken to celebrating Nowruz as a touchstone that unites the Persian sphere of influence everywhere from Armenia to Turkmenistan to Los Angeles.[15,16] Through such outreach, Iran has sought to establish itself as a new voice in the multipolar 21st century, alongside the African Union, ASEAN and UNASUR.

The Sunni Middle East, however, has no leading state. There, the process of regional union has stalled. A central theme in Islam is that of the *'ummah'*, the indivisibility of the Islamic nation. There is little about the current geography of Arab nation-states that reflects this. The region remains subdivided into weak, squabbling dictatorships seemingly incapable of the kind of unity desired by Muslims.

A survey taken in 2007 by World Public Opinion found that 65 per cent of Muslims wished to live under a unified Islamic Caliphate, a Muslim state with a single government. More than a third 'strongly' desired this. Polling by Pew in 2011 found that across the Islamic world, respondents considered themselves Muslims first; their nationality was secondary. This was the case everywhere except in that most eclectic of

Levantine states, Lebanon, where slightly more people viewed
themselves as being primarily Lebanese, although the high
proportion of people who failed to respond either way casts
some doubt even on this finding, given the violently polarized
nature of communal relations.

The concept of the nation-state has never embedded in the
Muslim world, and many Muslims would prefer to live under
some kind of unified government or Caliphate. Writing in
The Guardian newspaper, Inayat Bunglawala pointed out that
a new Caliphate could be like a democratic union between
Muslim states, like the European Union. Sadly, this was not
the only model on offer.

The Arabian Peninsula is the centre of the Islamic world. It
suffers acutely from the ailments of the wider *ummah*. Arabs
are divided from one another by lines on a map dissecting
them into Saudis, Jordanians, Yemenis, Qataris, Kuwaitis,
and – increasingly blurred – Syrians and Iraqis. Enforcing
these borders has been delegated to brutal dictatorships. Their
brutality has only bred resistance.

Iraq

The history of Iraq is instructive. In 1990, the country's
then-dictator, Saddam Hussein, ordered the invasion of
neighbouring Kuwait. Kuwait was a sheikhdom that had
split from Ottoman Mesopotamia in 1913, under a deal
between the British and the Ottoman High Porte. The rest of
Mesopotamia became Iraq after the end of the First World
War and, not without reason, Iraqi leaders tended to view
Kuwait as an alienated part of their own territory. They
were only deterred from invading in 1961 by British military
reinforcements – Britain relied on Kuwaiti oil.[17]

The expulsion of Iraqi troops by the US and its allies in 1991
did little to make the barriers between Sunni Arabs any more
credible. If anything, the war in Kuwait, and the failure of the
US to remove Saddam from power, added to the impression
that foreign powers had deliberately subdivided Arabs into
small, weak bantustans that relied on the West for protection,

and whose corrupt leaders would reliably export their oil in exchange for weapons and luxuries.

Such was the view of a Saudi jihadist named Osama bin Laden, a veteran of Afghanistan's revolt against Soviet occupation of the 1980s. After Iraq's invasion of Kuwait, bin Laden became incensed by the presence on Saudi soil of tens of thousands of non-Muslim troops he called 'filthy, infidel crusaders'. Bin Laden had offered to drive Iraqi troops from Kuwait using veterans from the Afghan conflict, but his offer was declined by the Saudi royal family.

Saudi Arabia is home to Islam's two holiest sites, Mecca and Medina. This desecration of Saudi soil, as he saw it, inspired bin Laden and al-Qaeda to stage a series of attacks on US nationals that culminated in the events of 11 September 2001. Those attacks saw the US lurch into wars in Afghanistan and Iraq that, in the case of the latter, were of questionable legality and stoked further accusations that the Americans were principally interested in securing control over desert oil supplies.

The invasion and occupation returned Iraq's oil to the market, lifting the Saddam-era sanctions at a huge cost in human life. In December 2011, after eight years of entanglement in Iraq's sectarian and nationalist bloodshed, US troops departed in a hurry, leaving behind a weak government in Baghdad that represented only the country's Shi'a Muslim majority, as well as a more effective but increasingly autonomous government in Kurdistan.

Never did the US seek to promote an EU-style regional union between Iraq and its neighbours, or to promote the 10 factors that brought peace to Europe. American experiences of pan-Arab co-ordination have not been happy ones. In 1973, the US considered invading Middle Eastern countries to seize their oil fields, in response to an OPEC-wide oil embargo that followed the Arab-Israeli war. After speaking to US Defense Secretary James Schlesinger, Lord Cromer, the British ambassador, reported:

...it was no longer obvious to him that the United States could not use force... The US government might consider that it could not tolerate a situation in which the US and its allies were in effect at the mercy of a small group of unreasonable countries.[18]

The US viewed a unified Middle East as a threat to its economy. Six of the world's top 10 oil exporters lie in the area, led by Saudi Arabia. Any political union between them would allow their joint government to exert vastly more pricing control over crude oil than even the OPEC cartel. They would grip the world economy by the throat.

Caliphates and the Islamic State

The sequel to the 2003 invasion of Iraq was more destabilizing still. It began in Syria in 2011. There, Bashar al-Assad's regime mirrored that of Saddam Hussein. Both men led Baathist parties that enforced a brutal but secular kind of dictatorship. Both had their power base in a religious minority: Saddam among Iraq's minority Sunni Muslims, Assad among Syria's Alawite Shi'a minority. The destruction of Saddam's government by the US had generated a wave of unrest across the Middle East and North Africa that became known as the Arab Spring. Eventually, it came to Syria.

Northern Syria was an incubator for all manner of revolutionary groups. One, however, discovered a winning strategy. It exploited the suppressed desire among Sunni Arabs for political unification, and it set about destroying the borders dividing them. In June 2014 the group's leader, known by his *nom de guerre* Abu Bakr al-Baghdadi, declared the creation of a Caliphate. He renamed his group the Islamic State (IS). In doing so his group removed the words 'Iraq and the Levant' from its branding, deleting any association with nation-states.[19]

IS was not the only organization dedicated to a Caliphate, but it soon became the most successful. As it overran and destroyed border checkpoints between Iraq and Syria, the group used the Twitter hashtag #SykesPicotOver to publicize its action.[20] The Sykes-Picot Accord was a secret understanding struck in 1916 between the British and French empires to divide the Ottoman empire – the last Caliphate – into zones of control that corresponded with the modern countries of Iraq, Syria, Lebanon, Jordan and Israel/Palestine.

At it pushed eastwards towards Baghdad, the so-called Islamic State captured economic resources commensurate to its claims of independence. By September 2014, the US Department of Defense admitted that Baghdadi's group controlled half of the territory of Syria and Iraq.[21] The US Air Force resorted to blowing up oil refineries in eastern Syria that were generating millions of dollars in revenue for IS.[22] One assessment suggested that the US had spent almost $1 billion on airstrikes against the group in just three months.[23]

Other entities seeking a Caliphate, such as the nonviolent Hizb ut-Tahrir (HuT), looked sceptically at these gains and the international response. HuT did not support IS, but it questioned why the US was so quick to bomb the group while refraining from bombing Assad, even after he crossed the 'red line' set by President Obama by using chemical weapons against civilians.[24] The group's UK spokesman Taji Mustafa noted that the US decision to launch airstrikes had united IS with a competitor group, the al-Qaeda-aligned Jabhat al-Nusra, thereby actually increasing its power.[25]

Militant jihadist groups were more enthusiastic about the new Caliphate. Although the Afghan Taliban denounced IS, the Pakistani Taliban offered moral support.[26] So too did Abu Sayyaf in the Philippines,[27] and Nigeria's Boko Haram.[28] Young Muslims around the world flocked to Turkish border towns such as Akcakale to join the IS fighters. Some were Muslim Chechens opposed to Russia's rule over their homeland, increasing the probability that those who survived their experiences in Iraq and Syria would return to Russia to continue their jihad.[29]

IS was fighting to fill the Sunni leadership vacuum that had existed since the fall of the Ottomans in 1923. In staking their claim, the militants exploited the pretensions of other claimants to that crown. They proved adept at exploiting the divisions between the governments of Sunni-majority countries, particularly those that saw themselves as pan-Sunni leaders.

Saudi Arabia

Of these pretenders, the Saudi king has perhaps the strongest claim to being paramount leader of the world's Sunnis. He controls the holy sites of Mecca and Medina and he is an Arab, as was the Prophet Mohammad. Saudi Arabia burnishes its credentials as the holiest state by imposing extremely strict and literal interpretations of Islam; women, for instance, are not allowed to drive a car or show their faces in public.

Moreover, Saudi Arabia has vast financial resources as a result of its oil, which it uses to spread its brand of Islam around the world. These very financial resources, however, have compromised the Saudis' ability to lead. Selling oil to the US and Europe requires co-operative relations with them. The Saudis are major buyers of Western arms, helping the West to balance its trade, but, as proven in the first Gulf War, the Saudis are still beholden to the US and its allies for their defence, much to the fury of Islamist groups.[30]

Such cordial relations are Saudi Arabia's Achilles' heel when it comes to claiming the mantle of Sunni leadership. Other pretenders can assert their own credentials through overt hostility to the West and to Israel, trumping Saudi Arabia's claims to piety and strength. Iran, although disbarred from pan-Muslim loyalty due to its Shi'a complexion, uses every opportunity to pronounce its desire to see Israel destroyed (although the modalities by which Iran would achieve this are rather less dramatic than the rhetoric.)[31]

Even relative pipsqueaks such as Qatar have used Saudi Arabia's compromised position to assert claims to pan-Sunni leadership. Qatar hosts Al-Jazeera, the leading Arabic-language news network. Al-Jazeera operates with a high degree of editorial freedom and issues many reports that are embarrassing to the Saudis, who closed down its Riyadh offices in March 2014.[32]

The reason for this act, according to the Saudis, was because the Qataris backed the Muslim Brotherhood, particularly in Egypt. The Brotherhood is a mostly peaceful Islamist movement that the Saudis and Egyptian elite nonetheless view as a threat. Qatar hosts the Brotherhood's exiled spiritual leader, Sheikh Youssef al-Qaradawi, despite pressure from the Saudis, Egypt and their allies, who withdrew their ambassadors in protest at the Qataris' regional antics.[33]

Sponsoring such pan-Islamic movements amplifies Qatar's influence far beyond its borders. Not only is the region unable to Resist External Interference, one of the 10 underpinnings of peace, but its members actively interfere with each others' security. Most egregiously, some wealthy Qataris sent money to IS in Iraq and Syria. Although Saudis also provided funds, US officials argued that Qatar's government made less effort to stop these transfers and that this failure reflected Qatari foreign policy.[34] Officially, the Qatari government denied involvement. As for the militants themselves, they claimed that by 2022 Qatar would be part of their Caliphate. They advised the organizers of the football World Cup, due to be held in Qatar in 2022, to find an alternative venue.[35]

The Gulf Co-operation Council

The self-styled IS Caliphate's brutal, top-down approach to Muslim political unity was a response to the failure of Sunni states to unite peacefully. The splits between the Qataris and the Saudis were despite both being members of the Gulf Co-operation Council (GCC), a transnational bloc drawn from only the wealthiest and most stable states on the Arabian Peninsula. The GCC was meant to be the Arabs' answer to the EU.

In theory, the GCC is committed to the creation of a single currency among its members. In reality, there are structural problems. Rodrigo de Rato, a former managing director of the IMF, made the point that for a GCC currency to be successful, there would need to be some degree of fiscal harmony, for instance on taxation.[36] Such harmony requires representative politics, something the GCC countries lack. Again, the Enshrined Democracy precondition is fundamental.

The lack of Enshrined Democracy is not the only obstacle to the GCC's monetary union. The crisis that beset the Eurozone after the 2008 financial crisis reduced their enthusiasm still further. The smaller members were also concerned by the extent to which Saudi Arabia dominated GCC arrangements.

If even the GCC, with its narrow membership, cannot agree, what hope is there for any larger union? The League of Arab States was founded after the Second World War. Like the GCC, political divisions between the League's 22 members limited its activities to general areas of mutual agreement, for instance in opposing Israel and supporting the Palestinians. The group's summits failed to create a unified front on most foreign policy issues, even though the League, being exclusively Arab, did not incorporate tricky customers such as Iran or Pakistan.

The Organization of Islamic Co-operation (OIC) is an even larger grouping. It is the world's second-largest multilateral after the UN. As a lobbying bloc within the UN, it has been quite successful, for instance by maintaining diplomatic pressure on Israel over its treatment of the Palestinians, but as a means of forging political or economic unity between its members, the OIC has failed. As is the case in the GCC, whose members are also members of the OIC, the splits within it are often more virulent than those found between members and non-members.

With governments unable to offer political change, Islamist groups gained momentum. The result is that today, the countries of the Middle East and North Africa are ranked as among the world's least peaceful.[37] This is despite the population of the Arab world being only around 370 million people,[38] less than half that of Europe or sub-Saharan Africa, and only a third that of South or East Asia.

Some have attributed this violence to the nature of Islam itself. The biologist Richard Dawkins has called Islam the 'greatest force for evil today'.[39] Yet there is a counter-example to this idea that Islam is inherently violent. On the other side of the world, there are almost 300 million Sunni Muslims – considerably more than the entire population of North Africa – who live lives that are peaceful and democratic when compared to their co-religionists in the Middle East and Africa.

Islam in South-East Asia

Arab merchants brought Islam to South-East Asia more than a millennium ago, to Indonesia and Malaysia, to the southern Philippines and to trading ports across Asia. Today, the modern states of Indonesia and Malaysia offer lessons to the Middle East and Africa, offering two separate models for peace. Malaysia is a federal union; Indonesia, a unitary state, albeit one experimenting with regional autonomy.

Malaysia's federation is an interesting model for the Middle East because it has united a disparate group of sheikhs and sultans of the kind that wield power in many Arab states. Malaysia's sultans and chiefs elect one of their own number to serve as Malaysia's titular leader, even as political power reposes in an elected prime minister and parliament. The monarchs are, however, allowed to dictate matters of religion and culture.[40] This has allowed for a diversity of religious observance within the new Malaysian state.

As a result, some of modern Malaysia's sultanates are more orthodox than others. The northern state of Kelantan, for instance, is led by a party that espouses the creation of an Islamic state and which bans the sale and consumption of alcohol. Other states are much more liberal, and as a result have attracted many non-Muslim tourists to their beaches. Malaysians are free to move around the federation to areas that best reflect their own values.

Indonesia has a population far larger than any Arab country, with about 250 million people, and is geographically less contiguous, being scattered across an archipelago. After spending much of its independent history as a unitary state under bloody military dictatorships, it too has shifted towards greater regional autonomy, a strategy that has yielded clear benefits for peace and democracy.

From 1999, Indonesia began to pass new laws allowing for regional autonomy.[41] In 2005, a peace agreement created the conditions for an end to the long-running insurgency in the province of Aceh, at the northern tip of the island of Sumatra, which gave extensive local powers to Aceh's government. Aceh is a former sultanate that practises a more conservative brand of Islam than the rest of Indonesia.

Since 2009, Aceh's government has moved to introduce stricter laws based on Islamic texts, some of which have attracted international condemnation for breaching human rights.[42] Nevertheless, the ceasefire has held. If this lasts, in the words of the scholar Antony Reid, 'Indonesia will have discovered through a bitter and painful route a formula that Malaysia adopted at the start.'[43]

It is unlikely that any functioning pan-Islamic union will abide precisely by human rights as the West understands them. Even liberal Malaysia has effectively revived the concept of the *dhimmi*, the status given to non-Muslims by the Ottoman Caliphate. Although *dhimmis* were sheltered by the Caliphate, they enjoyed fewer rights than Muslims. Today, modern Malaysia discriminates in favour of Muslim Malays and against the country's large ethnic Chinese and Tamil minorities.

Nevertheless, Indonesia and Malaysia prove that, human rights deficiencies notwithstanding, Sunni Muslims can live peacefully and coexist with other cultures so long as they are permitted a substantial degree of democracy and regional variation. The ingredient they have discovered, which the Middle East lacks, is representative government. Without the legitimacy conferred by a popular mandate, leaders are paralysed either from devolving powers downwards or, as is necessary for transnational unity, upwards.

Supporting democracy

The refusal of the West to support democracy in the Muslim world is a major contributing factor to the violence in the Middle East. The Obama administration's failure to oppose in any serious way the military overthrow of Egypt's elected Muslim Brotherhood government, and the subsequent military persecution of its members, was a depressing sight.[44] Washington's suspension of its annual $1.3 billion military aid to Egypt lasted barely a year.[45]

The West's extensive support for dictators across the Middle East and North Africa is a principal impediment to the political unity that so many Muslims desire. Ending this support for unelected despots, and holding themselves to their own democratic values, is an urgent requirement for the US and EU in their relations with the region. In the words of Condoleezza Rice, speaking in Cairo as US Secretary of State:

For 60 years, my country, the United States, pursued stability at the expense of democracy in this region, here in the Middle East, and we achieved neither.[46]

How the West supports democracy is, of course, a significant question. To date, the US approach has been to demand the democratization of enemy states (Syria, Saddam-era Iraq, Iran) and to quietly oppose it among its allies (Oman, Saudi Arabia, the United Arab Emirates, Egypt). A braver and more credible approach would be to exert peaceful pressure on the Gulf states to shift towards constitutional monarchy, with political power vested in elected ministers.

In order to apply such pressure, the West needs to ease its reliance on Gulf oil. This, thankfully, is already under way. Renewable energy, unconventional hydrocarbons, recycling, new discoveries outside the Middle East, environmental awareness and technology have changed the patterns of demand. The International Energy Agency says the world is nearing an inflection point, whereafter oil consumption growth will begin to decelerate.[47] If nothing else, this should focus minds in the Middle East on how to secure the region's future prosperity.

Without elected governments, the Muslim world lacks the building blocks of a successful transnational union. Weak, autocratic regimes simply do not have the legitimacy or the political will to pool sovereignty in a meaningful fashion, as the GCC, Arab League and OIC have demonstrated. This leaves the process of regional unification in the hands of radical movements such as IS.

Therein lies the risk. If the Muslim nation-state cannot be reformed along democratic lines, the only avenue to Muslim unity is the one espoused by Islamist militants – the forcible creation of a Caliphate. Even if the current generation of jihadists is defeated, such groups will continue to rise and to engage in brutal acts of terrorism and war, until a viable path towards Sunni Muslim unification materializes.

There is little reason to believe that Islam alone can form the basis of a functioning regional union. Without the Rules, Rights and Multiculturalism precondition, any such Caliphate is likely to exhaust its energies trying to impose a single version of the faith upon others who see the world differently. Unity, writ large, requires the toleration of difference. The Ottoman expansion after the fall of Constantinople made no great effort to convert other faiths to Islam; when Greece declared independence four centuries later, it was still overwhelmingly Christian. Albania was converted voluntarily to Islam over a long period under Ottoman rule and today is hailed as a model of religious tolerance, even as Islam enjoys a revival there after decades of enforced atheism.[48]

Such differences in orthodoxy can be reflected and managed within smaller federal units, as Malaysia and Indonesia demonstrated. The UAE provides another example. Despite their lack of democracy, the emirates are islands of peace, prosperity and relative social liberalism in a troubled region. United by a federation, they divide their powers into those that are best kept at a municipal level, and those that the constitution deems best pooled. The result is a group of city-states, united under a shared banner for defensive and economic purposes.

The UAE's model could be extended much more widely. Official projections suggest that, by 2050, 90 per cent of Saudis will be urbanized.[49] By threading together city-states in the manner of the UAE, or Malaysia's sultanates, a balance can be struck not only across the emirates but across the entire Arabian peninsula, creating a constellation of city-states that unites Abu Dhabi and Dubai with Muscat and Aden, Kuwait City, Riyadh and Jeddah, Bahrain and Qatar. As the world shifts away from its dependence on Middle Eastern oil, such a federation would help the peninsula overcome the transition to a new economy.

Increasing the autonomy of Arab cities would have the additional benefit of loosening the connection between the holy sites of Mecca and Medina and the kingdom of Saudi Arabia. Its absolute control of those two cities has driven radicalism, given the Saudi role as a political actor, its national-security preoccupations and the fact it is Sunni orthodox. Mecca and Medina are holy sites for all Muslims, including Shi'a. Complaints about the treatment of Hajj pilgrims from other sects are common.[50,51]

By contrast, the Vatican, the holiest site in Catholicism, operates on an autonomous basis from the city of Rome and from the Italian state. It offers an example of how peace can be enabled by allowing small, culturally sensitive units to manage their own affairs, while pooling sovereignty on issues such as shared infrastructure, finance, freedom of movement and defence to reduce costs for the whole.

This model makes particular sense for Arab and North African countries, which are often dominated by one or two major coastal cities trying to assert control over a barren hinterland of the kind often exploited by anti-government militants. Satellite pictures taken by night show the extent to which populations hug the North African coastline. Pooling sovereignty when it comes to defence and intelligence would make the southern areas more manageable.

The federal model offers another hopeful possibility. It maintains an important degree of unity while also preserving a productive rivalry. It was this spirit of rivalry that led Qatar to found Al-Jazeera, creating a kind of Arab-language journalism that transformed the media scene of the Middle East. Such cultural competition between city-states would do much to revive the Islamic traditions of poetry, literature, music and scientific discovery that have waned in the era of nation-states, replacing the religious one-upsmanship that larger countries have employed to justify their internal autocracies.

As for Israel and Palestine, a federal or confederated structure offers the most promising avenue for resolving the Israel-Palestine dispute. Writing for Al-Jazeera, John Bell, Director of the Middle East Programme at the Toledo International Centre for Peace in Madrid, noted that even Israel's founding prime minister David Ben-Gurion embraced this concept:

The regime [Palestine] must foster the rapprochement, accord and co-operation of the Jewish people and the Arabs in Palestine... [in] a federal state, comprising an alliance of cantons [autonomous districts], some with Jews in the majority, and some with Arabs.[52]

Such a solution would allow both Israelis and Palestinians their own geographically demarcated homeland, and allow both to call Jerusalem their capital. It would allow them both their own sets of institutions while acknowledging the economic symbiosis without which neither could survive. The factors of Open Borders, Economic Peace, Veto and Consensus, and perhaps eventually Mutual Trust, would be established.

In Iraq, the post-2003 federal experiment failed because the prime minister at the time, Nouri al-Maliki, concentrated more and more power in his own hands rather than respecting devolution to the Sunni and Kurdish areas. The Iraqi state's subsequent collapse into IS-held territory demonstrated that whereas devolving power strengthens a Muslim country, centralization weakens it.

Spreading this realization throughout the Muslim world is the best hope for resolving its many conflicts. The simultaneous process of devolution and regional unification would do much to satisfy Muslims at a local level that their demands were being met, while meeting their aspiration for a united voice on the world stage.

First, however, must come democratization, without which organizations such as the GCC will remain dysfunctional. For this, the West needs to be a better friend to the Middle East than it has been hitherto. It needs to recognize that regional unity in the region is no more 'extreme' an aspiration than it is in Europe or elsewhere, and that suppressing the desire for unity is likely to reduce stability rather than supporting it.

1 Obama, Barack, 2009, 'Remarks By President Obama to Turkish Parliament', The White House, 6 April. 2 Unnamed author, 2004, 'Bush rebuff to Chirac over Turkey', CNN, 29 June. 3 Unnamed author, 2004, 'Chirac chides Bush over Turkey', CNN, 29 June. 4 Unnamed author, 2010, 'US embassy cables: Future pope objects to EU membership for Muslim Turkey', *The Guardian*, 10 December. 5 Unnamed author, 2007, 'Nicolas Sarkozy, président, "s'opposera à l'entrée de la Turquie" dans l'UE', *La Dépêche*, 3 May. 6 Said, Edward W., 2001, 'The Clash of Ignorance', *The Nation*, 4 October. 7 Gracie, Carrie, 2014, 'The knife attack that changed Kunming', BBC News, 16 July. 8 Farrelly, Nicholas, 2013, 'The Myanmar-Kachin truce', New Mandala, 31 May.

9 Coughlin, Con, 2011, 'Sudan: A nation driven apart by Muslim bigotry', *The Telegraph*, 12 January. 10 Black, Ian, 2007, 'Fear of a Shi'a full moon', *The Guardian*, 26 January. 11 Cockburn, Patrick, 2012, 'Iran increases hold in Iraq as Shi'a militia enters politics', *The Independent*, 7 January. 12 Unnamed author, 2013, 'Hezbollah heartlands recover with Iran's help', BBC News, 12 June. 13 AP, 2011, 'Bahrain hints at Iranian role over country's Shi'a uprising', *The Guardian*, 21 March. 14 Schimitt, Worth, 2012, 'Aiding Yemen Rebels, Iran Seeks Wider Mideast Role', *New York Times*, 15 March. 15 Unnamed author, 2015, 'Rouhani congratulates regional leaders on Nowruz', Mehr News Agency, 21 March. 16 Unnamed author, 2013, 'President Ahmaninejad to attend Nowruz festival in Turkmenistan', Press TV, 20 March. 17 Gibson, Bryan R., 'Leave it to the League', Foreign Policy, 22 September 2014. 18 Alvarez, Lizette, 2004, 'Britain Says US Planned To Seize Oil in '73 crisis', *New York Times*, 2 January. 19 Unnamed author, 2014, 'ISIS jihadists declare 'Islamic Caliphate'', Al Arabiya News, 29 June. 20 Black, Ian, 2014, 'Isis breach of Iraq-Syria border merges two wars into one 'nightmarish reality'', *The Guardian*, 18 June. 21 Marshall Jr., Tyrone, 2014, 'Hagel: Clear Mission to Degrade, Destroy ISIL capability', US Department of Defence, 3 September. 22 Roulo, Claudette, 2014, 'Coalition Aircraft Disable ISIL Refineries in Syria', U.S. Department of Defence, 24 September. 23 Ernst, Douglas, 2014, 'Airstrikes against Islamic State cost US $1 billion in three months', *Washington Post*, 1 October. 24 Video, 2014, 'Islam Channel – Taji Mustafa debates UK airstrikes on Iraq, Syria, ISIS', Hizb

ut – Tahrir Britain, 26 September. **25** Chulov, Martin, 2014, 'Isis reconciles with al-Qaida group as Syria air strikes continue', *The Guardian*, 28 September. **26** Unnamed author, 2014, 'Pakistan taliban vow support for IS in Syria and Iraq', BBC News, 5 October. **27** Moore, Jack, 2014, 'Malaysia Declares 'Red Alert' in Sabah as Filipino Terror Group Abu Sayyaf Pledge Allegiance to Isis', *International Business Times*, 22 September. **28** Unnamed author, 2014, 'Boko Haram voices support for ISIS' Baghdadi', Al Arabiya News Africa, 13 July. **29** Dearden, Lizzie, 2014, 'Chechen IS fighters under Omar al-Shishani threaten to take fight to Putin', *The Independent*, 10 October. **30** Mehta, Vijay, (2012), *The Economics of Killing*. London: Pluto Press. **31** Haaretz, 2014, 'Iran's Khamenei proposes plan for Israel's elimination – on Twitter', *Haaretz*, 9 November.

32 Cockburn, Patrick, 2014, 'Saudi Arabia closes local al Jazeera office over Qatar's backing for the Muslim Brotherhood', *The Independent*, 10 November. **33** Black, Ian, 2014, 'Arab states withdraw ambassadors from Qatar in protest at "interference"', *The Guardian*, 5 March.

34 Windrew, Robert, 2014, 'Who's Funding ISIS? Wealthy Gulf "Angel Investors", Officials Say', NBC News, 21 September. **35** Smith, Mikey, 2014, 'ISIS threaten Qatar World Cup terror attacks if FIFA don't cancel tournament', *The Daily Mirror*, 10 July. **36** Trenwith, Courtney, 2014, 'GCC single currency comes down to politics, says ex-IMF boss', ArabianBusiness.com, 25 November.

37 McKelvey, Dana, 2012, 'World Grows More Peaceful – Except for the Middle East', *Diplomatic Courier*, 28 June. **38** The World Bank Data, Arab World. **39** Taylor, Jerome, 2013, 'Atheists Richard Dawkins, Christopher Hitchens and Sam Harris face Islamophobia backlash', *The Independent*, 12 April. **40** p.148, *Federalism in Asia,* eds: He Baogang, Brian Galligan, Takashi Inoguchi, Edward Elgar Publishing, 2007. **41** p.154, *ibid*. **42** Unnamed author, 2014, 'Indonesia: Aceh's New Islamic Laws Violate Rights', Human Rights Watch, 2 October. **43** p.156, *ibid*.

44 Barsoum, 2014, 'El-Sisi and Obama discuss ISIS threat, Libya crisis', Ahram Online, 26 September. **45** Ackerman, Spencer, 2015, 'Obama restores US military aid to Egypt over Islamic State concerns', *The Guardian*, 31 March. **46** Unnamed author, 2005, 'Rice calls for Mid East democracy', BBC News, 20 June. **47** International Energy Agency, 'Medium Term Oil Report 2014', p.12. **48** Squires, Nick, 2014, 'Pope Francis hails Albania as model of religious harmony in attack on religious extremism', *The Telegraph*, 21 September. **49** Country Profile/Background, 'Demographic Profile of Saudi Arabia', Permanent link: www.escwa.un.org/popin/members/ SaudiArabia.pdf **50** Unnamed author, 2013, 'Anti-Shi'a sectarianism on Hajj is a worrying trend', Islamic Human Rights Commission, 22 October. **51** Malik, Nesrine, 2012, 'Treatment of female Nigerian pilgrims embarrasses Saudis at the start of Hajj', *The Guardian*, 29 September. **52** Bell, John, 2014 'Israel and Palestine: Two states and the extra step', Al Jazeera English, 14 May.

Chapter 9 – Exorbitant Privilege

The current international system contains in-built advantages for those countries that constructed it, particularly the US. This chapter examines how the emerging powers such as Brazil, Russia, India and China are crafting their own multinational institutions to rival the Bretton Woods banks, and how their efforts intersect with moves to create EU-like structures on each continent.

It was as finance minister of France that Valéry Giscard D'Estaing coined the expression 'exorbitant privilege'. Giscard used it to describe the many advantages that came with issuing the world's leading currency. Thirty years earlier, the US dollar had wrested that status from the British pound, battered by the Second World War. Exorbitant privilege is a description that could be applied to many aspects of the United States' global leadership, but the perks of the dollar are particularly imposing.

In the modern world, a country's creditworthiness is assessed by how many dollars it holds in its vaults. Holding one's *own* currency does not impress the credit ratings agencies. It is the holding of dollars, sometimes along with precious objects such as gold bars, that shows whether a country can pay its bills. Oil, metals and other commodities are priced in dollars. Purchasing them requires hoards of US currency.

To gather more dollars, countries dispatch their real, valuable goods and services to the US in exchange for what, ultimately, are no more than pieces of paper. Nations that fail to do this, and which therefore have few dollars to hand, endure poor credit ratings and pay more to borrow. As it happens, the major sovereign ratings agencies – Moody's, Standard & Poor's, and Fitch – are all US-based.

Because creditworthiness is based on how many dollars you possess, and because the US can print its own dollars, the US credit rating is artificially strong. When other countries try to print their way out of debt, the value of their currency plunges against the dollar. They are no better off and, indeed, they risk hyper-inflation. But when, as is usually the case, the US government spends more than it earns in taxes, and when the US as a whole imports far more than it exports, it suffers no penalty. US politicians have little to fear even when they threaten to default on their national debt, as they sometimes do – only once has a ratings agency downgraded US credit-worthiness from its 'triple-A' status.[1]

The US government has no shortage of willing creditors. In order to generate a return on their dollar holdings, countries swap them for US government bonds, which count as a form of money. Washington DC therefore has an almost bottomless pit of demand for its debt. It has no need to offer generous interest rates to persuade people to buy US bonds. Furthermore, because the Treasury's interest rates underpin those of the whole US banking system, American businesses can themselves borrow artificially cheaply, allowing them to raise money to invest and buy up assets overseas. International trade is conducted overwhelmingly in dollars, so US businesses also have the convenience of transacting in their own currency.

These privileges have a bearing on war and peace. The ease with which the US government can borrow means it has no need to manage its finances prudently. This allows it to spend literally trillions of dollars on a military which, as we have seen, serves as an extremely inefficient welfare system for individuals and corporations. The vast military-industrial complex reinforces the dollar's status as the world's reserve currency, by creating the illusion that the US is safe from external threats and therefore always likely to honour its financial commitments.

Its control over the dollar makes it easier for the US to prevent its enemies from trading. This is especially true of enemies who rely on exporting dollar-denominated commodities such as oil. It also means the US can pick and choose its trading partners in a way that would bankrupt other nations. As described in 2012's *The Economics of Killing*, the trade imbalance between the US and China is due largely to Washington's refusal to sell China the high-tech and military goods that it wishes to buy.[2]

The current world order enforces a system of global economic inequality. Bretton Woods institutions (IMF, World Bank) were established 70 years ago to ensure that the rules regarding the present international financial system are rigged in favour of the wealthy and the powerful at the expense of everyone else. Today, 85 of the world's wealthiest people own more wealth than the bottom half of the global population, over three billion people. Oxfam has estimated that in 2016 the top one per cent of the world's population will own more wealth than the bottom 99 per cent.[3]

Europe and the US set the agenda for global institutions, and their priorities are to prevent poorer nations from 'catching up' with them economically. They are happy for industrializing powers such as India and China to manufacture low-technology products. They are much less happy to compete with them in the manufacture of the high-value, high-technology items manufactured by the West.

For that reason, the concept of intellectual property rights became central to membership of the World Trade Organization. The eminent Indian economist Arvind Panagariya was one of many who doubted whether this was good for developing countries, or whether it really had much to do with free trade at all. He argued that patents – in effect, monopoly rights on inventions – distorted markets in a way that disproportionately damaged the Global South.[4]

The concept of 'intellectual property' arose at a convenient historical moment for the West. Europe and then the US achieved global dominance based on two Chinese inventions – paper and gunpowder – for which they paid not a penny in royalties. The first military rockets were used by Indian forces, but they were adapted free of charge elsewhere. Arabs perfected the process for making soap, but they did not receive licence fees for it.

In the modern world, however, the rich countries expect poorer ones to pay them for using 'their' technology and brands. The game of chess originated in India before it spread across the globe, with a great variety of boards and pieces. However, any Indian who wishes to play Monopoly, the modern world's best-selling board game, can only do so legally on a board purchased from Hasbro, a US company. Europeans did not invent alcohol, but today the only people legally permitted to call their whisky 'Scotch' or their wine 'champagne' are from Scotland and France.

This insistence has even extended to medicine. The US requires poor countries to pay the patent-holder's premium rather than producing their own, cheaper versions of life-saving drugs.[5] Yet half of all prescription drugs are based on chemicals found in plants, some of which have been used in traditional medicine for centuries.[6] In a belated acknowledgement of this fact, in 2013 the EU parliament began debating a biopiracy law to compensate indigenous peoples for using their medical techniques.[7] The debate came after a German company, Schwabe, tried to patent the curative use of a plant that communities in South Africa had used for centuries.[8] This repackaging of traditional remedies even has a name: bio-prospecting.

Such double-standards are enforced by the trade-and-aid institutions controlled by the West. The most pernicious effect is perhaps psychological. European luxury brands have come to signify wealth and prestige, by dint of their association with wealthy countries. This perception of wealth and prestige is felt most powerfully in the world's poorer countries, where sales of such luxury goods have soared among those able to afford them.[9]

The irony is that the designer handbags and luggage are often manufactured in those very same poorer countries, for a fraction of their retail price. Any attempt to sell the same goods at a more reasonable rate is deemed 'piracy', because it lessens the huge profit margins remitted back to countries such as France and Italy, where the goods are designed. Thus, the rich countries stay rich, and the brands maintain their association with wealth and privilege.

In the short term, there is not much China and the other big emerging powers can do about the situation. A vast proportion of China's national wealth is tied up in US bonds, which would become worthless in the event of serious hostilities between the two. The argument peddled by US officials, that China need only de-peg its currency from the dollar to rectify the imbalance, has been widely discredited. Some economists even believe the peg now *over*-values the Chinese yuan, although China's double devaluation in August 2015 made that less likely.

In the longer term, however, China is working to end the dollar's special status in global trade. China is promoting its own currency, the yuan, as a rival medium of exchange. It has banded together with four other large countries – Brazil, Russia, India and South Africa – to overturn the existing system of Western-dominated international institutions, and replace it with a new world order. Their word for this is 'multipolarity'. Rather than a unipolar world led by the US, the BRICS (Brazil, Russia, India, China and South Africa) demand equality of influence.

A practical example of BRICS co-operation came in December 2014. As the US and its EU allies used sanctions to isolate Russia, Moscow found itself running out of dollars and unable to purchase more, as the value of the Russian rouble slumped. China, however, was on hand to help. It offered to swap billions of Russian roubles for Chinese yuan.[10] This meant that even without dollars, Russia could purchase Chinese goods directly from China.

China has swapped currencies with dozens of other nations. The US-based ratings agencies spent much of 2012 and 2013 predicting that Pakistan would go bust due to large repayments it owed the EU-led International Monetary Fund.[11] Such financial pressure was strategically useful to the US government, which was demanding that Pakistan sacrifice even more of its troops against the Taliban and was withholding aid until it did so.

But Pakistan did not default on its debt. In late 2013, it swapped rupees for $1.6 billion worth of Chinese yuan.[12] Because Pakistan buys more goods from China than it does from anywhere else, its lack of dollars suddenly became much less of a problem. China's help also reduced the IMF's ability to pressure Pakistan into privatizing its state-owned businesses and cutting energy subsidies.

De-dollarization also came to the rescue of Pakistan's next-door neighbour, Iran. Under heavy US-led sanctions, it worked to replace the dollar in its trade with other major countries such as Russia and Turkey.[13] The Iranians used this non-dollar trade as a negotiating chip to secure a deal to lift sanctions in mid-2015. Their ability to circumvent the sanctions regime was a significant reason why the US eventually came to terms in 2015. In under-reported comments by US Secretary of State John Kerry, he told an event in New York that:

If we turn around and nix the deal and then tell them, 'You're going to have to obey our rules and sanctions anyway,' that is a recipe, very quickly... for the American dollar to cease to be the reserve currency of the world.[14]

The exorbitant privilege of the dollar as reserve currency is intertwined with Western domination of other multilateral bodies. This too is under siege, however. A second strand of the BRICS' campaign has been to reform the World Bank and International Monetary Fund. The political domination of these two institutions by the US and EU comes at the expense of the developing powers. The BRICS account for only 11 per cent of the votes at the IMF, even as they represent a fifth of global economic activity.[15] Even when IMF chief Dominique Strauss-Kahn resigned in disgrace in 2011, he was replaced by another French nominee, Christine Lagarde.

With the Bretton Woods institutions seemingly determined to remain in Western hands, the BRICS were left with only one option. In July 2014, their leaders gathered in

Fortaleza, Brazil, to announce the creation of the New Development Bank (NDB). This institution would develop new infrastructure in emerging countries as an alternative to the World Bank. The BRICS would pay in an initial $50 billion to the bank, which would have its headquarters in Shanghai, China. The NDB's first regional office would be in Johannesburg, South Africa, suggesting that Africa would be a major venue for NDB projects.

At Fortaleza, the BRICS also created a competitor for the IMF. The Contingency Reserve Arrangement (CRA) was announced with $100 billion of capital; China was easily the largest contributor, with $41 billion. This capital would be swapped with the domestic currency of countries in financial distress, patching up the world's financial safety net. Some of the CRA's work would be linked to that of the IMF; some of it would be explicitly de-linked.[16]

One should not exaggerate the rivalry between the new BRICS institutions and the old Western ones. In truth, it was perfectly possible for the NDB and the CRA to coexist and co-operate with the World Bank and IMF, which already worked alongside regional bodies such as the Asian Development Bank and the Chiang Mai Initiative. Much of the new institutions' work would merely reproduce or replace the kind of support that China already offered the developing world.

At the same time, the BRICS offered strength to smaller countries under pressure from Western institutions. The EU itself is not immune from criticism in this regard. During Greece's debt crisis in the years after the West's 2008 financial implosion, a cycle was established whereby the other Eurozone states offered loans to Greece that were conditional on it delivering savage cuts to government expenditure. Plummeting economic output prevented the Greek economy from reviving, necessitating ever more loans, and ever more demands from Germany, in particular, for lower Greek public spending and higher taxation.

The Eurozone, led by Germany, maintained this punitive 'hair shirt' approach to discipline the Greeks for their perceived shiftlessness, even as it failed to rectify the situation. The bailouts kept Greek banks afloat, but unemployment soared and hardship multiplied. Eventually, even the IMF took the view that, without the cancellation of some Greek debt, the cycle of recession and bailout would never be broken. The European Commission and European Central Bank followed the IMF's lead.[17] For their part, the Greeks elected ever more radical governments to negotiate on their behalf.

Their negotiating position was strengthened by some outside help. Belying the familiar Eurosceptic argument that the EU first entraps and then reduces its members to helpless provinces, Greece found an outside benefactor in Russia, one of the BRICS. Although a member of the EU, Greece imported more goods from Russia than it did from any other country.[18]

Russia faced its own economic troubles at the time, amid a plummeting oil price and Ukraine-related sanctions. It was unable to offer its own cash bailouts to Greece, although these in any case had proven ineffective. What Russia offered was more important: a reminder that should Greece leave the Eurozone, or even the EU itself, there were other teams it could join. With complementary economies, a shared interest in controlling shipping into the Black Sea and a Christian Orthodox majority, Greece could just as easily align with Russia and its Eurasian Economic Union.

This consideration, with its attendant strategic consequences, was enough to concentrate minds in Washington and London. The US and UK have bases in Crete and Cyprus that are vital staging posts for military operations in the Middle East. Greece is a member of NATO. It was therefore no surprise that the US asked the Germans to soften their position over Greek debt, even as Greece struck a deal with Russia to allow construction of a gas pipeline opposed by US and EU strategists.[19,20]

This state of affairs might lead some to view Greece's EU membership as a mistake in the first place, but this is to forget the country's history before it joined. Immediately after the Second World War, Greece was the focus of another strategic tussle between the West and Russia, but one which plunged it into a civil war between US-backed generals and Stalinist communists in which tens of thousands of people died. That war was followed by decades of coups, dictatorships, the mass imprisonment of political dissenters, and a war with Turkey in Cyprus.

All this violence came to an end in 1981, when Greece joined the forerunner to the EU, the European Economic Community. In return for membership, it committed to democracy, the observance of human rights and freedom of speech. As a direct result of the pan-European embrace, Greece's next three decades were vastly more peaceful than the previous three. By the same token Turkey, which also wanted to join the EU, made great strides towards peaceful democracy.

What counts as a crisis within the calm waters of the EU is very different from what counts as a crisis elsewhere. If a human reminder of this were needed, during its debt crisis Greece became the landing point for boats carrying refugees across the Mediterranean from North Africa. Many of those who risked the perilous journey were fleeing Syria's civil war, a conflict that, like Greece's 70 years earlier, demonstrated the consequences of outside powers supporting rival factions within a state. By contrast, the clear patterns of alignment represented by the EU, and potentially by the Eurasian Economic Union, ensure that the Resistance to External Interference factor is maintained.

As the new regional blocs became stronger, so power ebbed from the old structures of the 20th century. The most dramatic example of this new world order went curiously unnoticed. In the decade after the 2003 invasion of Iraq, the UN Security Council – hitherto the arbiter of global war and peace – simply ceased to matter.

Little fuss was made. The Council's sudden, unheralded irrelevance was met with indifference by India and Brazil in particular, which had long complained about their exclusion from permanent, veto-wielding membership of the panel. Whereas the Security Council has three permanent members from Europe – Russia, France and the United Kingdom – there is not a single representative from Africa and South America, and only one (China) from Asia's three billion-strong population.

The Security Council's drift into obscurity could be traced directly to the US-led invasion of Iraq in 2003. That adventure was preceded by a lengthy squabble over whether or not the Council had granted the US legal permission to invade. Russia and France insisted that it had not. China was uneasy but noncommittal. The UK said that it was legal to invade without a second resolution, but only after its Attorney General appeared to change his mind.[21]

In the absence of any higher arbiter, the sides accused each other of interpreting the law according to their own national biases. The US, for its part, did not seem to care a great deal about the Council's deliberations. As history records, it invaded without a clarifying resolution. One of the many consequences of this decision was that, henceforth, the Security Council's veto powers all but evaporated. Where once its authorization was needed to attack a sovereign state without its permission, unilateralism became the norm.

Examples mounted. Outraged by the invasion of Iraq, Russia's Vladimir Putin staged his own unilateral invasion of Georgia in 2008. In 2013, a Security Council resolution authorizing a no-fly zone over Libya was transformed by the US and its allies into a full-scale military operation involving some 10,000 air strikes; the BRICS denounced this a massive overreach of UN authorization.[22] The same year, the US initiated air strikes in Syria, again with no covering Security Council resolution.[23] With lawlessness now the norm, Putin invaded Ukraine and annexed Crimea.

The world had entered a new era. Might was right. Old games were played anew. The giants resumed the standard practice of securing allies on the borders of their rival superpowers. Ukraine's tilt towards the EU, deemed a US-backed putsch by Putin, was one example. Vietnam's flourishing and surprising friendship with the US was another.

Although the Vietnam War was still a painful living memory in many households in both countries, the former enemies forged a close partnership against China, cemented by US politicians such as John Kerry and John McCain who were veterans of the Vietnam War.[24]

Allowed to continue, this new system of mutually belligerent superpowers would create a chessboard of buffer states, shifting alliances and proxy wars, setting neighbour against neighbour and giant against giant. The inevitable end of the dollar's reserve currency status will cause a massive readjustment of US spending priorities and a commensurate shift in the world order. Smaller countries, seeking temporary advantage, would play one superpower off another, but throughout human history this tactic has ended in war. No longer fearing a UN veto, the superpowers would invade their smaller neighbours with impunity.

In order to build on their early successes, the BRICS must become the champions of regionalism. India, China and Russia can learn from Brazil when it comes to uniting their smaller neighbours. Brazil has championed the cause of UNASUR in South America, and has succeeded in this regard because it does not believe its own size merits it any special treatment. If the other BRICS can harness the Brazilian mind-set, they too can witness the peaceful transformation of their immediate neighbourhoods.

As matters stand, the BRICS embody the best hope of reforming the international system in order to give a voice to the planet's poor majority. Despite the differences between them, the BRICS countries have delivered a message to the old institutions of international government: democratize, or die. Now their task is to ensure that those institutions are reformed or replaced in such a way as to ensure that peace is prioritized, paving the way to disarmament.

1 Brandimarte and Bases, 2011, 'United States loses prized AAA credit rating from S&P', Reuters, 6 August. 2 See Mehta, Vijay, 2012, *The Economics of Killing*, London: Pluto Press. 3 Slater, Jon, 2015, 'Richest 1% will own more than all the rest by 2016', Oxfam, 19 January. 4 Panagariya,

Arvind, 'TRIPs and the WTO: An Uneasy Marriage', paper based on a seminar presentation at the WTO on 20 July 1999. **5** Pipes, Sally, 2013, 'India's War On Intellectual Property Rights May Bring With It A Body Count', Forbes, 16 September. **6** Unnamed author, 2008 'Medicinal plants "facing threat"', BBC News, 19 January. **7** Hall, Marc, 2013, 'EU debates biopiracy law to protect indigenous people', *The Guardian*, 1 May. **8** Groenewald, Yolandi, 2010, 'Town like Alice takes on German "biopirate"', *Mail & Guardian*, 22 January. **9** Paton, Elizabeth, 2013, 'Asian route to the top at luxury brands', *Financial Times*, 30 September. **10** Li, Zhou and Andrianova, 2014, 'China Offers Russia Help With Currency Swap Suggestion', Bloomberg Business, 22 December. **11** Byrne and Oosterveld, 2012, 'Moody's downgrades Pakistan government bond ratings to Caa1, outlook negative', Moody's, 13 July. **12** Zaidi, Erum, 2013, 'Pak-China currency swap accord implemented', TheNews.com.pk, 8 May. **13** AA/AA, 2015, 'Iran, Turkey to trade in own currencies', Press TV, 3 May. **14** Strobel, Warren, 2015, 'Dollar could suffer if US walks away from Iran deal: John Kerry', Reuters, 11 August. **15** Eichengreen, Barry, 2014, 'Do the BRICS need their own development bank?', *The Guardian*, 14 August. **16** 2014, Treaty for the Establishment of a BRICS Contingent Reserve Arrangement, Fortaleza, Portal Brazil, 15 July. **17** Robinson, Duncan, Wagstyl, Stefan, and Milne, Richard, 2015, 'Brussels backs IMF over Greek debt relief', *Financial Times*, 13 August. **18** See Hellenic Statistical Authority 2015. **19** Jopson, Barney and Donnan, Shawn, 2015, 'Jack Lew and Christine Lagarde urge debt relief for Greece', *Financial Times*, 8 July. **20** Maltezou et al, 2015, 'Greece, Russia to cooperate on Turkish Stream pipeline', Reuters, 19 June. **21** Sengupta, Kim, 2010, 'How Goldsmith changed advice on legality of war', *The Independent*, 1 July. **22** Unnamed author, 2011, 'UN Security Council votes to end Libya operations', BBC News, 27 October. **23** Arimatsu and Schimitt, 2014, 'The legal basis for the war against Isis remains contentious', *The Guardian*, 6 October. **24** Stout, David, 2014, 'The US Is Finally Making a Friend of Vietnam', *Time*, 22 May.

Chapter 10 – The Anglo-Paradox

A fact often lost on the European debate in Britain is why, for so many years, the UK advocated the rapid eastward expansion of the EU. Today, this has resulted in a mass inward migration from new members of the EU that is among the primary causes of British Euroscepticism. Opponents of the EU say that Britain should instead be partnering with other English-speaking nations such as the US. What this argument misses is that it was Britain's alliance with the US that prompted the UK to champion the cause of EU expansion. By treating the EU as the civilian arm of NATO, however, British leaders set the scene for the multiple crises the EU now faces, not least in terms of its relationship with Russia.

On top of a hill in southeast London, surrounded by the village that bears its name, sits Blackheath. As London parks go, it is curiously empty; a flat expanse of grass with none of the artful majesty of the adjacent Greenwich Park. On the heath's southern edge stands a fine 19th-century church, but otherwise Blackheath gives an impression of sparseness, as if it exists for a purpose no longer required.

There is a common myth that the heath was used as a mass burial site during the Black Death, the bubonic plague that swept London in the 14th century. This is not true; the 'black' in Blackheath refers to the darkness of the soil. Nevertheless, death has often come to the hilltop. Its tactical position overlooking London has on several occasions turned it into a battlefield.

By 1497, the people of Cornwall had had enough. Their impoverished peninsula was being taxed to the hilt so that England's king, Henry Tudor, could pay for a war against Scotland. Henry was marching an army northwards because the king of the Scots, James IV, was supporting a young man named Perkin Warbeck. Warbeck claimed to be one of two young princes suspected to have been murdered in the Tower of London by their uncle, the former English king Richard

III. Henry had defeated Richard in battle 13 years earlier and taken his crown. Now, Henry's legitimacy as monarch was threatened by Warbeck's appearance.

The Cornish were an ethnic minority who for the most part still spoke a Brythonic language related to Welsh and Breton. They failed to see why they should pay for a conflict in the far north of England. In their view, it was the northern nobility who needed defending from the Scots, and thus it was they who should pay for it.[1] Thousands of Cornish protesters, many of them tin miners, marched on London to petition the king. As they marched, they attracted followers from other southwestern counties.

By the time they reached Blackheath, looking out along the Thames to London, their numbers had swelled to over 10,000. Residents of the capital were alarmed. The king, it is said, moved his family to the Tower for safe-keeping, including his son, the future Henry VIII. He recalled his forces from the north and mustered another army to assist them. The sides met at Blackheath on 17 June.

The battle was entirely one-sided. The Cornishmen were led by a lawyer and a blacksmith who were no match for Henry's seasoned commanders. Afterwards, one of these commanders, a man named John Seymour, was knighted by the king on the field. His daughter Jane would become queen, as Henry VIII's third wife. Otherwise, the Cornish revolt was little more than a footnote in English history.

Yet it epitomized how wars tended to start in Europe. With no Enshrined Democracy and Rule of Law, the political legitimacy of rulers was dubious and subject to violent contention, and there were few mechanisms to align the aspirations of rulers with those of their subjects. Without Resistance to External Interference, enemy states could sponsor their own preferred candidates in a power struggle, as did the Scots with Perkin Warbeck. Without Open Borders and Human Ties, there was little empathy between the Scots and the English, and without Permanent Discussion, Dialogue and Diplomacy, the English and Scottish negotiators failed to defuse the mutual antagonism. Without a permanent Economic Truce, trade was insufficient to act as a brake on hostilities, and without Soft Power and Common Purpose, the Cornishmen had little bond even with their fellow Englishmen in the northern counties.

The absence of Rules, Human Rights and Multiculturalism meant that England's government had little compunction in treating its Cornish minority worse than the rest of the country. The lack of Financial Incentives and Support meant that Cornwall's relative poverty could not be monitored or alleviated by central authorities, sensitizing the population to economic inequality. Without the Veto and Consensus function there was no way that the English and Scots could peacefully scotch each other's schemes. And without the Mutual Trust that flows from the other nine factors, Henry Tudor assumed that the Cornish march on London intended him harm.

The defeat of the Cornish at Blackheath did little to secure England's stability. Later that year, Warbeck landed in Cornwall to take advantage of the locals' dismay over their treatment. Warbeck rallied another Cornish army, but he later deserted and was captured by Henry's forces, who took him to London and executed him. The next Cornish revolt would come 52 years later, in protest at the looting of monasteries by the state to fund wars against Scotland and France.[2]

Today, there is little prospect of the Cornish marching on London, and certainly not of them encountering such a brutal response. This is not because Cornwall has suddenly become rich. It remains the poorest part of England, and is poorer than areas of new European Union members such as Poland, Lithuania and Hungary, according to EU per capita statistics.[3] Central London, by contrast, is the wealthiest place in Europe.

That the EU measures such things is one reason why the Cornish are unlikely to revolt again. London realizes that it is very wealthy relative to other parts of Britain and this ensures that taxation does not target poorer areas. Nor is England likely to fight a war against Scotland, because for the past three centuries they have been part of the same United Kingdom.

The United Kingdom, as its name suggests, is a regional union of its own. It unites the kingdoms of England and Scotland with the principality of Wales and the six counties of Northern Ireland. England and Scotland were themselves slowly constructed from ancient Saxon and Pictish kingdoms such as Lindsey and Fife. As rival kingdoms, the English and Scots fought dozens of wars until 1603, when the two crowns were united.

After that, the wars ceased. Until it was integrated into the British Royal Navy in 1707, the Royal Scots Navy co-existed peacefully with the English fleet for another century, rather as the navies of the European Union co-exist peacefully today. This is not for any lack of disputes in the EU: maritime boundaries and fishing rights continue to vex European relationships, and resulted in the so-called 'Cod War' violence between Britain and Iceland in the 1970s.[4]

The political unification of Britain came during a period when the island was dominated by European culture. Christianity was the pan-European context. Latin was the language of scripture and scholarship in Britain and Ireland as much as elsewhere. French was the *lingua franca* in which royal courts communicated. England, Scotland, Wales and Ireland were intimately entangled in the same pan-continental movements that gave rise to Protestant forms of Christianity and to the Enlightenment.

Exiles circulated. Before arriving in Scotland, Warbeck was a guest at the French and Burgundian courts. William Tyndale, who translated the Bible into English – then a heresy – found refuge in Germany and the Low Countries. European leaders were related by blood and marriage. Henry Tudor and James IV waged war on each other, but then James married Henry's daughter, Margaret. James was later killed in battle against the English army of Margaret's brother, Henry VIII, after being called into war by Scotland's ally, France, under the pact known as the Auld Alliance. The Scots ensured that

England could never concentrate its forces against France without being attacked from the rear; in return, France guaranteed Scotland's independence. Scottish kings would typically marry French princesses. French was the language of the Scottish court for centuries; even Scots words such as 'haggis' and 'hogmanay' are actually corruptions of French expressions.

There was no sense in which the countries of the British Isles were anything other than a part of Europe, or 'Christendom' as it was then. The viral spread of ideas, thinkers and royal bloodlines marched across Europe alongside the armies that championed them. The modern British monarchy changed their surname to Windsor only in 1917, before which it was Saxe-Coburg Gotha, a name redolent of their German origins. The dawn of the Windsors came as Britain's understanding of its cultural geography began to slip away from the continent.

The rise of the United States diverted the British gaze westwards. From the 1920s, Hollywood was not merely the centre of the US film industry but that of the Anglophone world. Actors such as Australia's Errol Flynn and the Englishman Charlie Chaplin were among the earliest Hollywood superstars, and behind the camera British directors Alfred Hitchcock and David Lean availed themselves of the concentration of talent and finance that they found in Los Angeles.

As the 20th century progressed, this Anglophone knot tightened. Technology shrank the Atlantic to a manageable size. The Beatles and the Rolling Stones shared the musical limelight with Elvis Presley and the Beach Boys. Even the small screen and newspapers began to bleed into a single Anglophone mass; television dramas poached actors from Hollywood's global pool, while national newspapers transformed themselves into global news websites. By the 21st century, CNN and the *New York Times* found themselves competing for readers with *The Guardian* and the *Daily Mail*.[5]

Continental Europe could not compete with the US

juggernaut for British affections. This was not least because that juggernaut drew so much of its talent and inspiration from Britain, Ireland and the Antipodes. As the 20th century progressed, British appreciation for contemporary European novels, cinema, theatre and music was increasingly confined to intellectuals, who embraced continental culture often for the express purpose of distancing themselves from what they saw as the crassness and conservatism of commercialized Anglo-American offerings.

Only on the football pitch did British culture remain focused on Europe, but sport tended to emphasize national and regional identities and rivalries, rather than fostering a sense of European commonality. At the insistence of the footballing authorities, club teams could not pioneer a European league structure, and were instead required to ply their trade in the old national leagues. Football hardened boundaries, rather than softening them.

Just as the UK was integrating economically and politically with continental Europe, culturally it was falling out of it. This fact was not lost on European leaders. During the 1960s and 1970s, as Britain lobbied strenuously to gain membership of the European Economic Community, France's President Charles de Gaulle twice blocked British accession. He suspected that the British would be little more than agents of Washington in Europe. Many Britons viewed his *non* as a betrayal, given de Gaulle's reliance on British and US forces to recover his country in the Second World War.

As Hollywood's soft power cast its spell over the British, appreciation for Britain's historical role in Europe dwindled to an educated elite. The classic British political comedy of the 1980s, *Yes, Minister*, embodied this mind-set in the character of Sir Humphrey Appleby, a serpentine Whitehall mandarin. In one episode he argued that Britain needed nuclear weapons not because the Russians had them, but because the French did:

...they've been our enemies for most of the past 900 years!

In Sir Humphrey's view, Britain only supported the EEC's expansion because 'the more members it has, the more arguments it can stir up, [and] the more futile and impotent it becomes'. This represented an important strand in British military-strategic thinking. Describing Britain's historical role in her famous Bruges Speech to the College of Europe in 1988, Prime Minister Margaret Thatcher noted that:

Over the centuries we have fought to prevent Europe from falling under the dominance of a single power.[6]

Put another way, Britain's interest in the continent was essentially negative. Its goal was simply to prevent the emergence of a single European giant – a Napoleonic empire, a Nazi Reich – able to overwhelm the British Isles. De Gaulle suspected that the British only wanted to join the EEC as a spoiler, to ensure that it never became too unified or too threatening to British – or US – interests. This, after all, had been its strategy for centuries.[7]

It would be incorrect, however, to ascribe such cynical motives to modern British Eurosceptics. They desire Britain to leave the EU altogether, without standing in the way of the bloc's integration *per se*. Whereas under de Gaulle and Konrad Adenauer the French and the Germans resisted British membership, today they appeal to the British to remain within the union.

Philosophical divide

One must ask why the British, within the space of a generation, have gone from demanding admission to the European club to staring at the exit. Today, the philosophical divide between those who support British membership of the EU and those who oppose it is often reducible to their attitude to what some call the 'Anglosphere'. It was Winston Churchill, the son of a British aristocrat and an American heiress, who wrote this movement's foundational texts. In the 1950s he published his four-volume work, *A History of the*

English-Speaking Peoples, which envisaged North Americans, Australians, New Zealanders, Britons and the Irish as a league of democracies with a unique responsibility for world freedom.

Anglospheric thinkers ask why the UK should be integrating with Europe at all, when its language, legal system and culture are more closely aligned with other English-speaking countries. Opinion polls suggest that the British view Australians, Canadians and Americans far more favourably than they view their fellow members of the EU.[8] The choice is often presented in binary terms. The Anglosphere often extends to former British colonies such as Israel and India that have a tradition of democracy.

This is the view of the UK Independence Party (UKIP), which is campaigning for Britain's exit from the EU and which attracted almost four million votes at the UK's 2015 general election. UKIP argues in favour of stronger links between Britain and its ex-colonies, to replace the links it wishes to sever with Europe.[9] Its French equivalent, the Front National (FN), takes a similarly paternalistic approach. In the words of FN leader Marine Le Pen:

France must assume its role as mother of the French-speaking world... It is time for France to rebuild its networks of influence and to build on the assets bequeathed by history, together with our overseas territories and those countries that speak the French language.[10]

Whereas such a 'Francosphere' would be led by France, the Anglosphere is the latest iteration of an older concept that saw the UK as the '51st State' of the US. When de Gaulle vetoed Britain's attempts to join the European common market for a second time, the response of the then prime minister, Harold Wilson, was to consider applying to become part of the US.[11] According to his press secretary, the US government resisted this notion because it wanted to retain Britain's influence within Europe.

It is a paradox that the rise in UKIP's support can be traced precisely to the way in which US strategy has played out in Europe. In March 2014, shortly before his party won a resounding victory in elections to the EU parliament, UKIP's leader made some surprising comments about Russia. Nigel Farage condemned not Vladimir Putin but rather the EU as 'imperialist', even though at that moment Russia was locked in a deadly battle with the US and EU over the future of Ukraine.

Farage's comments offered a more sophisticated insight than his many detractors realized.

The rapidity of the EU's eastwards expansion was not only unpopular in Moscow, but also among many Western European voters. The shift in British public opinion tapped by UKIP was not so much against EU membership, but against the sudden surge in net immigration after 2004, following the accession of countries such as Poland and the Czech Republic.[12] Given that most EU countries teach English in their schools as the principal foreign language,[13] and that speaking the local language improves job prospects, Britain became a magnet for immigration.

Although some surveys showed a majority in favour of quitting the EU, the urge to limit or reduce immigration was far more clearly established in polling.[14,15] The two issues are, of course, linked. The free movement of persons is a fundamental right accorded to EU citizens. Open Borders and Human Ties is one of the 10 factors that created peace in Western Europe. As the bloc expands, so too does the number of people with that right, although it is not conferred immediately after accession.

Herein lay the central contradiction in Anglospheric thinking. What Farage did not address is *why* the EU had spread east so quickly. It did not occur to him to mention that the United States, the Anglosphere's leader, might have been instrumental in Poland and other Eastern Bloc countries being assimilated into the EU a mere decade after the European Union was formed in 1993.

The reality is that, if the British needed someone to blame for mass immigration from Eastern Europe, they should look to their friends in Washington DC. American pressure for EU enlargement was relentless. Like most aspects of US strategy, it made no difference whether Republicans or Democrats were in the White House. Often, the statements made by senior US officials gave the impression that they had as much right to be involved in this process as actual EU members.

Speaking about Croatia's planned accession, US Secretary of State Hillary Clinton said in 2011 that 'Europe will not be complete until all of the countries of the Western Balkans are full EU members'.[16] She described 'European and Euro-Atlantic integration' as if they were synonymous. In the US strategic mind, membership of the EU goes hand in hand with membership of NATO, the military alliance built to confront Soviet communism but which lumbered on even after that threat had vanished.

In an effort to explain why NATO still existed, another US Secretary of State, Colin Powell, said it was 'hard to shut down a club when people keep trying to get in'.[17] He was referring to the new EU members of Eastern Europe, countries he candidly admitted were 'once on my target list' as a US general. In words that confound proponents of the Anglosphere, Powell explained why the US involved itself so heavily in EU enlargement:

We are a European power, a European nation just as much as we are a North American nation. We are linked in so many ways: by history, by tradition, by commerce, by shared values.

He argued that the US deserved some credit for the EU's success and expansion, due to the security and economic support provided by Harry Truman and every subsequent US president. Nevertheless, Powell, one of the most decorated officers in the US army, acknowledged that the EU had brought peace to a continent that 'for so many hundreds of years had been awash with blood and war'. He argued that its enlargement would expand the benefits of that peace to millions more people. He quoted US revolutionary Benjamin Franklin: 'If we do not hang together, then we most certainly will hang separately.'

Not all of Powell's Republican colleagues were so enlightened. Speaking in 2003, Donald Rumsfeld, then US Defense Secretary, divided the EU into 'old' and 'new' Europe. He dismissed Germany and France as 'problems' but hailed the new Eastern European members: 'They're not with France and Germany... they're with the US.' He was talking specifically about support for the US invasion of Iraq.[18]

Powell's Democratic predecessor Madeleine Albright voiced the US interest even more boldly. Writing about NATO expansion in *The Economist* in 1997, she said that:

...EU expansion is vital. Though the United States has no vote in the process, we do have an interest in seeing it happen as rapidly and expansively as possible.

Albright gave an alternative explanation for NATO's continued existence. She said it didn't matter if NATO members faced no actual threats; the alliance should be permanent 'to prevent a threat from ever arising'. As for Russia, she said that 'few ordinary Russians express concern about an alliance that many of their leaders concede poses no actual military threat to Russia'.

A few years later, the US would start negotiating with Poland to install a missile shield, a move seen by Russia as an attempt to neutralize its own nuclear arsenal. Russia also saw the eastwards spread of NATO as a direct violation of promises made by the West not to exploit the end of the Soviet Union and the Warsaw Pact for security purposes.[19]

The view from Washington was that the EU was the political wing of NATO, a velvet glove of soft power around the alliance's hard steel fist. The US was determined that it should control security in Europe. NATO was the vehicle through which it would maintain that control. A major US strategy report issued in 1995 listed as a key objective:

...preserving and enhancing the effectiveness of European security

organizations, especially NATO, as the principal vehicle for continued United States leadership and influence on European security issues.[20]

Here it is possible to see another explanation for why the US was so eager to keep Britain, one of its most co-operative allies, inside the EU. Without the British veto, the EU was likely to develop its own, independent military force, ending the US control over European security created by NATO's structure. Pro-Europeans were keen on this idea. In May 2015, the president of the EU commission, Jean-Claude Juncker, called for the creation of just such a European force, saying it was the only way the bloc could force a common foreign and defence policy.[21] His words were endorsed by German politicians.

The response of the British was immediate. A UK government spokesperson ruled out any EU-wide military units, instead saying that defence was the responsibility of individual nations.[22] Two years earlier, the UK had blocked efforts to streamline and integrate the EU military.[23] This was even though, as an EU report pointed out, vast resources were being squandered by European nations duplicating military functions at a national level.[24]

By this point, the Anglosphere concept begins to look tenuous. Asked about British plans to hold a referendum on EU membership, US President Barack Obama made it clear that the US wanted Britain to stay within the union.[25] He advised that the UK instead attempt to 'fix' those aspects of EU membership that create political opposition, and indicated that Britain's international standing rested on its being part of the EU.

British membership of the EU is critical to US strategy. The US continues to support the expansion of NATO into areas previously held by Russia, and it needs Britain to stay within the EU to prevent the bloc creating a rival military force that could 'declare independence' of the Pentagon and conduct operations of its own accord, without first consulting Washington.

The US also needs Britain to cheerlead the eastwards expansion of the EU. Britain has been a stalwart supporter of this process, even as far as Turkey.[26] As recently as December 2014, official British documents described the country as 'a long-standing, strong supporter of EU enlargement' which has been 'highly influential in driving the enlargement process' throughout both Conservative and Labour governments.[27] Curiously, this bipartisan support for EU enlargement is rarely mentioned by British political commentators, even as Europe has risen to the top of the policy agenda.

The UK supported US military-strategic goals by bringing former Eastern Bloc countries into the union. It gained influence with them as a result. So too did Washington. As Rumsfeld noted, the entrance of countries such as Poland and Lithuania diluted the power of France and Germany and, being more nervous of Russia, were stronger supporters of NATO's continued dominance of European security planning.

In other words, the great wave of Eastern European immigration to Britain was largely a result of the UK's relationship with the US. Had successive British governments taken a stronger line with their American counterparts, and called for a more gradual EU expansion, UKIP would have little to complain about. The British would have found supporters in France and Germany, who were far cooler towards enlargement and more sceptical of US demands.[28]

Once this fact is acknowledged, a simple solution to the political strains of EU enlargement presents itself. Before accepting further members, the British and other major EU powers should require the US to offer working visas to people from accession countries. Croats, Serbs and Romanians would then have the option of working within the giant US economy, where population densities are low and where there are already well-established Eastern European communities. The US and European halves of Samuel Huntington's single 'Western' civilization would come together to ease the EU's growing pains.

The political dynamic in Washington would not necessarily

be a problem. Much of the US opposition to immigration boils down to thinly disguised racism towards Hispanics; a fear that their numbers are becoming proportionally too large. Those with this mind-set might actually welcome new immigrants from Eastern Europe as a way of maintaining the racial status quo. More enlightened US leaders would recognize the benefits that skilled, hard-working artisans bring to the American economy.

A deal over US visas, extending the Open Borders and Human Ties condition for peace, would go much of the way to diffusing the sense of national anxiety surrounding the question of East-West immigration. Soon, workers from the poorer parts of the UK and France would not be undercut by Poles and Hungarians – who in many cases would be moving to the US – but instead stand to reap the many employment benefits of being part of an ever-wealthier economic giant.

It would also reassure the British that they had something to gain from their 'special relationship' with the US. For decades, the Anglosphere has boiled down to the UK being little more than Washington's cat's paw within the EU. British leaders have supported almost any US-backed policy in return for a photo opportunity with the president of the day. Reciprocity on migration would reward this unquestioning British loyalty, while giving the US an opportunity to prove it is willing to share the EU's growing pains.

Immigration and the Anglosphere are not the only wrinkles in British relations with Europe. There are signs that membership of the EU is tearing at the very fabric that keeps the United Kingdom united. There is a sense in some quarters that pan-European regional union has replaced the need for the pan-British regional union that brought Scotland and England together. Many Scots now feel that they should resume their role as an independent country, with Brussels replacing London as the union capital.

Scotland's independence referendum of 2014 was closer than initially anticipated. It sent shockwaves through Europe. Spain's Prime Minister Mariano Rajoy said that had Scotland voted for independence, it would have been 'a torpedo below the waterline for European integration'.[29] Spain has refused to allow Catalonia to run a similar exercise for fear that Catalan separatists might actually win.

This kind of secessionism is potentially devastating to the EU project. If Scotland and Catalonia were to win independence within the union, this would redouble the momentum of dozens of other separatist movements across Europe. In India, as we saw in Chapter Four, a political cottage-industry exists to champion the creation of new provinces. Its demands have multiplied with every new state created.

If Scotland and Catalonia were permitted to become new countries within the EU, many other similar movements would be strengthened. New ones would be launched. If this seems far-fetched, consider the following. The Scottish and Catalan separatists share an EU parliamentary bloc with parties seeking an independent Corsica and Brittany (France), Frisia (Netherlands), Åland (Finland), Bavaria (Germany), South Tyrol (Italy), Silesia (Poland and Czech Republic), to name only a few.[30]

If the nation-states begin to disintegrate, it is likely they will attempt to leave the EU in order to preserve their territorial integrity, threatening European convergence in its entirety. Scotland is one of the most pro-EU parts of the UK; had it voted for independence, this would have greatly increased the likelihood of the remainder of Britain voting to quit the EU.

The EU must make it clear, therefore, that a declaration of independence from a member state is also a declaration of independence from the EU, with no guarantee of fast-tracked future accession. The ambiguity over whether this is or is not the case was a feature of Scotland's referendum campaign. Devolution within existing nation-states is a better solution, one that does not jeopardize the peaceful gains of European cohesion.

Part of the reason for the Scottish nationalists' success in the 2015 UK general elections was the weakness of the 'No' campaign in the referendum debate. It sought to present an independent Scotland as economically destitute. Not only was this insulting to a country that survived independently for centuries, and a dispiriting message around which to campaign, it also neglected the fact that within an EU context, many small countries have prospered. Part of this is because they spend less of their national wealth on defence. The nationalists, for instance, have made it clear that they would not tolerate the UK's nuclear submarines being based in an independent Scotland.

A better argument for the 'No' campaign would have been to cite the example of the US state of Texas. Like the Scots, Texans have a strong sense of distinctive identity and, like the Scots, they control a huge amount of oil wealth. The Republic of Texas existed as an independent country for a decade after its separation from Mexico in 1836, before its annexation by the US. An independent Texas would be a wealthy country. This does not mean, however, that an independent Texas is necessarily a sensible idea.

Today, the Texas Nationalist Movement (TNM) campaigns for full independence from the US.[31] Just as the Scottish National Party excoriates politicians in Westminster for being disconnected from the concerns of ordinary Scots, so too does the TNM depict Washington DC as a haven of detached insiders who are unable to solve Texan problems. The TNM points out that recent opinion polls have shown that over a third of voters in southwestern states want independence from the US.[32] Even the state's Republican governor, Rick Perry, has at times refused to rule out Texan secession.[33]

Texans' and Scots' ideas of their own national distinctiveness are often lost on foreigners, who view them as being scarcely different from other Americans or Britons. What drives both movements is a feeling of detachment from the centre of power, and a retreat into localism as a means of reasserting control. In both cases, resentment has been fuelled by the national election of national parties – Democrats, Conservatives – that are disliked in Texas and Scotland respectively.

This suspicion of the central authorities, indeed, reflects the attitude of many British Eurosceptics towards the EU capital of Brussels. This they view as an opaque bureaucracy dedicated to expanding its own powers and perks, and with a political culture that is alien. Returning full sovereignty to London, they argue, is the answer to Britain's problems, rather as Scots nationalists see salvation in their own parliament.

Addressing this existential angst is not a simple matter. In the case of the US, devolving more powers to state governments is, as we have seen, vital to ending the federal government's inefficient and militarized approach to tackling unemployment and social care. In the case of Europe, it is essential to ensure that member states retain real and significant powers and that they are not sucked into a US-style super-state.

The case of the UK, however, presents particular difficulties. If the Westminster government devolves further powers to Scotland, while simultaneously pooling a greater proportion of its own sovereignty with the EU, there is a risk that London may become an irrelevant intermediary between Edinburgh and Brussels. This is one reason why, for instance, the UK is so reluctant to envisage a pan-European military force. Defence is one of the areas where London is determined to protect its power.

A better solution would be to address why Scots, and indeed many other Britons, feel that the Westminster government no longer understands them. One part of the problem is the geography of power. The UK is unique in the Anglosphere for concentrating its political, cultural and financial capitals in a single city: London.

To draw a comparison with the United States, if Hollywood and Wall Street were to be found in Washington DC, rather than in Los Angeles and New York, it is likely that resentment against the US federal government would be so great that states such as Texas would indeed break away. Most major countries are careful to strike a geographic balance of power. Canada's economic capital is Toronto, but its political capital is Ottawa and its cultural capital Montreal. New Delhi hosts India's political centre, but the financial capital is Mumbai and the cultural capital is Kolkata (formerly Calcutta). South Africa's political capital is Pretoria, but its financial centre is Johannesburg and its cultural capital is Cape Town.

London, however, hosts the Houses of Parliament, the City of London, the Royal Opera House and Ballet, the National Theatre and Wembley Stadium, the Olympic Park, the headquarters of the BBC, one third of Premier League football teams, every state ministry and department, the Crown Court and Supreme Court, any number of professional bodies, and no fewer than five international airports. At the UK general election in 2015, all three of the major party leaders hailed from London or the surrounding counties. It was perhaps no surprise, then, that the Scottish National Party (SNP) took almost a clean-sweep of Scottish parliamentary constituencies.

Relocating Britain's administrative centre would do much to reassure the British that their politicians are not in the pockets of financiers, and that they do not confuse life in London for life in Britain as a whole, which is poorer and less diverse than the capital. There is historical precedent. London only established itself as England's capital after the Norman conquest of 1066, before which the capital was the town of Winchester. That the government faces a £3 billion ($4.3 billion) bill to refurbish the Houses of Parliament is another good reason to explore new localities.[34] The BBC has already shifted much of its establishment to the northern city of Salford.

In Europe, the only other major country to centralize so much in one city is France, but at least Paris has the advantage of being geographically central. Around the world, countries such as Brazil, Pakistan and Nigeria have purpose-built new administrative capitals that are centrally located and thus better able to unite the country. Brasilia, Islamabad and Abuja are oases of relative peacefulness and security in a way that the cities they replaced – Rio de Janeiro, Karachi and Lagos – are not.

Such internal arrangements relate back to the question
of European migration and the UK's national cohesion.
Southeast England is now one of the most crowded places in
Europe, with 450 residents per square kilometre.[35] The over-
centralization of the British economy in London has acted
as a magnet for workers from across Europe, while drawing
younger people from other regions of England.

Scotland, by comparison, is sparsely populated and has
watched itself become a progressively smaller share of the
UK's total population. Its leaders have a very different
attitude towards immigration. In the words of Scotland's pro-
independence government, 'the Westminster government's
policy for the whole of the UK is heavily influenced by
conditions in the southeast of England'.[36] Whereas England is
trying to keep migrants out, Scotland welcomes them.

By shifting the seat of government northwards, the UK
would lessen the overcrowding around London and encourage
migration to Scotland, fulfilling the aspirations of the country
as a whole and lessening demands for Scottish independence.
This would seem a more productive approach than blaming
EU bureaucrats, who simply do not have the power to rectify
the UK's internal imbalances.

For pro-Europeans, it is essential to refute Eurosceptic
attempts to hold Brussels responsible for policies that are either
a function of the UK's relationship with the United States,
such as rapid EU enlargement, or are a product of Britain's
internal arrangements, such as the over-centralization of
national life in one corner of the island. So long as voters
blame the EU for such problems, it is unlikely they will ever be
resolved.

Rather, the UK should use its membership of the EU to
counterbalance its relationship with Washington. It should pay
more attention when its European partners counsel against,
say, the invasion of Iraq, or when they suggest a slower pace
of EU enlargement. Far from diluting British sovereignty, by
reasserting its status as a European nation the UK can achieve
a greater measure of autonomy from US strategic objectives,

while at the same time preserving an influential voice within the EU.

More generally, it is incorrect to draw some vast distinction between Europe and the 'Anglosphere'. As many senior US officials have noted, their country is a European state transposed to North America, and it sees itself as such. The EU therefore has as much right to counsel the US on matters of mutual interest as vice-versa. Simply subordinating its own national interests to those of the US has served Britain poorly. Paradoxically, by declaring its independence of the Anglosphere within an EU context, the UK could be far more influential than it finds itself today.

1 Fletcher, Anthony, *Tudor Rebellions*, 3rd edition, London. Longman, 1983. **2** Mills, Jon, 'Ethnocide and Genocide: The Suppression of the Cornish language' in *Interfaces in Language*, 2010, ed. Partridge, Jon, Cambridge Scholars Publishing, p.197.   **3** 2014, 'GDP per capita in the EU in 2011: seven capital regions among the ten most prosperous', Eurostat Newsrelease, 27 February. **4** Unnamed author, 1975, '1975: Attack on British vessels heightens Cod War', BBC On This Day, 11 December. **5** Sweney, Mark, 2014 'The Guardian overtakes New York Times in comScore traffic figures', *The Guardian*, 21 October. **6** Thatcher, Margaret, 1988, 'The Bruges Speech', Speech to College of Europe, 20 September, Bruges. **7** This strategy also accounted for Britain's heavy investment the Royal Navy after 1588, when England narrowly defeated an armada of 130 Spanish warships. The Spanish fleet were protecting an invasion force intended to overthrow Henry Tudor's granddaughter Elizabeth I. In London's eyes, protecting the waters around England's southern coast became of paramount importance. Britain's colonial and trade expansion after the 16th century was a by-product of this defensive investment in the Royal Navy. **8** Raines, Thomas, 'Internationalism or Isolationism', The Chatham House, YouGov Survey, January 2015. **9** Reynolds, Owen R, 2015, 'UKIP and the "new relationship" with the Commonwealth', UKIP Daily, 29 March. **10** '*La France se doit d'assumer son rôle de Nation mère de la francophonie... Il est temps pour la France de rebâtir les réseaux de son influence et de s'appuyer sur les atouts légués par l'Histoire, via la France d'outre-mer et via l'ensemble des Etats dans le monde ayant le français en partage.*' **11** Little, Alison, 1999, 'Wilson wanted UK to be US State', *The Independent*, 24 January. **12** 'Migration Statistics Quarterly Report, February 2015', Office for National Statistics. **13** Joseph, Marion, 2011 'Premiers cours d'anglais, les pratiques en Europe', *Le Figaro*, 27 January. **14** Helm, Toby, 2014, 'British people favour leaving the European Union, according to poll', *The Guardian*, 21 June. **15** Blinder, Dr Scott, 2014, 'UK Public Opinion toward Immigration: Overall Attitudes and Level of Concern', The Migration Observatory, 3 July.

16 Clinton, Hillary Rodham via Press Statement, 'Croatia: Conclusion of EU Accession Talks',

US Department of State, 30 June 2011. **17** Powell, Colin L., 1 May, 'Fifty Years of Formal United

States and European Union Relations and European Union Accession', 2004. **18** Unnamed

author, 2003, 'Rumsfled: France, Germany are 'problems' in Iraqi Conflict', CNN, 23 January.

19 Ruhle, Michael, 'NATO enlargement and Russia: myths and realities', Nato Review.

20 Perry, William, J., 'America's enduring interests in NATO', *Security Strategy for Europe and

NATO*, Chapter 1. **21** Balzli, Von Beat, 2015, 'Juncker will EU-Armee', *Die Welt*, 8 March.

22 Unnamed author, 2015, 'We need a European army, says Jean-Claude Juncker', BBC News, 9

March. **23** Unnamed author, 2013, 'EU to boost joint military projects', BBC News, 19 December.

24 2013, 'Communication from the Commission to the European Parliament, The Council,

The European Economic and Social Committee and the Committee of the Regions', European

Commission, 24 July. **25** 2013, 'Press conference: PM and President Obama', GOV.UK, 13 May.

26 HM Government article, 2012, 'Minister for Europe renews UK commitment to EU

enlargement', GOV.UK, 12 December. **27** HM Government report, 2014, 'Review of the Balance

of Competences between the United Kingdom and the European Union: EU Enlargement'.

28 Vucheva, Elista, 2009, 'France, Germany remain cool on EU enlargement', EU Observer, 30

March. **29** Unnamed author, 2014, 'Scottish or Catalan vote "torpedoes EU", says Spain's Rajoy',

BBC News, 17 September. **30** European Free Alliance, 'Member Parties', permanent link:

www.e-f-a.org/whos-who/member-parties/ **31** www.thetnm.org **32** Malone, Scott, 2014,

'Exclusive: Angry with Washington, 1 in 4 Americans open to secession', Reuters, 19 September.

33 Mooney, Alexander, 2009, 'Texas governor says secession possible' CNN Political Ticker,

April 16. **34** Kuenssberg, Laura, 2014, 'Parliament repair bill "could top £3bn"', BBC News, 20

November. **35** 'Regional Profiles – Population and Migration – South East, March 2013', UK

Office of National Statistics. **36** p.267, 'Scotland's Future: A Guide to an Independent Scotland',

white paper, first published by the Scottish Government, November 2013.

Postscript
Better Together – 10 Steps to Global Peace: Making It Happen

An analysis of what the world risks if the EU is allowed to unravel and be discredited. As we enter an age of chaos, in which defensive security has no hope of keeping track with unconventional and asymmetric warfare, weapons will not protect us. For that, we need to build institutions that pre-empt conflict before it erupts into violence. With the British referendum on EU membership at hand, it is vital to explain why the EU model is the last, best hope for achieving peace in our time.

In Egypt, Anubis was a death-god in the old religion that preceded Christianity and Islam. Depicted as a man with the head of a jackal, Anubis would lead the living to the underworld and guard their graves. In his honour, Egyptians mummified animals, particularly dogs, and lay them in catacombs beneath the desert sands. At the vast subterranean necropolis of Saqqara, beneath the ancient capital of Memphis, archaeologists found the remains of an estimated eight million animals.

In 2008, Anubis lent his name to another deathly mission, a secretive project undertaken by the US Air Force. Project Anubis was to create the perfect assassination device. At the Air Force Research Laboratory in the mid-western state of Ohio, researchers developed a Micro-Air Vehicle (MAV) with the ability to track and 'engage' high-value targets – in other words, to attack human enemies of the US government.[1]

Small, hand-held aircraft have been used for reconnaissance by US soldiers in Afghanistan and Iraq. Some of their development took place under the auspices of a programme to prevent US enemies, such as Iran, from developing weapons of mass destruction. One of the programme's accomplishments in 2011, according to budget documents, was the testing of an

MAV that would follow up air-strikes by videoing the damage and sending it back to the command centre.[2]

Reconnaissance is not the end-purpose of the MAVs, however. A presentation in 2009 by David Deptula, a US Air Force general and intelligence staff commander, suggested that 'nano-drones' would have deadlier applications. One was what he called 'indoor lethal'.[3]

To show what he meant by a 'nano' MAV, Deptula illustrated his presentation with a picture of a hornet-sized drone sitting in the palm of a man's hand. The US is researching such devices. One budget document, from 2006, described 'nano-robot fabrication' and 'ultra-small sensors' as a 'major programme area'. The project's goal was to create 'infrared cameras small enough to fit into mini-unmanned aerial vehicles'.[4] Worldwide, there are many projects to build tiny aircraft modelled on insect flight propulsion.[5,6]

General Deptula's presentation did not explain how such tiny flying devices could be 'indoor lethal'. They are too small to carry a deadly payload of explosives. Poison seems the only possibility. A microgram of the radioactive element polonium-210 is enough to be fatal. No larger than a speck of dust, such a dose could be delivered by an insect-sized MAV. The Russian defector Alexander Litvinenko was murdered with polonium in London in 2007, after his assassins slipped it into his cup of tea.

In theory, such a tiny drone could fly into any building in the world and murder any leader, no matter how well defended. Collectively, they could change the battlefield. Deptula's presentation mentioned 'swarming'. The US Navy has developed 'swarm' MAVs that can be fired from a cannon and then descend upon enemies like a plague of insects.[7] According to a US Navy video provided to CNN, the swarm drones would surveil a target before destroying it.[8] The initiative was codenamed Project Locust.

Other applications listed by Deptula included espionage and cyber-attacks. Many countries keep their most sensitive information on 'air gapped' computers disconnected from the internet. To penetrate them, hackers must arrange for a memory stick to be plugged into the air-gapped system in order to infect it with spyware. They must wait for their enemy to make a mistake, as did the US and Israeli spies who infected Iran's nuclear computer systems with the Stuxnet worm. Stuxnet destroyed nearly 1,000 of Iran's 6,000 enrichment centrifuges.[9] It went on to infect a number of other untargeted facilities, including a Russian nuclear power plant.[10] A nano-MAV would make it much easier to infect computers with hostile software. It could simply fly into a facility, unnoticed, and interface with a computer directly.

Project Anubis and its many imitators demonstrate the illusory nature of 'security'. Hiring a guard with a gun, or many guards with many guns, will soon offer no more personal protection than the spears and halberds carried by ceremonial beefeaters at the Tower of London. The preservation of secrets will become impossible in an era of electronic bugs more mobile and bug like than ever before. Technology is far outstripping a state's ability to defend itself from those who wish it harm.

In reality, the armed definition of security has always been an illusion. True security is based on goodwill; on the mutual agreement to respect the life, liberty and privacy of others. How one arrives at that situation is a political question, not a military one. Goodwill and its absence are the difference between peace and war.

Without peace there can be no prosperity, or human development, or hope of a stable and just society. Without it, questions of economics and public policy become inconsequential. It is remarkable that in a world where only one continent is free of extreme and persistent violence – Antarctica – so much energy is dedicated to the discussion of finance and economics, and so little to the structures of peace.

This book offers a pacifying framework that has been proven to work in the European Union. Of the 30 most peaceful countries in the world in 2015, 20 were in Europe.[11] The 10 factors that brought internal peace to Europe must be applied to other continents. Enshrined Democracy and Shared Values; Economic Truce; Open Borders and Human Ties; Soft Power and Common Purpose; Permanent Discussion, Dialogue and Diplomacy; Financial Incentives and Support; Veto and Consensus Building; Resistance to External Interference; Rules, Rights and Multiculturalism; Mutual Trust and Peaceful Coexistence. These are the factors that bind nations together in a way that preserves goodwill.

This is why the British referendum on whether to leave the EU is of such paramount importance. It is why Greece's fate within the Eurozone is so important. There are many who seek to step into the past, into the old certainties of a bygone era. They justify their arguments in economic terms. Greece needs its own currency to be prosperous, they claim, and the British need to sign their own trade deals, rather than waiting on a cumbersome pan-European process.[12]

The trouble with economics is that it can be enlisted to support almost any argument. Often, the best guide to an economist's views is simply whoever pays them. Those who work for state-subsidized universities tend to emphasize income inequality, which supports calls for higher taxes that ultimately benefit their own institution. Economists who work for large corporations, or privately funded think-tanks, tend to stress the importance of low tax rates for GDP growth, again in line with their employer's interests.

These biases filter into the political debate. As the noted economist John Maynard Keynes once said:

Practical men who believe themselves to be quite exempt from any intellectual influence are usually the slaves of some defunct economist.

Pro-Europeans argue that the single currency is a good thing, economically speaking. The ups and downs of foreign-exchange markets mean that a shipment that is profitable one week can be loss-making the next. By eliminating the risk of currency fluctuations, a single currency reduces the risks for companies, especially small ones, to trade across borders. But by making this argument, they entangle themselves in the selective quotation of statistics, with each side citing figures that support their side of the cost-benefit equation.

The analysis of peace is a more definitive way to win the argument over prosperity. There are thankfully few economists who claim that war-torn countries are more prosperous than peaceful ones, with builders benefiting from shattered homes and where unnecessary luxuries are eliminated. Most thoughtful people accept the strong connection between peace and prosperity.

A continent bound together by the EU's 10 peace-promoting factors is very much more likely to be peaceful – and thus prosperous – than one divided into nationalistic, mutually belligerent nation-states pursuing their own interests without reference to those of their neighbours. Arguing against this statement is theoretically possible, but to do so risks stepping out of the bounds of sanity.

This process of uniting across borders is called regionalism. It mirrors the idea of federalism, whereby very large countries subdivide power to localities in order to ensure harmony. In 1946, Winston Churchill gave his famous speech in praise of a United States of Europe (USE), which he imagined along the lines of the British Commonwealth. The Commonwealth had replaced the British Empire with a multilateral organization of nation-states united by the English language, common law and democracy. In Churchill's eyes, just as the Commonwealth sought to preserve the best aspects of the British Empire, this USE would become the guarantor of peace in Europe.

Churchill's comparison with the United States of America was ultimately to prove unfortunate. As Europe moved towards regionalism, the US regressed into a super-state in which individual state governments have their authority perpetually usurped by federal lawmakers and judges. Today, Eurosceptics seize on the 'United States of Europe' concept, likening Brussels to the overbearing centrism of Washington DC.

With this in mind, there is a valid criticism of the EU, in

that it has allowed itself to be a tool of US military-strategic posturing. That Barack Obama, George W Bush and the British were so insistent on rapid EU expansion pointed to a paradox at the heart of the modern EU, one that now threatens its very future.

On one hand the EU, by crafting a team from the nations of Western Europe, brought the continent unimaginable peace and prosperity. Before the Second World War, adults could be certain of multiple conflicts between European neighbours over the course of their lifetimes. On the other hand, Europe squandered the chance for reconciliation after the Cold War ended. The EU began to fulfil the prophecy of Samuel P Huntington, picking and choosing its members not against objective criteria – which Greece, for instance, never met – but against the schemes of military strategists and 'civilizational' thinkers. Slamming the door on Russia sowed the seeds for future conflict.

This civilizational thinking has propelled violence in the Middle East and North Africa. As Muslims watched other 'civilizations' agglomerate into peaceful and powerful blocs, they became painfully aware of their own division and weakness. The inability of their Western-backed dictators to pool sovereignty fed enthusiasm for ever more violent groups seeking to unite Muslims around a single flag. The rise of Islamic State and the rise of the EU flow from the same unifying impulse.

It is vital, then, that the EU's frameworks for peaceful unification be transplanted to every continent, before people of violence establish a very different model. To prevent war, education is essential for elites as well for as the masses. Rather than seeking advice from officials whose careers depend on the identification of new enemies and threats, leaders must instead ensure that peace is the first priority for their advisers.

It is also essential that the new regional blocs do not close their doors to new members based on arbitrary notions of shared 'civilizations', but instead are ready to include any country that meets the political and economic criteria for entry. To do otherwise risks hardening boundaries and attitudes, rather than softening them. This is all the more dangerous as the world enters a new era in which devastating, anonymous attacks can bypass conventional defences, rendering obsolete much of the ruinously expensive military-industrial complex.

Immanuel Kant, the great German philosopher of the 18th century, argued that 'humankind learns from history and war, but only the hard way'. There are no more lessons that can be sensibly drawn from armed conflict. The architecture for global peace is now within our grasp through the spread of EU-like regional unions, working within a reformed United Nations. They are the last, best hope for peace in our time.

1 Hambling, David, 2010, 'Air Force Completes Killer Micro Drone Project', *Wired*, 5 January.

2 p17, 'Department of Defense Fiscal Year (FY) 2013 President's Budget Submission', Defense Threat Reduction Agency Justification Book, February 2012. **3** Slides 15 and 16, 'Air Force Unmanned Aerial System (UAS) Flight Plan 2009-2047', Deptula, Lt Gen David, Deputy Chief of Staff, Intelligence, Surveillance and Reconnaissance, US Air Force. **4** p160, 'Department of Defense Performance and Accountability Report FY 2006', Section 3: Financial Information. **5** http://robobees.seas.harvard.edu/ **6** http://mavlab.lr.tudelft.nl/ **7** Unnamed author, 2015, 'US Navy develops cannon-launched "swarming" drones', BBC News, 16 April. **8** Video footage, 2015, 'U.S. Navy testing swarm "locust" drones', CNN, 15 April. **9** Nakashima, Ellen and Warrick, Joby, 2012, 'Stuxnet was work of US and Israeli experts, officials say', *Washington Post*, 2 June. **10** See comments by Eugene Kaspersky, Press Club 2013, Canberra, Australia. **11** Global Peace Index 2015. **12** See Clements, Ben, 'Britain outside the European Union', IEA Brexit Prize 2014.

INDEX